Happy Birth) Dad

To my

be beach

I attribute much of my health
to following the seasonal eating
of this book.

may you have health, happiness,
& great realization ☺

— Cameron

Healthy Eating

Traditional Chinese Medicine-Inspired Healthy Eating Guides for All Four Seasons plus 240+ recipes to Restore Health, Beauty, and Mind

TRACY HUANG

Disclaimer

Please note that I am NOT a medical doctor; and make no claims to be. The information provided in this book is provided for general information purposes; and does not constitute medical, legal or other professional advice on any subject matter. The author of this book does not accept any responsibility for any loss which may arise from reliance on information contained within this book or on any associated websites or blogs.

Contents

Introduction

Spring is a blossoming season, a time when people easily develop hay fever. It is also a windy season; as a result, your skin may become dry, rough, and itchy, potentially causing you to have a dry mouth, a dry tongue, and a sore throat.

When you seek solutions to keep your skin moisturized, besides applying thick and creamy moisturizers on your face and using a lip balm on your lips for protection, did you know that consuming foods like whole grains, pears, and lotus seeds also helps? And, did you know that, if you easily have hay fever in this season, it is important to cut down the intake of seafood, alcoholic beverages, and pungent foods?

In summer, the season with vibrancy and energy, trees grow the fastest at this time, which suggests growth and reaching one's potentially.

At the same time, this season also comes with a series of challenges. For example, the increasing temperature can decrease your appetite; if you have oily or combination skin, your skin may become oiler, which can clog pores and cause breakouts; what's more, one can get moody or easily agitated in hot summer days.

As you can see, changes in nature can lead to changes in how your body functions internally, in skin health, and even in your temperament as well.

Yes, you could consider appetite-enhancing drugs to deal with loss of appetite, antibiotics for acne breakouts, and drugs to soothe an anxious and agitated mind. These are, however, medicines only remove the symptoms and may not be able to address the root causes.

Did you know that, to protect your digestive system in this season, it is recommended you minimize the intake of raw and cold foods as they are hard to digest and can cause extra burden to digestion? And, did you know that consuming mung beans and bitter melon soups can help heal breakouts, and that foods like millet, rose petals, and lotus seeds can calm the mind?

When autumn arrives, temperatures slowly drop and weathers gradually get drier and drier. You may again start to suffer from dry skin, a few coughs, and a sore throat. If you don't pay attention to taking good care of the body, these minor issues can be turned into more serious problems like skin disease and respiratory infection.

To prevent a worse scenario from happening, did you know that it helps tremendously if you could consume more lungs-moistening foods such as pears, lily bulbs, lotus seeds, white fungus, and lotus roots, and hydrating foods such as brown rice congee, pumpkins, Chinese yams, herbal tea, and skin-nourishing soups?

At last, when it comes to winter, you may start to have cold digits throughout the season. Besides wearing more warm clothes and thick gloves, have you ever realized that these can be a sign that your body is calling for attention and care from the inside?

Did you know that, by consuming foods like black sesame seeds, black beans, black rice, black fungus, seaweed, ginger, astragalus (a type of Chinese herbs popular with the Chinese that can promote energy flow throughout the body), fish with cooking wine and ginger, and lamb, you can also warm up the body and your hands?

These are just quick examples of showing you how adjusting the way you eat can help you heal diseases and keep you staying healthy. In fact, this is partially the essence of Traditional Chinese Medicine – it's about forming the dietary habits that your body needs at a particular time.

TCM sees that different symptoms like dry skin, breakouts, an agitated mind, and cold digits can be signs that your body is calling for attention and care from the inside.

As well, it believes that our body is a piece of sophisticated and well-designed machine; different parts of the body are working closely with and for one another. That means if you carefully listen to what your body needs and take care of it from the inside by consuming nourishing foods with different healing properties, your external conditions could be healed naturally.

This can be perfectly summarized in the following sentences: "you cannot heal selectively. If you truly heal, everything heals", a quote by Charlotte Gerson, daughter of Dr. Max Gerson who was a German-born American physician and developed the Gerson Therapy, an alternative dietary therapy which he claimed could cure cancer and most chronic and degenerative diseases.

Such healing benefits in foods are rarely discussed in the west. On the contrary, therapeutic properties in foods have been recognized, talked about, served as dietary guidelines for the Chinese people, and benefited many people for over 2,000 years.

As I learn more about Traditional Chinese Medicine, I find it is important for you to also understand how TCM views foods and therapeutic benefits in different kinds of whole foods – a different way to approaching eating to help you restore health, beauty, and mind.

That's why I wrote this book. I want to share with you how

different foods can be served as medicines to help you live throughout the year with a healthy body, glowing skin, and a calm mind.

In this book, you will learn:

-   Basic guidelines and best practices for eating in spring, summer, autumn, and winter
-   How each season with a three-month period can be divided into six shorter periods of time (each period describing a subtle change in atmospheric characteristics and animal behaviors) and how ancient Chinese used this type of categorization to plan for what to eat to promote health
-   More than **240 recipes** to choose from to get started with healthy eating in different seasons

This book is a collection and summary of my personal experience with Traditional Chinese Medicine and experiments based on the teaching of Chinese Food Therapy, what I learned from my Chinese doctor, Fang-Tsuey Lin, Licensed Acupuncturist who has been practicing since 2001 in Lexington, Massachusetts, as well as key insights from a series of books written by Traditional Chinese Medicine practitioners.

I am constantly learning more about Chinese Food Therapy and may update this book in the future. If you wish to get free updates about this book, please feel free to subscribe to my mailing list.

By doing so, you will also be receiving my personal insights, experiments, and learnings on Traditional Chinese Medicine and Food Therapy along the way. In addition, you will also get a bonus chapter that helps you understand your own body and how to find the right foods that fit only your body type.

Here's where to sign up: http://bit.ly/sign-up-for-bonus-chapter.

I very much look forward to having you on the journey and growing with you.

Without further ado, let's get started!

Part 1: Seasonal Eating Basics

Before we dive into details on what to eat in each of the four seasons, I have created this part to help you understand seasonal eating in general, the basic terms and concepts that reveal the ancient Chinese people's way of viewing nature, and of deciding when and what to eat. Because I will refer to these terms and concepts regularly in Part 2, this part gives you the preparation to help you understand and absorb knowledge from Part 2 more easily, so that you can better understand the principles and recipes from Part 3 and start your experiments in the kitchen right away.

Simply put, seasonal eating is all about finding the right time to consume the right food. Thus, you need to know both the "timing" and the "food" to reap the benefits from this traditional practice.

Specifically, in Chapter 1, I will first cover the benefits of seasonal eating. Then, we'll move on to the "timing". Chapter 2 teaches you how the Chinese people have their own ways of viewing the seasons.

The Ancient Chinese created a concept called *jieqi* (pronounced as che-chi) to divide the seasons into even smaller time units, grouped together by the same atmospheric characteristics and animal behaviors; I will walk you through what these *jieqi* are and why Chinese people have divided up the seasons in this way. Once you understand that, at last, it's time to learn more about the "food".

You will find the Chinese ways of distinguishing different foods in Chapter 3 and Chapter 4. Chapter 3 introduces you to the Chinese five elements, and how they connect to the seasons, and will help you to decide what foods to eat. In the last chapter of this part, I will briefly touch upon food properties, which you can observe from the outside of foods, to help you discover the healing benefits in whole foods.

Chapter 1: An Introduction to Seasonal Eating

Changing the types of foods that you eat, according to the change of seasons, is a key concept, and a traditional practice derived from Chinese food therapy, which believes that each kind of whole food has its own therapeutic properties and, therefore, the process of consuming whole foods can be seen as a process which heals the body, prevent diseases, restores natural glow, and strengthens health.

Since Chinese food therapy is a part of Traditional Chinese Medicine, seasonal eating also reflects TCM's core philosophies, one of which is that human beings and nature should be connected as one. In other words, we need to respect, and follow, the law of nature. When natural environments change, the body starts to react to external changes. Then, food therapy comes in to nourish or fuel the body and to help it better cope with the different conditions. For example, your appetite may be decreased when hot summer weather strikes.

According to TCM, it is then recommended that you consume more sweet whole foods to increase the appetite and to improve digestion. On the other hand, in cold winter days, you may feel that your appetite is increased. That's a signal that your body is telling you that it needs to store more energy, to cope with the cold weather. As a result, foods with dark colors (such as black sesame seeds, black beans, and black rice) are recommended, because Chinese medicine believes that the darker the color a type of whole food has, the more energy and nutrition it gives the body, to fight against coldness.

Choosing what to eat according to the different seasons is a way to listen to the body, to heal it naturally, to strength your immunity, and to minimize the chance of the body becoming imbalanced because of seasonal changes. The key difference between western medicine and Traditional Chinese Medicine is that western medicine is used to cure diseases, whereas TCM focuses more on preventing sickness from starting. Carefully choosing what to eat in different seasons plays a key role in keeping you looking healthy and energetic, your skin glowing, and your body away from illness.

In Chinese, seasonal eating is also known as a way of "nourishing life in different seasons", from which you can tell that it is not just about "eating", but about living a wholesome life as well.

The first step to nourish your body is to find the right time to do the right thing. The next chapter will be teaching you how ancient Chinese came up their own way to figure out the timing for eating different foods.

Chapter 2: *Jieqi* (Che-Chi), Chinese People's Unique Way to Divide Seasons to Smaller Units

Thanks to science, we now know that the earth moves around the sun in its own orbit. It is this sun-earth relationship that causes the four seasons that we now know. This also means that, within one year's time (about 365 days), the sun is format a constantly changing angle to the earth.

In fact, over two thousand years ago, the ancient Chinese also discovered that the sun's position, relative to the earth, has been changing all the time throughout the year and they came up with their own way of understanding and measuring the associated changes in nature. This chapter teaches you how *jieqi* is formed and how it is used to help the Chinese understand nature and guide their own activities based on *jieqi*.

The ancient Chinese lived in an agricultural society, and they relied on climate changes, from season to season, to plan their farming activities. Because of this, they needed to find a way to precisely predict climate changes due to their importance as guidance for developing agriculture.

With such an intention, they found out that, as the sun's position relative to the earth changes, it leads to changes in atmospheric characteristics and in animal behaviors. Additionally, they concluded, through thousands of years of observation, that there are variations in nature – such as the change in humidity, temperature, wind, precipitation, and animal activities – every 15 days or so. In other words, they found out that each pattern in nature lasts about 15 days and that there are twenty four 15-day periods that each individually describe a particular pattern in nature.

How could they specifically separate one pattern from the other? That is when the concept of *jieqi* was created. Each *jieqi* serves as a landmark to tell the beginning of a new pattern or the end of an old pattern.

Considering that there are 24 patterns evenly spread out through a year, this means that there are six patterns led by six different *jieqi* in each of the four seasons that you know as spring, summer, autumn, and winter (24 patterns in a year / four seasons = six patterns).

Since Traditional Chinese Medicine is all about respecting and following the law of nature, and living according to Mother Nature's changes, the creation of the concept called *jieqi* was very important. It was used to effectively help the ancient Chinese understand the gradual and subtle changes in nature, plan their daily activities, and take care of their body accordingly.

As this book aims to teach you how to eat appropriately in each of the four seasons, I will briefly walk you through all six of the *jieqi* in each season. Below is a high-level summary of all of the 24 *jieqi* in all four seasons.

In spring, there are *lichun, yushui, jingzhe, chunfen, qingming,* and *yushui.* If you feel that you are reading Martian language here, don't worry. I am about to explain each *jieqi* to you. In Chinese, each of the *jieqi* has its own meaning which reflects what changes you can expect to see, in that particular time of the year. After I explain each term, each *jieqi* will make more sense to you.

The translations of these six *jieqi* are: arrival of spring (*lichun*), increase of rains (*yushui*), awakening from hibernation (*jingzhe*), official spring (*chunfen*), freshness and clarity (*qingming*), and more rains and benefiting for growing crops (*guyu*). I hope that you find them as interesting as I see them!

These six *jieqi* all have a common pattern that there are warmer weathers, more greens, and more winds in the air. Details of these six *jieqi* will be discussed in Chapter 6, where you will learn when each *jieqi* usually takes place, the climate characteristics and the animal behaviors that you can expect from the 15 days following that particular *jieqi*, and the expert's dietary advice for those days.

In summer, there are *lixia, xiaoman, mangzhong, xiazhi, xiaoshu,* and *dashu*. The translations of these six *jieqi* are arrival of summer (*lixia*), fruits starting to appear but not fully ripe (*xiaoman*), grains becoming mature (*mangzhong*), official summer (*xiazhi*), weather becoming hotter (*xiaoshu*), and weather becoming the hottest (*dashu*). They all have a common pattern that there are hotter weathers and crops grow rapidly during this time. Details of these six *jieqi* will be discussed in Chapter 8.

The six *jieqi* in autumn include: *liqiu, chushu, bailu, qiufen, hanlu,* and *shuangjiang*, for which the translations respectively are: arrival of autumn (*liqiu*), hot summer almost gone (*chushu*), dew starting to form (*bailu*), official autumn (*qiufen*), dew becoming colder (*hanlu*), and frost starting to appear (*shuangjiang*). The common pattern of these six *jieqi* in autumn is that there are lower and lower temperatures and drier and drier weather during this time. You can find all the details regarding these six *jieqi* in Chapter 10.

In winter, the six jieqi are *lidong, xiaoxue, daxue, dongzhi, xiaohan,* and *dahan*. The translations of these six *jieqi* go: arrival of winter ufor more details on these *jieqi* and dietary advice.

One thing worth pointing out is that this is just a general pattern and for reference only. What the actual natural scene looks like should depend on where you are located, too. For example, trees in my hometown Shenzhen, which is in the south of China in a subtropical area, are green all year round and there is no snow at all. But people in Shenzhen still use *jieqi* as their reference to plan for what to eat and how to best take care of the body.

As you progress in this book, always remember that the whole point of the creation of *jieqi* is to help you develop the awareness to feel the changes in nature more attentively. That way, you will be able to listen to what your body needs more carefully, give it what it looks for, and truly take care of it.

Chapter 3: Relationships between the Chinese Five Elements, the Different Seasons, Your Internal Organs, and What to Eat

In the last chapter, we discussed about the timing that should guide you to seek dietary advice.

Chapter 3 and Chapter 4 in Part 1 both show you the Chinese understanding of foods. Once you grasp the key concepts, you will easily digest the dietary advice that follows in Part 2, where you will learn all the details on healthy eating in four seasons.

To understand the importance of why you need certain foods, we will go deeper into why your body (or your internal organs) needs them at a particular time of the year. We will even dig deeper and explore how the different seasons are connected to different organs, and how the different seasons and organs are linked with the Chinese five elements.

The ancient Chinese regarded the five elements as the foundation that forms all things in nature, and as the theoretical guideline to explain the relationships between natural objects (such as human beings and animals) and natural phenomenon.

Let's start from Chinese five elements.

The Chinese Five Elements and Their Interrelationships

The ancient Chinese used five elements – metal, wood, water, fire, and earth –to understand nature. They believe that these five elements are the building blocks that shape the world and use them as the theoretical foundation to explain all natural phenomena, to understand human bodies and human activities, and to figure out solutions.

For example, the ancient Chinese discovered that each season is linked to one particular element; and every human being, depending on the time, date and location of their birth, has characteristics that belong to one of the five elements. We need to first recognize what the element is that applies to the particular season or individual person; then we design solutions for lifestyle changes or improvements based on the characteristics of this element, and the interrelationships between all five elements.

Since this book is about seasonal eating, we will dig deeper into how all of the seasons are connected with all five elements.

What are the relationships between metal, wood, water, fire, and earth? The ancient Chinese found out that one element can send positive or negative energy to another element, depending on what two elements you place together. As a general rule, metal sends positive energy to water, water to wood, wood to fire, fire to earth, and earth to metal. On the contrary, metal weakens wood; wood, earth; earth, water; water, fire; and, fire, metal.

Maybe you feel a little bit overwhelmed by now, but when you relate all the strengthening and weakening relationships to nature, things might start to make more sense.

In the wild, trees cannot grow without water, from which you can understand better why the element water strengthens the element wood. Similarly, the following natural phenomenon can help you better understand the strengthening relationships between particular elements: pieces of wood are used to start the campfire (wood supporting fire); fire burns wood to ashes which becomes a part of soil and fertilizes soil (fire supporting earth); the earth's crust contains metals (earth strengthening metal); and tools made of metal are used to dig into the ground for water (metal strengthening water).

By looking into nature, you can also find clues on how one element inhibits the growth and development of another element. Because planting enough trees can prevent soil erosion, trees can minimize the movement of soil (wood limiting earth); soil, if shaped in a specific form, can trap water and restrict its flow (earth limiting water); water is used to put out fire (water restricting fire); fire can melt a piece of metal (fire restricting metal); and metal-made knives and swords can cut wood into pieces (metal restricting wood).

Thus, the relationships between these five elements can be best visualized as shown in the chart below.

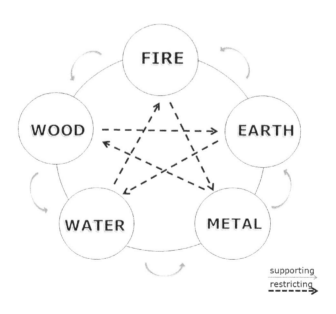

[Side note: if you cannot view it clearly, you could visit here for a color version of this chart - http://bit.ly/5-elements-1.]

How to Match the Five Elements with the Different Seasons and Internal Organs

Now that you understand the five elements are and the relationships between them, let's move onto how to match these elements with the different seasons.

Spring is a wood element; summer, a fire element; long summer, an earth element; autumn, a metal element; and winter, a water element. Yes, there are five seasons in the year, according to the ancient Chinese way of understanding nature.

As a side note, "long summer" has not been clearly defined. Some experts say that long summer refers to summer days that slowly transition to autumn, while others believe that "long summer" means the transitional stage between spring, summer, autumn, and winter. In other words, according to my research, what "long summer" refers to still remains a debatable area.

For my current understanding, I stick with the first explanation: "long summer" means the season right before autumn.

Since the five elements have been used to interpret everything in nature, including human bodies, the Chinese believe that, if you know the relationships between the different organs and these five elements, you will be able to take care of your organs more effectively as well.

Specifically, liver belongs to wood; the lungs, metal; the heart, fire;

the spleen, earth; and, the kidneys, water.

When you consider the season and the organ(s) that belong to the same element together, you will get a general picture of the organ(s) that you should primarily pay attention to when it comes to a particular season. Below is a chart to help you go over what you have learned so far.

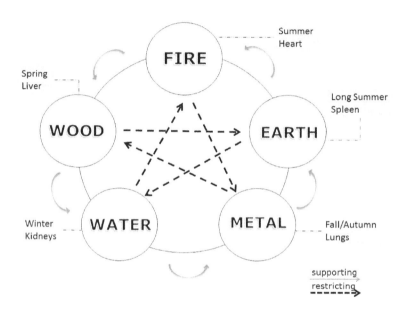

[*Side note: if you cannot view it clearly, you could visit here for a color version of this chart - http://bit.ly/5-elements-2.*]

Using the Five Elements to Explain the Importance of Keeping Your Organs in Balance

You now understand that there are supporting and restricting relationships between the five elements, and that different organs have their own associated elements.

What can you infer when you combine both areas?

The answer is that you need to constantly keep your internal organs in balance, because an imbalance in one organ, which belongs to a particular element, may inhibit the functions of another organ with an element that the first element restricts. As an example, if there is excess energy in the kidneys (water elements), it can weaken the heart (a fire element).

This book teaches you how to avoid energy imbalance in all primary organs, and which organs you should pay attention to in each of the four seasons (yes, in every season there is a particular organ, or a pair of organs, that you need to especially take care of, to maintain the internal balance of the body).

It also teaches you what to do in each season if the primary organs are not in balance, in order to strengthen the functions of the organs which can be potentially weakened. For example, in autumn (a metal element), the lungs (metal elements) are the primary organs that you should pay the attention to; at the same time, you also need to pay attention to the liver (a wood element) which can be potentially weakened by the lungs.

In conclusion, there are, in fact, two types of organs you should primarily pay attention to in each season: one type that shares the same element with the particular season that you are in and the other type belonging to an element which the former element restricts.

The Relationship between Internal Organs, Flavors, and Natural Food Colors

After learning what organs you need to pay the most attention to in the different seasons, the next step is to understand how to take care of them. According to TCM, different flavors from natural foods have healing benefits for different organs.

Simply speaking, sweetness nourishes the spleen; sourness, the liver; bitterness, the heart; pungency, the lungs; and, saltiness, the kidneys.

Through thousands of years of observation, the Chinese have also discovered that whole foods with specific colors have special healing benefits for particular parts inside the body. Although it may not always be the case, you can use this theory as a reference to help you choose what to eat.

The relationships between the colors in foods and the internal organs go like this: foods with red colors (such as watermelons and rose petals) nourish the heart; green foods (such as dark leafy greens) are believed to cleanse and detoxify the liver; white foods (such as white radishes and lotus seeds) can moisten the lungs; yellow foods (such as millet and rolled oats) are especially good for the spleen; and black foods (such as black beans and black sesame seeds) provide a rich supply of nutrition to the kidneys.

You can find example foods with five flavors in "Appendix B: Foods of Five Flavors", and more example foods with five colors in "Appendix C: Foods of Five Colors".

Putting Everything Together

With all of the knowledge that you have learned, here are three key takeaways which you should remember before we move on.

First, by using the five elements, you can find out the key organ(s) that you should pay the most attention to in a particular season; next, you refer to the supporting and restricting relationships between the elements and find out the other organ that can potentially be weakened in the same season; after figuring out the organs that you should primarily focus on, you then look into what foods you need to choose by using as a reference natural flavors from whole foods and natural food colors. Below is a chart to help you refresh your memory.

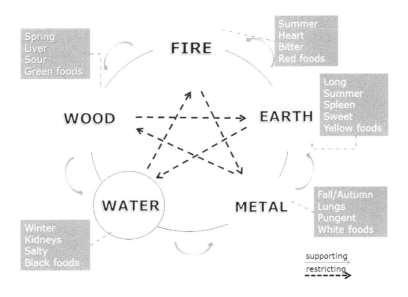

[Side note: if you cannot view it clearly, you could visit here for a

color version of this chart - http://bit.ly/5-elements-3.]

Chapter 4: Food Energies, Actions, and Movements

In Chapter 3, I mentioned that you can roughly tell the healing benefits of whole foods from food flavors and colors. Besides this, there are three other important food properties that you should know – energies, actions, and movements – to help you pick what to eat in the different seasons.

Let's talk about them one by one.

Food Energies

The five energies of foods are cold, cool, neutral, warm and hot. Make sure that you don't mix these adjectives – "cold", "cool", "neutral", "warm" and "hot" – with the actual physical temperatures of the foods that you can feel. The five words described here measure the energies given to the body inside, after the foods are digested.

The ancient Chinese believed that each kind of food has its own energy, and will have an effect on the body accordingly. To improve health, it is important to understand the different energies of different foods and to keep the energies inside the body in balance.

So, how do you achieve balance in the energies inside?

Simply put, to achieve balance means to consume foods that can bring the energies inside your body to a neutral state. Our bodies are usually not in balance; and the Chinese believe that the human body can be classified into two basic imbalanced categories: cold types (or yin types) and hot types (or yang types).

In other words, it is likely that you tend to have either more yin or yang in the body. To improve health and to achieve internal balance, you first need to find out what body type you have and then identify the kinds of foods, with the right energies, that you should have to balance out the excess yin (if you have a cold body type) or yang (if you have hot body type).

Let me give you a quick definition of what cold and hot body types mean (I've included details on what body types mean, why they are important, how to identify your own body type, and how to incorporate this concept into seasonal eating in the Bonus Chapter: http://bit.ly/sign-up-for-bonus-chapter).

If you constantly feel cold and not thirsty, and prefer hot or warm drinks, chances are you might have a cold physical constitution (or, yin body type) and excess yin. On the other hand, if you tend to feel hot and thirsty all the time and prefer drinking cold drinks, you might have a hot body type (or, yang body type) and excess yang.

So far, you've learned what the five energies are and how they can help the body to achieve balance on a theoretical level. Here's a specific example that demonstrates the healing benefits in foods: if you have a cold body type, it is suggested that you consume more ginger, ginseng, and wine, all of which have warm energies that can balance out your excess yin inside the body.

You can find more about foods of five different energies in "Appendix A: Foods with Five Energies".

Food Actions

There are two types of actions of foods: organic actions and common actions of foods.

Organic actions of foods refer to benefits for specific internal organs on which the foods can act. The Chinese focus on ten internal organs for dietary treatments: the liver, the gall bladder, the heart, the small intestine, the spleen, the stomach, the lungs, the large intestine, the kidneys, and the bladder. Each food is believed to be able to act on one or more internal organs. Additionally, food flavors serve as an important benchmark to determine the organic actions of foods, as you can tell from the last chapter.

Here are some examples for you: brown rice and millet act on the stomach; black sesame seeds and black rice act on the kidneys; white fungus and lotus seeds act on the lungs; and dark leafy greens act on the liver.

The second type of actions – common actions of foods – refers to the general benefits that foods can bring to you without referring to any specific internal organ. For example, to deal with heat stroke in the summer, you could consider having bitter melons; meanwhile, the same food can be also used for relieving constipation; and mung beans and Chinese barley are good for reducing breakouts and removing acne marks.

In "Appendix E: Foods with Different Organic and Common Actions", you will find a list of examples for foods with organic actions and common actions.

Food Movements

This is a rather complicated subject. I will describe this to you in these three areas: what are they, how to tell food movements, and how to use this property to heal the body and promote health.

1. What Are They

Food movements simply describe how the food energies move inside the body.

You can first think of the body divided into four regions: inside (internal region), outside (skin and body surface), upper body (above the waist), and lower body (below the waist). Based on these four regions, TCM has discovered that the energies of foods have a tendency to move inside the body in four directions: upwards, downwards, inwards, and outwards.

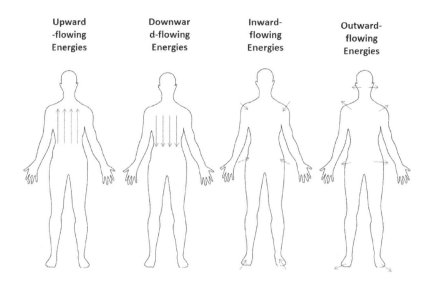

[Side note: if you cannot view it clearly, you could visit here for a larger version of this chart - http://bit.ly/food-movements.]

To move upwards means to move from the lower region to the upper region, whereas a downward movement means to move from the upper region to the lower region; moving from outside to inside means moving inwards, whereas moving from inside to outside indicates an outward movement.

Besides the four directions mentioned above, there are also two characteristics associated with food movements: glossy (sliding), and obstructive.

2. How to Tell Food Movements

You can tell a food movement by the direction a particular type of foods grows and by the flavors of the foods.

To give you a few examples, leaves and flowers, once consumed, tend to develop energies inside the body that move upwards; whereas after you consume roots, seeds, and fruits, the energies they produce may have a tendency to move downwards. But this is only a very general principle; and there are a lot of exceptions, according to Dr. Henry C. Lu, Traditional Chinese Medicine practitioner since 1972 and author of *Chinese System of Food Cures: http://bit.ly/chinese-system-to-food-cures*.

Additionally, as a general rule, sweet and pungent foods tend to have upward and outward movements, whereas sour and bitter foods tend to have downward and inward movements.

3. How to Use This Property to Heal the Body and Promote Health

According to TCM, to heal a certain health issue, you must first observe the direction that this particular health issue develops towards; then you use foods with movements in the opposite direction to restore the balance.

For example, foods with upward movements can relieve diarrhea, prolapse of the uterus, and falling of the stomach (which have downward movements). Foods with downward movements may relieve vomiting and hiccupping (both of which indicate upward movements). Foods with inward movements can ease abdominal swelling (which showcases an expanding motion). Finally, foods with outward movements can induce perspiration and reduce fever – to expel the internal heat out of the body (fever is considered to have an inward movement).

What's more, glossy foods (such as honey and spinach) can facilitate movements and are good for constipation, and internal dryness. On the other hand, obstructive foods (such as guava and olive) can prevent movements and are good for stopping diarrhea.

Lastly, TCM sees that the different seasons have their own movements, too. For example, winter has an inward movement (think about some animals choosing to hibernate). Because TCM believes it is important to follow the law of nature, it is important to enjoy foods with the same movements as the movements of the season that you are in. If it is winter (which has inward movements), it is recommended that you have more foods with the same movements.

Examples of foods arranged by their different movements are listed in "Appendix D: Foods of Four Movements".

As you will soon find out, from Part 2, these three basic food concepts are fundamental to help you understand what to eat in all seasons. At any point later on in this book, if you feel confused about these concepts you can revisit this part to refresh your memory and to enhance your knowledge of these three fundamental concepts.

Part 1 Summary

Through long-term observation, the ancient Chinese discovered that one year (about 365 days) can be equally divided into twenty four 15-day periods separated by 24 *jieqi*, and that each period describes a unique atmospheric pattern or a series of similar animal activities at that particular point in time.

Your body is, in fact, sensitive to environmental changes. This means that when there is a change in the environment after the arrival a particular *jieqi*, you need to especially pay attention to the body and listen to what it needs.

So, how can you take care of the body at different times and what foods should you give to the body?

Chinese food therapy, an over-two-thousand-year-old practice, can give you the answer.

First and foremost, it helps you to find out which organs tend to be out of balance and which organs you need to pay the most attention to at a particular time of the year, so that you know the parts inside your body you should give priority to.

Second, it summarizes the kind of foods that different parts of your body like and maps out in detail what kinds of foods have healing benefits for what particular parts inside the body.

Finally, it teaches you how to become a food expert and to be able to tell the healing properties of whole foods by looking at the food flavors, colors, energies, actions, and movements.

Now that you know all of the basic concepts and terms related to seasonal eating, let's move on to Part 2, where I share with you details about how to take care of the body in different seasons, general eating principles in each season, and specific eating tips for each *jieqi* and 15 days that follow.

Part 2: Seasonal Eating Details

Welcome to the juiciest part of this book!

Part 2 contains four sections ("Part 2-1: Spring Eating Details", "Part 2-2: Summer Eating Details", "Part 2-3: Autumn Eating Details", and "Part 2-4: Winter Eating Details") with each section dedicated to discussing eating guidelines for one season exclusively. Specifically, each section covers characteristics for one season, overall health guidelines for that particular season, and specific dietary practices based on these given health guidelines.

I will also talk about what each *jieqi* means, their characteristics, which explain why they are named this way, and key guidelines for taking care of the body for each particular *jieqi* and the 15 days the follow.

You may discover that how the Chinese are calculating the different seasons is quite different from when you think these seasons should start and finish. There is no right or wrong way to group days into seasons. To me, the formation of different seasons is just a summary of how nature behaves differently at different times.

The creation of *jieqi* can not only show you how nature behaves, but also invites you to pay more attention to the gradual changes around you, to listen to your body more closely, and to feed it with the right food at a particular time of the year.

Therefore, I recommend that you truly be aware of the difference in your body, while using the information below as a reference only. The last thing that you want to do is to follow the dietary advice given below for the sake of following the advice.

Make sure that you know that you need a change in diets because you can feel that your body is telling you to do so, not because it reaches a certain date on a calendar when you are told that you are supposed to do certain things.

Another thing that you should pay attention to is that the dietary suggestions listed for each 15-day period following each *jieqi* (you can refer to "Chapter 6: Specific Eating Guidelines in Six *Jieqi* in Spring", "Chapter 8: Specific Eating Guidelines in Six *Jieqi* in Summer", "Chapter 10: Specific Eating Guidelines in Six *Jieqi* in Autumn", and "Chapter 12: Specific Eating Guidelines in Six *Jieqi* in Winter") are the recommended priorities for you to pay attention to; this, however, doesn't mean that you should *only* pay attention to what's listed.

Instead, the general guidelines for each season (you can refer to "Chapter 5: General Eating Guidelines in Spring", "Chapter 7: General Eating Guidelines in Summer", "Chapter 9: General Eating Guidelines in Autumn", and "Chapter 11: General Eating Guidelines in Winter") still apply to all *jieqi* in that particular season. It is just that the main focus should be on the priorities given.

Enough said, let's get started.

Part 2-1: Spring Eating Details

I will walk you into spring where you are going to feel the freshness and energy of the season. In two chapters' time, you will learn the atmospheric characteristics of this season and of each of the 15-day periods led by the six different *jieqi* of this season; more importantly, I will clearly lay out a list of principles and dietary practices that you need to follow as a general guideline, and walk you through each *jieqi* to show you all of the fundamental dietary suggestions for the 15 days following each *jieqi*.

Specifically, in Chapter 5, I will talk about general spring eating principles where I will describe the overall climate in this first season of the year, and the overarching dietary suggestions based on Traditional Chinese Medicine.

Chapter 6 gets into details of each of the six *jieqi* in spring. By then you will know, though all of these six *jieqi* are in the same season, how they actually slightly differ from one another, if you pay attention to them closely, and what the priorities are for each 15-day period following each *jieqi*.

Chapter 5: General Eating Guidelines in Spring

Spring Characteristics

From time to time, I like to pay attention to the birds singing, right outside of my bedroom window, first thing in the morning as I open my eyes. There is a huge difference between what you can hear on a typical cold winter morning and the sounds that go into your ears on an early warmer spring morning:

There is only dead silence on a winter morning, when even the sun feels too cold to climb up to the sky; as spring slowly arrives, you gradually feel the spirits of birds eagerly wanting to clear their throats after their long silence over a cold winter. Sometimes, the singing scene is as boisterous as a crowded farmer's market on a sunny Saturday afternoon.

Usually, when there is a scene with lively spirits, warmer weather and a brighter morning sky, you can tell that spring has arrived.

Besides, Chinese medicine also sees that the energy in the season moves upwards and outwards. When you see small plants grow taller, or fresh green seedlings climb out of the soil and grow towards the sky, these scenes signify upward energy. Meanwhile, when you see budding flowers on trees or animals slowly move out from their caves to participate in all kinds of activities on earth, this is outward energy according to TCM.

As you see, movements and energy are not as mysterious or incomprehensible as you think. Instead, when you observe closely how objects grow or behave in nature, you can figure out the directions of movements in different seasons and where the energy is growing towards, too.

Another thing that you should pay attention to in spring is that there are stronger winds in this season, which can cause health concerns in various ways, if you don't take good care of yourself. To minimize the impact of strong winds on your health, I will include how to eat properly to protect yourself as well.

Spring Overall Health Guidelines

Specifically, there are four major principles to follow in this season:

First, you should consume foods with the same kind of energy and movements that spring has. Because the energy and movements associated with spring are both upwards and outwards (as mentioned above), you should consume more foods with upward and outward movements and energy as well.

Next, as you have learned from Chapter 3, in each season there is one particular organ that you need to pay close attention to, that the liver is the organ that you should focus on in spring, and that both spring and liver belong to the same element, wood.

From the same chapter, you have also learned that, to take care of your body in spring, you should not only pay attention to the liver, which shares the same element with spring, but also nourish the organ belonging to the element that wood restricts – earth. Chinese medicine believes that, if there is excess energy in the liver (a wood element), it can inhibit the functions of the spleen (an earth element). Thus, in spring, you should especially take good care of both the liver and the spleen.

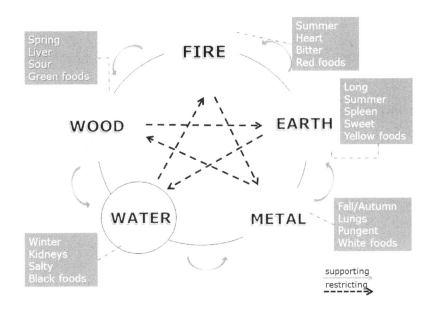

Spring
Liver
Sour
Green foods

FIRE

Summer
Heart
Bitter
Red foods

WOOD

EARTH

Long
Summer
Spleen
Sweet
Yellow foods

WATER

METAL

Fall/Autumn
Lungs
Pungent
White foods

Winter
Kidneys
Salty
Black foods

supporting
restricting

[Side note: if you cannot view it clearly, you could visit here for a color version of this chart - http://bit.ly/5-elements-3.]

Usually, in the winter right before spring, you eat a lot of warm foods with high calories to protect yourself from coldness, because your body needs it. Some people even consume a lot of strong alcoholic drinks or too much animal meat to keep the body warm. In the course of the entire winter, there may be excess internal heat buildup in your body, slowly causing the body to be out of balance.

That's why the third principle – eating light and clean – in the spring becomes important. It is an opportunity to rebalance the body by driving out internal excess heat.

Last but not least, it is wise to take dietary precautions to minimize health risks caused by the winds in spring. The windy season can cause dry skin, dry tongue, coughing, a sore throat, and other chronic diseases. One effective way to avoid, or alleviate, symptoms is to consume the right foods to nourish the skin, moisten an irritated throat, and to improve your immunity.

In conclusion, TCM recommends you follow these four key guidelines to ensure that you have a healthy body, strong immunity and good skin in spring: consuming foods with upward and outwards movements and energy, choosing to eat foods that especially take care of the liver and nourish the spleen, eating light meals, and protecting yourself from winds in this season.

Eight General Dietary Practices in Spring

In this section, I am about to share with you more specific suggestions for how you can put these four guidelines above into practice in your daily life.

1. Consuming Pungent and Sweet Foods with Warm Energies

So, what are the foods with upward and outward movements and energy?

If you still remember what I have mentioned in Chapter 4, you will quickly find the answer: usually sweet and pungent foods have upward and outward movements, while sour and bitter foods tend to have the opposite movements.

That's why it is recommended you enjoy more pungent and sweet foods in spring. Meanwhile, according to TCM, it is important to harness the yang energy in the season. In other words, consuming foods with warm energy – which protects the yang energy inside you – should also be in your dietary practice at that particular time.

Example pungent foods are: scallion, onion, garlic, ginger, radish, daikon, leek, and chives. Examples of sweet foods are: honey, sweet fruits, nuts, seeds, yams, sweet vegetables such as bamboo shoots, lotus roots, taro, beans, carrots, peas, and potatoes, and whole grains such as brown rice, millet, and barley.

You can find examples of foods with warm energies from pungent and sweet foods, as Chinese medicine has discovered that, in most cases, foods with pungency or sweetness have warm energy.

2. Consume More Vegetables

Green is the color of spring, and green foods are believed to act on the liver and strengthen its functions, according to TCM. Dark leafy green vegetables can detoxify the liver, and therefore cleanse the body. Additionally, a lot of skin-related problems – such as stomatitis, night vision problems, and glossitis – which are usually seen in spring – can be avoided, or effectively treated, by consuming more vegetables.

Example vegetables are: sprouts, chives, spinach, mustard greens, scallions, lettuce, asparagus, broccoli, cauliflower, garlic, leeks, eggplant, Chinese cabbage, celery, mushrooms, white fungus, black fungus, seaweed, potatoes, sweet potatoes, coriander (also known as cilantro, which is one of my favorites), and bok choy.

3. Consume Foods with Cooling and Calming Effects

If you find yourself easily becoming emotional or irritated in spring, chances are that you have developed imbalances or excess heat in the liver, which is commonly seen at this time of the year. In this case, sweet foods with calming and cooling properties are believed to be able to soothe emotions such as anger and impatience.

Recommended options are coconut milk, black sesame, celery, kelp, spring onion, and leafy greens. You could also try chrysanthemum tea with goji berries. Both chrysanthemums and goji berries are known for improving vision and for nourishing the liver. The herbal tea made of both ingredients has effective calming and cooling properties to help drive out excess heat in the liver.

I know that a lot of people are amazed by chrysanthemum tea's unique refreshing smell. Among the people I know who have enjoyed the tea for the first time, they have wished that they had been introduced to this tea sooner!

Another reason to consume this type of food is to balance out the excess heat that you might have accumulated from the previous winter. Normally, in a cold winter season, you wrap yourself up under warm jackets, spend as much time as possible staying in a heated room, sit close to the fireplace while enjoying a movie with your loved one, consume all kinds of warm foods, and maybe drink some glasses of red wine or even stronger alcoholic beverages.

These are all necessary activities to give you warmth and energy to fight the severe coldness of the winter. On the other hand, since TCM believes that there should be a balance in everything, constantly giving warmth to the body can lead to excess heat buildup inside and cause imbalance in the body. When spring arrives, this kind of imbalance can be manifested as dizziness and discomfort in four limbs.

As a result, Chinese medicine sees spring as the season to internally deal with energy imbalance and help the body recover from winter. To do this, consuming foods with cooling properties, as mentioned earlier, also helps.

4. Pick the Right Foods to Nourish Blood and Promote Blood Flow

Besides eating more vegetables and foods with cooling and calming effects to take care of the liver, another way to strengthen liver functions is to nourish the blood inside your body and to promote blood flow.

Example foods that nourish the blood and promote blood flow are: black rice, sesame seeds, goji berries, walnuts, mulberries, and vegetables such as spinach, mustard greens, soy-bean sprouts, mung-bean sprouts, cilantro, bamboo shoots, celery, and dandelion. If you are not a vegetarian or a vegan, you could try a small amount of beef, pork, and animal livers as well.

5. Increase the Intake of Sweet Foods but Reduce the Amount of Sour Foods

You already know that spring is the primary season to take care of the liver, and that sour foods can nourish the liver; but it doesn't mean that the more sour foods the better. Consuming too many whole foods with sour flavors can cause the liver to become too active. The overly active liver (a wood element) will restrict the functions of the spleen (an earth element).

The truth is: you'll want the spleen to perform properly at its best, because it is a very crucial organ inside the body – it helps to digest your food and absorb nutrients, and serves as part of the immune system, with roles like recycling old red blood cells and storing white blood cells.

Therefore, it is important to help the spleen function normally and to keep it in balance. To take care of the spleen, you can start from choosing foods with the right flavors. Remember to moderate the intake of sour foods and to consume more sweet foods as they can nourish the spleen.

You can find example sweet foods above. As for example sour foods, try plums, lemons, limes, apple cider vinegar, tomatoes, grape tomatoes, and pineapples.

6. Moderate or Avoid the Intakes of Hard, Sticky, Raw, Cold, and Oily Foods or Foods with Rich Flavors

Another tip to take care of the spleen is to be considerate and thoughtful by not consuming too many foods that are hard to digest. Foods that are hard to digest will cause more burden on the spleen. Think twice before you consume hard, sticky, raw, cold, and oily foods or foods with rich flavors. It's recommended that you moderate or avoid the intakes of those kinds of foods for better digestion. Examples are sticky rice, rice cakes, sashimi, sushi, fried foods, and creamy curry.

For hard foods, think about raw nuts. My Chinese doctor advises me to slightly cook or roast nuts, like walnuts and almonds, in the pan before I consume them. Alternatively, you could add nuts into whole grains and cook them together, which is what I usually do when I prepare my morning congee for breakfast.

7. Eat Foods that can Moisten the Mouth and Throat

Spring is a windy season that can cause dry, rough and itchy skin, dry mouth, dry tongue, and sore throats. That's why foods that can nourish the skin and moisten the mouth and throat are highly recommended such as whole grains, oranges, honey, white fungus, sesame seeds, sugarcane, Chinese yams, pears, Chinese dates, and lotus seeds.

8. Eat Foods that can Improve Your Immunity

There are not only more winds in spring, but unpredictable weather in this season as well. Additionally, warmer environments provide favorable conditions for bacteria to grow and spread. All of these factors combined explain why spring is often a time for multiple illnesses and diseases. This makes eating the right foods to improve your immune system particularly important.

Below are several tips to help you improve your immunity in spring. First, don't forget that breakfast should be the most important meal of your day. So, make sure that you have breakfast each morning and add protein to your diet.

Next, drinking enough water to stay hydrated is another great option.

Other great sources include green vegetables (such as mustard greens, spinach, celery, and scallions), seaweed, mushrooms, tomatoes, strawberries, oranges, and carrots.

Additionally, you can try Chinese herbs known for improving the immune system such as royal jelly and reishi mushrooms.

After learning the general characteristics about spring, let's now turn to the next chapter to go deeper into this season to uncover how the six *jieqi* in spring are different from one another, how they can affect your health, and how to eat accordingly, based on the differences.

Chapter 6: Specific Eating Guidelines in Six *Jieqi* in Spring

Do you still remember the six *jieqi* in spring?

To refresh your memory, let's go over them together. Specifically, they are: arrival of spring (*lichun*), increase of rains (*yushui*), awakening from hibernation (*jingzhe*), official spring (*chunfen*), freshness and clarity (*qingming*), and more rains and benefiting for growing crops (*guyu*). Below are details on the characteristics of the different *jieqi* in spring and how that can influence what you should eat in the days that follow.

Lichun (Arrival of Spring): Focus on Consuming Pungent and Sweet Foods and Foods with Warm Energy

Lichun starts from around February 5 of every year (if you reside in the southern hemisphere, it will be around August 5 of every year).

The Chinese name this "the arrival of spring" because usually you begin to feel more wind, more rain, more daylight, and warmer weather; you also see that ice starts to melt and that animals slowly become more active (for example, you see more fish swimming in the river; or, a few bugs climb out of their caves to receive sunlight).

By now, I believe that you have some ideas of what "movements" mean (otherwise, you can revisit Chapter 4 to familiarize yourself with the concept). With the scene described above, can you guess what energies there are at the start of spring? Because the energy is slowly being built up in early spring and animals gradually become active again by seeking more activities out of their caves, *lichun* already begins to demonstrate upward and outward movements.

As TCM believes that you should follow the law of nature and eat foods with the same movements as those in each *jieqi*, pungent, sweet foods and foods with warm energy are recommended. Pungent and sweet vegetables are believed to be especially good and should be your top choice at this time. You can consider having scallions, cilantro, Chinese red dates, peanuts, carrots, cauliflowers, broccoli, bok choy, green peppers, white radish, and chives. If you like seafood, you can try shrimps.

Yushui (Increase of Rains): Focus on Nourishing the Spleen

Yushui begins from around February 20 of each year (this will be around August 20 for people who reside in the southern hemisphere). As you can tell from its Chinese meaning, at this time there is slowly more precipitation, and there is more melting of ice into water.

As it is warm and not dry, TCM believes that it is a good opportunity to nourish the spleen, which is believed to be the foundation of good health and the secret to longevity. According to Traditional Chinese Medicine, if you nourish the spleen, you replenish and harness qi (flow of energy) inside the body, which then leads to an optimal state of health and well-being.

You've learned this from last chapter already: there are two ways to take care of the spleen. First, increase the intake of sweet foods; next, reduce the amount of sour foods and moderate the amount of foods that are hard to digest such as hard, sticky, raw, cold, and oily foods. So, these two aspects become your focus for *yushui* and the 15 days the follow.

Jingzhe (Awakening from Hibernation): Focus on Eating Light and Improving Your Immunity

From March 5 begins *jingzhe* (or September 5 in the Southern hemisphere).

The temperature continues to increase. At this time, more animals become active and spend more time outside for their own activities. Different organisms (including bacteria) start to reproduce and grow. That's why a lot of people easily get sick at this time. Thus, the key focus in *jingzhe* is to improve your immunity.

To strengthen your immune system, you need to include more variety of food choices into your diet, eat light meals, and consume more foods that can strengthen your body.

So, what does variety means? Ideally, you will include whole grains, vegetables, nuts, and seeds into your meals every day. In my book, *Food as Medicine: Traditional Chinese Medicine-Inspired Healthy Eating Principles with Action Guide, Worksheet, and 10-Week Meal Plan to Restore Health, Beauty, and Mind (http://bit.ly/food-as-medicine)*, I've specifically laid out details, and an action guide, on how to make sure that you incorporate a variety of choices into your diet.

For now, in order to get started, I would recommend that you begin by introducing whole grains (such as barley, millet, and brown rice), dark leafy green vegetables, seeds (such as black sesame seeds, hemp seeds, chia seeds, flax seeds, and pumpkin seeds), nuts (such as walnuts and almonds), and sauerkraut (I will include a recipe for you in Chapter 17).

Additionally, eating light means reducing the amount of oily foods and foods with strong flavors, such as creamy curry. Instead, consume more vegetables, whole grains, bean curds, and fish.

To improve your immunity, consume more foods rich in vitamin C such as chili peppers, bell peppers, bitter melons, broccoli, cauliflower, spinach, fungus, cilantro, bamboo shoots, oranges, papaya, and pomegranates.

Chunfen (Official Spring): Focus on Maintaining Your Internal Balance

Chunfen starts from March 21 (for people in the southern hemisphere, *chunfen* begins on around September 21).

On this day, the night and day hours each last 12 hours long. After March 21, the daytime on the northern hemisphere gets longer and nighttime gets shorter, while on the southern hemisphere the days get shorter and nights become longer.

TCM sees that when day and night share an equal amount of hours on March 21, this signifies that it is time to start paying more attention to restoring the yin and yang balance inside the body.

To get started, you will first need to know more about your body before seeking dietary solutions. In other words, you should know your body type first. After spending more than 30 years of research, Qi Wang, a well-respected professor at Beijing University of Chinese Medicine, who is one of the 500 most recognized Traditional Chinese Medicine practitioners selected by the Ministry of Personnel, the Ministry of Health, and the State Administration of Traditional Chinese Medicine, has concluded that there are nine basic body types and that there is at least one body type that applies to every person (yes, one can have multiples body types at the same time).

Below is a quick overview of the different body types – from which you can quickly find out if you belong to any of the body types – and the basic recommended dietary solutions. A summary has been laid out for you in "Appendix F: Foods for Nine Body Types". For now, let's briefly go over these nine body types.

1. If you constantly feel weak, tired and easily get sick, you may have a **qi deficiency** body type. You will first need to follow all of the basic guidelines laid out in Chapter 5 and perform more physical activities to nourish internal qi.

2. If you tend to have cold hands and feet, chances are that you might have a **yang deficiency** body type. It is recommended that you consume more foods with warm energy (such as sweet and pungent foods).

3. If you have a **yin deficiency** body type, then it is likely that you have dry skin, warm hands and feet, a red face, dry eyes, and dry stool. You tend to easily get thirsty. In this case, consider consuming more duck lotus root soup, lily bulbs, and sesame seeds.

4. A **blood stasis** person usually has dark eye circles, and easily gets bruises even if the person is only mildly hurt. If this applies to you, try seaweed, black beans, grapefruit,

and hawthorn berries.

5. A **dampness heat** person would usually have acne-prone skin and may have bad breath. If you belong to this body type, consider trying winter melons, watermelons, mustard greens, cucumbers, bitter lemons, and water spinach.

6. If you are a **qi depression** person, you will usually feel depressed and suffer from insomnia. In this case, you could try oatmeal, cilantro, radish, scallion, and rose tea.

7. If you have a body type of **phlegm dampness**, chances are that you might be overweight and feel heavy in all four limbs. For dietary solutions, consume more winter melons, radish, seaweed, and Chinese barley.

8. Last but not least, if you have a **special diathesis** body type, you will easily get allergies and are sensitive to environmental changes. Make sure that you cut down the intake of seafood, alcoholic beverages, and pungent foods.

Make sure you find out your own body type(s) and try out the dietary and lifestyle suggestions here to help bring your body back to a balanced state.

If you want to know even more, I've also included a bonus chapter (http://bit.ly/sign-up-for-bonus-chapter) to help you understand body types, how to accurately identify your body type, and basic lifestyle suggestions. I hope you'll enjoy it.

Qingming (Freshness and Clarify): Continue to Focus on Improving Your Immune System

Qingming arrives on April 4 (this is around October 4 if you live in the Southern hemisphere).

From its Chinese translation, you can tell this is a *jieqi* that makes you feel refreshed. That's because the weather continues to be warmer, grass and trees continue to grow, and flowers blossom. What's more, after rain you will be able to see rainbows at this time.

The difference in temperature is distinct in *qingming*. It is recommended that you keep yourself warm, and continue to focus on strengthening your immunity around this time.

Guyu (More Rains and Benefiting for Growing Crops): Focus on Driving out Dampness inside the Body

Guyu begins from around April 21 (around October 21 for people in the Southern hemisphere).

During this time, there is an increase in the amount of rain and the temperature climbs up more quickly. *Guyu* is believed to be a good time for the farmers to become more actively engaged in farming, as the heavier rains can be used to irrigate the crops to help them grow.

Due to the increase in humidity in the air, TCM sees that this can increase dampness inside the body, which leads to poor digestion, heaviness in the head and the whole body, joint pains, and sore muscles. Therefore, removing dampness is the priority of this *jieqi*.

Foods that can help to treat, and relieve, the symptoms include Chinese barley, Chinese yams, lotus leaves, winter melons, white radishes, lotus roots, bamboo shoots, and soy bean sprouts.

Part 2-1: Spring Eating Details Summary

Spring is a season of hope and new lives. There is warmer weather, longer daylight hours, stronger winds, more rain, and a growing number of animal activities on earth.

Seasonal changes lead to changes in the body. This means that you need to adjust your lifestyle accordingly – particularly what you choose to eat – to take care of the body to maintain and improve health.

To maintain a strong and healthy body in spring, choose to eat foods by following four guidelines:

Consume foods with upward and outward movements, such as pungent and sweet foods, and foods with warm energy; consume foods that nourish the liver and the spleen, enjoy light meals that are easy to digest, and eat more foods that can nourish the skin, moisten the throat, and improve your immune system.

There are different priorities that you need to pay attention to in six *jieqi*:

In *lichun* (arrival of spring), focus on consuming pungent and sweet foods and foods with warm energy; in *yushui* (increase of rain), place more emphasis on nourishing the spleen; in *jingzhe* (awakening from hibernation), pay more attention to eating light and improving your immunity; in *chunfen* (official spring), focus on restoring your internal balance; in q*ingming* (freshness and clarity), you should continue to focus on improving your immunity; and in the last jieqi in Spring – *guyu* (more rains and benefiting for growing crops), you need to focus on driving out internal dampness.

By now you have learned all of the basic dietary principles for spring. Let's continue on the journey and discover summer eating guidelines.

Part 2-2: Summer Eating Details

Summer is a time when you are going to feel the dynamic vibrancy of the season. In the following two chapters, I will show you the atmospheric characteristics in this season and in each of the six *jieqi* of summer; you will find a list of seven principles to follow, as a general guideline and all of the fundamental dietary suggestions for those 15 days after each *jieqi*.

Specifically, in Chapter 7, I will talk about general summer eating principles where I describe the overall climate in this second season of the year and the overarching dietary suggestions for this season, based on the teaching of Traditional Chinese Medicine.

Chapter 8 gets into the details of each of the six *jieqi* in summer and the dietary priorities that you need to give to each *jieqi* and the 15 days that follow.

Chapter 7: General Eating Guidelines in Summer

Summer Characteristics

Summer is the most vibrant season of the year. It is the time when plants grow the fastest and start to produce fruits.

It demonstrates abundant outward and upward energy in nature. As you learned from the "food movements" section in Chapter 4, this means that the temperature rises and plants grow tall more rapidly (which showcases upward movements), plants yielding fruits and more people seek different kinds of outdoor activities like surfing, swimming, and enjoying concerts at an open-air venue (both of which demonstrate outward movements).

As the temperature goes up, summer is also the time of the year when you can easily associate the season with air-conditioning, iced tea, tank tops, shorts, and sandals. Hot summer weather drives you to seek different activities to expel heat and helps you to determine what to wear to stay cool.

Besides, there is also high humidity in the air, which can keep the summer heat from being released from the body, making you feel uncomfortable and triggering a series of potential health issues such as inflammation in the joints and heart diseases.

Summer Overall Health Guidelines

Specifically, there are **seven** major principles to follow in this season: first, you should consume foods with the same kind of energy and movements summer has. Because the energy and movements associated with summer are both upwards and outwards, you should consume more foods with upward and outward movements. In other words, summer is a time to harness the yang energy inside you, by performing various kinds of activities.

Next, as you have learned from Chapter 3, in each season there is one particular organ that you need to pay close attention to. Since both summer and the heart belong to the same element, fire, TCM sees that the heart is the organ that you should focus on in summer. You have already learned that, in order to take care of your body in summer, you should not only pay attention to the heart, which shares the same element with Summer, but you should also nourish the organ belonging to the element that fire restricts – metal.

That's because the process of nourishing the heart (a fire element), can lead to a weakening in the functions of the lungs (metal elements). Chinese medicine believes that, if there is excess energy in the heart (a fire element), it can inhibit the functions of the lungs (metal elements). Thus, in essence, summer is the time when you should especially take good care of both the heart and the lungs.

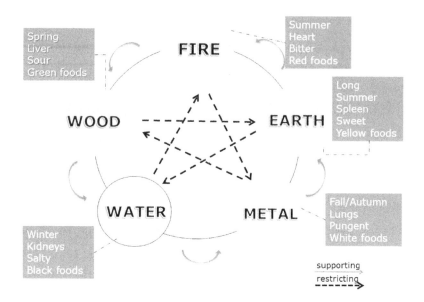

Spring
Liver
Sour
Green foods

FIRE

Summer
Heart
Bitter
Red foods

WOOD

EARTH

Long
Summer
Spleen
Sweet
Yellow foods

WATER

METAL

Fall/Autumn
Lungs
Pungent
White foods

Winter
Kidneys
Salty
Black foods

supporting

restricting

[Side note: if you cannot view it clearly, you could visit here for a larger version of this chart - http://bit.ly/5-elements-3.]

Besides the heart and the lungs, the other two organs that you need to take care of are the spleen and the stomach. Since summer has high humidity, which can lead to a series of health problems. One of them is restricting digestive system functions. This can be manifested as poor appetite and digestion, diarrhea, bloating, dizziness, and nausea. Therefore, it becomes particularly important to strengthen the functions of both the spleen and the stomach by eating the right foods and avoiding certain foods.

By now, you know that the energy in the lungs (metal elements) can be restricted by the heart (a fire element), the organ that you should primarily pay attention to in summer. In fact, the energy in both the liver and the kidneys is also weakened in summer, according to TCM. As a result, your task is not only to take care of the heart and make sure that its energy does not become excess, but also to make sure that all of these organs – the lungs, the liver, and the kidneys – are properly nourished and strengthened.

A fifth area that you should pay attention to is staying hydrated. This is easy to understand: summer is a season when you often get thirsty because you sweat easily at this time of the year. Even some of the mildest movements can cause you to sweat in hot humid weather:

I have a body type that tends to not perspire easily, which means that I can have no sweat at all or shed only a few drops of sweat even when I play tennis in the winter. But, in summer, when I do yoga with some mild movements involving a few poses that enhance upper and lower body strength (like five push-ups and warriors poses), I can easily sweat while doing them.

The tricky thing is how to keep yourself hydrated. For some people, drinking ice tea or cold water makes them feel good and stay cool. That's why they keep doing so whenever they feel thirsty. Some people do not drink water for a whole day in a hot summer and then suddenly drink a lot of water at one time, to relieve excessive thirst, as soon as they get home at the end of the day.

In fact, *neither* way is recommended.

Besides, staying hydrated in the summer is important to keep the body functioning normally; at the same time, *how* you consume water is also important.

In the next section "General Dietary Practices in Summer", I will explain why it is not good to consume too much ice water or suddenly drink a large amount of water all at once; from the same section, you will also learn how to drink water more scientifically.

The sixth and seventh areas are eating foods that can drive out excess heat and dampness internally. According to Traditional Chinese Medicine, hot summer weather means heat and dampness can be easily accumulated inside the body, leading to excess heat buildup. Expelling the heat and dampness out of the body becomes important to keep the body and internal organs in balance.

This is particularly important for people with acne-prone skin. TCM sees that people of this kind have a body type that belongs to dampness heat, which means that they often accumulate excess heat and dampness inside the body.

Not clearing excess heat and dampness in summer can worsen the situation, and lead to more breakouts. My body type belongs to dampness heat. That's why I particularly pay attention to selecting foods that can bring down the heat and remove the dampness inside my body in summer.

The takeaway here is to focus on consuming foods that can bring down internal heat and expel dampness, especially for those who have a dampness heat body type.

In review, TCM recommends that you follow these seven key guidelines to ensure that you have a healthy body, strong immunity and good skin in summer:

- Consuming foods with upward and outward movements and yang energy
- Choosing to eat foods that especially take care of the heart
- Selecting foods that can strengthen the stomach and the spleen
- Consuming foods that can improve the functioning of the

weakened liver, kidneys, and lungs in this season

- Staying hydrated in a scientific way
- Eating foods that bring down internal heat
- Choosing foods that remove internal dampness

General Dietary Practices in Summer

In this section, I am about to share with you how you can put these **seven** guidelines above into practice in your daily life with more specific suggestions.

Consuming foods with upward and outward movements and yang energy

One way to harness yang energy inside the body is to **consume warm foods**. For example, drinking congee in the morning and in the evening helps to relieve thirst, to expel heat from inside the body, and to nourish the body.

By mixing different foods into the congee and cooking them together, you can achieve different health benefits from properties of each type of food, while replenishing and circulating yang energy. As an example, if you mix red beans with brown rice and make the mixture into a congee, it can improve kidney functions and relieve swelling.

Consuming congee has now become my everyday habit; it helps to nourish my skin and to keep my body hydrated. I highly recommend that you try it. I will share with you my favorite congee recipes in "Part 3: Seasonal Eating Recipes", so that you can also start benefiting from congee.

As a reminder, you can find more food choices with upward and outward movements in "Appendix D: Foods with Four Movements".

Choosing to eat foods that especially take care of the heart

According to TCM, the heart and your mind are closely connected. Therefore, summer is a time to take care of the heart as well as the mind (in fact, the Chinese character used to describe "heart" can also be referred to as "mind"). Specifically, below are two ways that you to take care of the heart in this season.

It is important to **consume foods that can calm your mind**. In summer, TCM sees that high temperatures can easily cause excess heat accumulation inside the body, which leads to heat imbalance in the heart (TCM calls this "heart fire"). Symptoms can be that you easily feel impatient or irritated.

Consuming foods that soothe your mind can definitely help here. Foods known for soothing your mind include millet, rose petals, lotus seeds, and longan.

Next, make sure that you also **consume foods that can strengthen your heart functions**. Consider such foods as ginger, blackberries, blueberries, strawberries, and raspberries.

Selecting foods that can strengthen the stomach and the spleen

In Chapter 3, I mention that there are five seasons in a year, according to TCM. After summer, Chinese have figured out that there is also a "long summer" right before autumn. This is a time where there is an increased amount of humidity in the air, which can lead to an excess amount of dampness accumulated in the spleen and the stomach and, therefore, cause energy imbalance in these two organs, and restrict their functions.

To improve and support the functions of both organs, I've collected five suggestions for your reference:

First, since an increased amount of dampness is the number one issue that can cause deteriorating stomach and spleen functions, **eating foods that can expel dampness from the body becomes the key**. Example foods that can remove dampness include millet, Chinese barley, winter melon, red beans, mung beans, and black beans.

Next, it is important to **minimize the intake of raw and cold foods**. It seemingly makes sense to consume cold foods to cool down the body in hot summer weather. But, consuming too many cold and raw foods on a regular basis can hurt the digestive system and may cause more harm than good.

For example, consuming cold foods can cause irregular contractions inside the stomach, which can lead to stomachache, diarrhea, poor appetite, and a series of disorders in the stomach and spleen function.

Also, **watch out for food contamination,** particularly in this season, because warmer temperatures provide a favorable environment for bacteria to grow. Here is an example showing how bugs and bacteria are more active in summer:

Have you noticed that there are more fruit flies in summer than in winter? In summer, I would usually buy greenish yellow bananas. They become ripe (with yellow color and a few dark spots) in just a few days; and then you start discovering fruit flies flying and dancing happily around. But in winter, bananas can stay fresh yellow for an entire week without attracting any fruit flies!

Make sure that you keep your food in a safe and clean place that can best keep it away from bugs or flies. Also, I know from personal experience that it is best to try to avoid leftovers in summer, as foods can easily go bad or stale around this time.

Another way to protect your stomach and spleen is to **control your food intake**. Overeating can cause too much burden on these two major organs in the digestive system and can lead to bloating, constipation, obesity, and other health issues.

A good practice is to stop eating as soon as you feel eighty percent full. Studies show that it takes about 20 minutes for the signals sent by the stomach to reach the brain.

Therefore, what you are feeling at the moment while you finish eating does not necessarily show how your stomach *truly* feels. When you become eighty percent full, chances are you might be very full already. You just need some 20 minutes for your brain to receive this message from your stomach.

Lastly, make sure that you **minimize the intake of fried and greasy foods**. These foods are hard to digest and cause extra burden to the stomach and to the spleen as well. Consuming too many of these kinds of food can also deplete your energy, making you feel drowsy and tired all day long.

If possible, always opt for eating lights foods like vegetables (especially dark leafy greens), whole grains, fruits, and lean protein such as hemp seeds, and organic chicken breast.

Consuming foods that can improve functions of weakened liver, kidneys, and lungs in the season

Traditional Chinese Medicine sees that bitterness can strengthen and nourish the heart. Yet, too much bitterness can cause the heart (a fire element) to become overactive, which also leads to weakening of the lungs (metal elements). Since pungency is believed to strengthen and nourish the lungs, it is recommended that you **consume more foods with pungent flavors while cutting down the intake of bitter foods**.

Example pungent foods are ginger, scallions, garlic, onions, and chili peppers. Example bitter foods are bitter melons, broccoli rabe (also known as rapini), lettuce, arugula, and turmeric.

This, however, doesn't mean that I am suggesting that you avoid bitter food at all. Rather, you do need to eat a proper amount of bitter food each day. It's just that you need to find a fine balance and intentionally consume more pungent foods in this season to maintain the balance.

The next tip is to be sure to **cut down your intake of raw and cold foods** for the health of your kidneys. Not only can raw and cold foods hurt both the stomach and the spleen. In fact, they can also restrict kidney functions. From this, you can see that there is only very little benefit from consuming cold or raw foods too often.

Then, what about foods that can nourish the kidneys? As a general rule, whole foods that contain dark colors – such as black sesame, black beans, black rice, and black fungus – can all nourish the kidneys and should be consumed on a regular basis for supporting and improving kidney functions. So, **enjoy more foods that are black in color**.

To nourish the liver, it helps to **strengthen the liver functions when you consume more sour foods**. Lemon is a great option here. I highly suggest drinking 500ml of warm water with the juice from a half or a whole lemon as the first thing that you do in the morning. This is what I do every morning to detoxify the body, stimulate bowel movements, and nourish the liver.

Another way to protect the liver is to **eat lots of dark leafy green** to help detoxify the organ.

Staying hydrated in a scientific way

Earlier, I mention two ways of drinking water which are not recommended: drinking ice or cold water all the time (or regularly), and consuming a large amount of water at one time, to relieve excessive thirst.

Usually, a better way of helping the body to stay hydrated is to **drink a small amount of water multiple times throughout the day**, which helps to slow down sweating and the evaporation of your skin' moisture.

Most people do not drink water until they feel thirsty. The fact is that, when you feel thirsty, it can be a sign that the cells inside your body are already severely dehydrated, which may start to cause negative impacts in different parts of the body in various ways. So, make sure that you proactively allocate the time for drinking water throughout the day, instead of waiting until the point at which you feel thirsty.

If you are very athletic, and sweat a lot while performing your preferred sports, **consider adding some salt into your drinking water to replenish electrolytes after physical activities**. Juice from young coconut water is a great natural source of electrolytes, which can be your post-workout drink.

Eating foods that bring down internal heat

There are two things that you need to pay attention to here. The first thing is, of course, to **eat foods that can balance out internal heat**. Suitable foods include millet, rose petals, lotus seeds, longan, bitter melons, Chinese barley, winter melon, and green tea.

Additionally, make sure that you **moderate the intake of cold drinks**. Constantly consuming cold drinks can inhibit digestive system functions and lead to bloating, discomfort in the stomach, and diarrhea.

Here is a second reason: the cold drinks that you buy in grocery stores or supermarkets usually contain sugar. This means that the more you drink, the more dehydrated you will be, and the more thirsty you will feel.

As you see, consuming cold drinks does not help with relieving thirst at all.

Choosing foods that remove internal dampness

By now you know that it is important to drive out the dampness inside your body to support spleen functions (you may revisit the section above regarding what to eat to nourish and strengthen the spleen for reference).

After learning the general characteristics about summer, let's now turn to the next chapter to go deeper into this season to uncover how the six *jieqi* in summer are different from one another, how they can affect your health, and how to eat accordingly based on the differences.

Chapter 8: Specific Eating Guidelines in Six *Jieqi* in Summer

To refresh your memory, let's go over them together. They are: arrival of summer (*lixia*), crops almost mature but not fully ripe (*xiaoman*), grains becoming mature (*mangzhong*), official summer (*xiazhi*), weather becoming hotter (*xiaoshu*), and weather becoming the hottest (*dashu*).

As you can see from the common pattern across all six *jieqi*, the key theme is that there are rising temperatures and increasing humidity day by day. While the key dietary principles are the same – to bring down internal heat and to drive out dampness, you switch the priority in each *jieqi* as the level of humidity increases and as temperatures continue to rise.

In addition, as autumn approaches day by day, your priority should be directed to starting to prepare for the next two seasons: autumn and winter.

Personally, I really enjoy these subtle changes between *jieqi*, as it guides you to pay closer attention to nature and to feel its dynamism and vibrancy, helping you stay with nature as one.

Lixia (Arrival of Summer): Focus on Protecting and Nourishing the Heart

Lixia starts from around May 5 of every year (if you reside in the Southern hemisphere, it will be around November 5 of every year).

The Chinese name this "the arrival of summer" because usually you start to notice that the temperatures are continuing to go up and that there is more rain (in some places there are even rain storms); you will also see that trees are growing more rapidly at around this time.

It's a time to concentrate on taking care of your heart and mind, since TCM associate these two together. As you learned from the last chapter, there are two ways to do so: consume foods that can calm your mind, and eat more food that can strengthen heart functions.

Make sure that you incorporate these two tips into your daily life at the start of summer, set them as your priority, and revisit Chapter 7 if you want to refresh your memory on specific details.

Xiaoman (Crops Almost Mature but not Fully Ripe): Focus on Preventing Diseases

Xiaoman begins from around May 21 of each year (this will be around November 21 for people who reside in the Southern hemisphere).

Summer season crops grow rapidly at this time. They have almost become mature but are not yet fully ripe, hence the name *Xiaoman*, the direct translation of which is "a little bit full". For most of the time, this *jieqi* provides especially favorable conditions for crops to grow: plenty of rain, lots of sunlight, and warm temperatures.

As there are warmer temperatures and more rain, it can easily trigger various health issues such as join pains and skin problems. As a result, it is important to take care of the body, to strengthen the body's immune system, and to take all precautions possible to protect yourself from diseases.

According to Traditional Chinese Medicine, if you wait until you get sick before starting to pay attention to treating your body, it can be too late to cure a disease. TCM believes that a wise way to stay strong and healthy for the long term is to notice any trace of discomfort at an early stage and start treating it before it worsens and becomes a disease. In other words, TCM focuses on disease prevention.

That's why in *xiaoman*, a time when you are likely to get joint pains, skin problems, or a series of other health issues, it is crucial to do the right things to help the body to digest well, function better, and stay in balance.

The way you eat contributes a lot to helping to make a stronger body. In *xiaoman*, make sure that you are on a plant-based diet, and eat foods that can expel heat, and drive out dampness accumulated at this time.

Mangzhong (Grains Becoming Mature): Focus on Sun Protection, Dampness Prevention, and Improving Immunity

From June 5 begins *mangzhong* (for people in the Southern hemisphere, *mangzhong* begins on around December 5).

At this time, farmers start to harvest the summer season crops, most of which are grains. It is also a time when the air is very heavy, moist, and sultry. It is not uncommon to see foods, utensils, and clothes easily get moldy at this time.

When you look closely at both *xiaoman* (crops almost mature but not fully ripe) and *mangzhong*, you will see that there actually aren't that many differences. In *mangzhong*, there are also more rains and warmer temperatures. So, it makes sense that you should continue to work on eating the rights foods to drive out dampness, and to improve immunity to strengthen your body.

As temperatures get even hotter, sun protection becomes more and more important. Therefore, pay special attention to eating the right foods that can effectively remove excess heat in the body, and particularly in the heart.

Xiazhi (Official Summer): Focus on Expelling Excessive Heat in the Heart and Moderating Intake of Cold Foods

Xiazhi starts from around June 21 (this is around December 21 if you live in Southern hemisphere).

The direct translation of *xiazhi* to Chinese is that "summer has officially arrived". Starting from *xiazhi*, temperatures become extremely hot. It is believed to be the time when the crops grow the fastest.

I think that the message is clearly expressed here – because the temperatures become extremely hot starting from *xiaozhi*. All heat-removing activities should become the focus on this *jieqi*.

One thing worth mentioning is that, in today's modern world, people like to seek direct and quick ways to achieve results. This can be seen in the fact that a lot of people enjoy cold water, ice cream, or ice cream cakes, hoping to quickly bring down body heat and to help the body feel more comfortable.

But, as I mentioned in Chapter 5, consuming cold foods and drinks, on a regular basis, can trigger a series of health issues. That's why it is important to become a little disciplined with yourself to control your intake of the myriad of cold dietary options out there, for the sake of your long-term health.

Xiaoshu (Weather Becoming Hotter): Focus on Heatstroke Prevention and Consuming More Water

Xiaoshu arrives roughly on July 7 (around January 7 for people in the Southern hemisphere).

At this time, temperatures continue to become higher and higher; however, it has not yet reached the hottest time of the year. The direct translation for *xiaoshu* can be "a small amount of summer heat".

Usually at this time, you may see that trees grow so many leaves that they are able to provide shade for people who stand underneath. Because of rising temperatures, you will that the heat is gradually becoming more and more intense.

As temperatures become even higher, it is time to really focus on heatstroke prevention. Dizziness, headache, insomnia, feeling easily agitated, becoming impatient, and nausea – these are all symptoms showing that you are "attacked" by excess heat on this *jieqi*. As you may have noticed already, the focus has been slightly shifted to preventing and bringing down internal heat.

Dashu (Weather Becoming the Hottest): Focus on Cooling Down Your Body and Strengthening It to Prevent Illnesses You Are Prone to in Winter

Dashu begins from around July 22 (or, January 22 in the Southern hemisphere).

Welcome to the hottest time of the year! From *lixia* (arrival of summer), the temperature constantly climbs up in each *jieqi*; in *dashu* that the temperature reaches its peak. If you directly translate *dashu* from the Chinese, it is "a large amount of summer heat".

Heat can be the most intense at this time, making you feel very uncomfortable. From time to time, there will be big rain storms during this *jieqi*.

Needless to say, with *dashu* being the hottest *jieqi* of the year, the top priority definitely goes to preventing summer heat and cooling down your own body.

One thing that I would also like to particularly point out here is this: because *dashu* is the last *jieqi* in summer right before autumn, TCM sees that it is also a time when you start thinking about taking care of the body to get ready for the coming seasons.

One of the key characteristics in TCM to keep the body away from diseases is that you need to treat your winter illnesses in summer, with a mindset of preventing a problem before it happens.

Some people tend to develop certain diseases at the same time every year. TCM believes that it can help this type of people alleviate, or even avoid, these diseases if they start early to strengthen and nourish the body under a practitioners' guidance.

While this – how to strengthen the body to prevent illnesses that you are prone to in winter – is beyond the scope of this book, I think it is important enough to bring this to your attention, to help you become more aware of how to take care of yourself from a new and fresh angle. You can visit a TCM practitioner for further details if you would like to know more about this.

Part 2-2: Summer Eating Details Summary

Summer is a season with lots of dynamism, vibrancy, and energy for growth. There is warmer weather, more sunlight, more rain and rain storms, and a growing number of animal activities on earth.

To maintain a strong and healthy body in summer, choose the food you eat by following the **seven** guidelines:

Consume foods with upward and outward movements and yang energy; eat foods that especially take care of the heart; select foods that can strengthen the stomach and the spleen; consume foods that can improve the function of the weakened liver, kidneys, and lungs in the season; stay hydrated in a scientific way; eat foods that bring down internal heat; and choose foods that remove internal dampness.

There are different priorities that you need to pay attention to in the six *jieqi* in summer:

In *lixia* (arrival of summer), focus on protecting and nourishing the heart; in *xiaoman* (crops almost mature but not fully ripe), place more emphasis on preventing diseases; in *mangzhong* (grains becoming mature), pay more attention to sun protection, dampness prevention, and improving immunity; in *xiazhi* (official summer), focus on expelling excessive heat in the heart and moderating your intake of cold foods; in *xiaoshu* (weather becoming hotter), you should focus on heatstroke prevention and consuming more water; and in the last *jieqi* in summer – *dashu* (weather becoming the hottest), you need to focus on cooling down your body and strengthening it to prevent any illnesses that you are prone to in winter.

By now you have learned all of the basic dietary principles for summer. Let's move on to discover healthy eating guidelines for autumn, the golden season.

Part 2-3: Autumn Eating Details

We are about to walk into a fruitful and golden season. The following two chapters talk about atmospheric characteristics in autumn and in each of the six *jieqi* at this time; more importantly I have summarized general guidelines and best practices and will walk you through each *jieqi* to show you all of the fundamental dietary suggestions for the 15 days after each *jieqi*.

Specifically, Chapter 9 talks about general autumn eating principles where I will describe the overall climate in this third season of the year and the overarching dietary suggestions, based on Traditional Chinese Medicine.

Chapter 10 gets into the details of how to take care of the body differently in each of the six *jieqi* in autumn and on the days that immediately follow these *jieqi*.

Chapter 9: General Eating Guidelines in Autumn

Autumn Characteristics

For some people, autumn is a beautiful and fruitful season. It is a time when most crops become mature and it is the golden time for harvest. It is also a time when the leaves on the trees start changing colors, forming a picturesque scene, as if Mother Nature puts on an oil-painting art exhibition to show off her talents in capturing mesmerizing moments in the season.

Some others find autumn less pleasant, perhaps depressing or even annoying. Temperatures start to drop more rapidly, as it gets closer to winter; flowers begin to wither; night hours get longer and longer; the weather get drier and drier; in some places, leaves are falling from the trees and continue to do so until the trees are bare and look completely "dead"; and there are fewer activities out on the street.

Whatever you feel emotionally, or whatever you see through the filter of your eyes, may vary; yet, the pattern of changes that go through autumn stay the same: matured crops, golden colors, colorful leaves, dropping temperatures, withering flowers, longer night hours, dry temperatures, falling leaves, and fewer outdoor activities. All these little facts together make up the word that you now know called "autumn".

According to Traditional Chinese Medicine, the movements associated with this season are downward and inward.

Autumn Overall Health Guidelines

Specifically, there are **three** major principles to follow in this season: first, you should consume foods with the same kind of energy and movements that autumn has. Because the energy and movements associated with autumn are both downward and inward, you should consume more foods with downward and inward movements. In other words, autumn is a time to harness the yin energy inside you by performing various kinds of activities.

Next, by now you know that, in each season there is one particular organ that you need to pay close attention to. Since both autumn and the lungs belong to the same element, metal, TCM sees that the lungs are the organ that you should focus on in this season.

To take care of your body in autumn, you should not only pay attention to the lungs, which share the same element with autumn, but should also nourish the organ belonging to the element that metal restricts – wood. That's because the process of nourishing the lungs (metal elements) can lead to weakening of the liver (a wood element). In other words, if there is excess energy in the lungs (metal elements), it can inhibit the functions of the liver (a wood element).

Thus, in essence, autumn is the time when you should especially take good care of both the lungs and the liver.

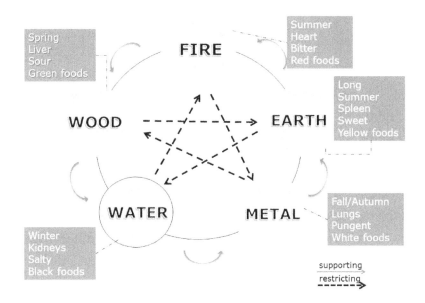

[Side note: if you cannot view it clearly, you could visit here for a color version of this chart - http://bit.ly/5-elements-3.]

Besides the lungs and the liver, other organs that you should pay attention to are the spleen and the stomach. Here's why.

For a lot of the people, summer is the time when you consume a lot of energy from the body either by sweating or performing different kinds of physical activities. As you move into autumn and the temperatures start to drop, your body might start to crave for more nourishing foods to replenish nutrients and to store more energy inside the body. In fact, you may notice this signal by having an increased appetite, too.

It is then recommended to consume foods that are more nourishing which, according to my experience, usually contain larger amounts of fats (think about black and white sesame seeds, all sorts of nuts), carbohydrates (for example lotus seeds, whole grains, pumpkins, or sweet potatoes), and animal proteins (such as chicken and lamb).

In order to assist the body to better digest and absorb all of the foods that you consume, it is important to strengthen the functions of the spleen and the stomach, the digestive powerhouse in your body. That's why taking good care of the spleen and the stomach should also be a focus in autumn.

Here's a side note for you: due to the dropping temperatures and improving appetite, some people may immediately start seeking to consume more nutrient-dense foods such as lamb and warm chicken soup on a constant basis. As a matter of fact, this is not recommended, according to TCM. Instead, you should take it slowly by making the transition one step at a time.

So, what are the three key health principles that you've just learned?

In autumn, you should consume foods that can nourish your yin energy within, pay special attention to taking care of the lungs and the liver, and strengthen spleen and stomach functions to improve your digestion. By following these tips, you will efficiently turn what you eat into energy and power to help you perform your everyday tasks energetically and powerfully.

In the section that follows, I am going to explain in detail specific health tips guided by these three principles. Let's move on.

General Dietary Practices in Autumn

In this section, I will share with you how you can put these **three** guidelines above into practice in your daily life with more specific suggestions.

Consuming foods that can nourish your yin energy within

One way to harness yin energy inside the body is to **consume foods that can nourish the yin inside the body.** These are good options to replenish yin: millet, whole grains, hawthorn berries, fruits like apples, pears, bananas and grapes, loach, sesame seeds, walnuts, lily bulbs, sticky rice, honey, peanuts, fresh Chinese yam, white fungus, red dates, American ginseng, and sugar cane.

Taking care of the lungs and liver

In Chapter 3, we have talked about different food flavors and how they can act on the different organs inside you; you have further learned that pungent foods can especially nourish the lungs. While it is right that a proper amount of pungent foods, such as ginger, can strengthen lung functions, too many of them can lead to excess energy buildup in the lungs, leading to imbalance.

As a result, it is recommended that you **moderate the intake of pungent foods** (however, do not misinterpret this message as suggesting that you not consume pungent foods at all).

Next, it is important to **enjoy white foods on a regular basis**. Mother Nature has left you a lot of clues to look for real gems and to make sure that you don't miss them. If you look into nature, a lot of white foods have lung-nourishing and lung-moistening benefits. Examples are lotus seeds, Chinese yam, white radishes, lily bulbs, water chestnuts, white fungus, winter melons, tofu, and white chrysanthemum flowers.

As the weather gets drier and drier day by day in autumn, which can trigger a series of respiratory infections, consuming moisturizing white foods in this season becomes the key to maintaining good health, especially in the lungs.

A third way to nourish the lungs is to **consume whole foods that can replenish qi and improve qi circulation**. TCM defines the life-force energy circulating inside the body as qi and believes that: if there are no blockages that prevent qi flow, inside the body and if you focus on replenishing qi for your body, then all of your internal organs will be nourished and strengthened. Naturally, you will improve your overall health and well-being.

A very effective way to replenish qi, and improve qi circulation, is to consume congee as your breakfast. This can also support and strengthen your spleen and stomach functions, as well as improve your overall immunity.

As you will learn in Chapter 10, when the first *jieqi* in autumn – *liqiu* (arrival of autumn) – arrives, your immune system is weakened because of the changing temperatures and weather. Therefore, improving your immunity is particularly needed as you transition from summer to autumn.

Since consuming congee constantly can help strengthen the body (especially when you have it in the morning), I highly recommend you pick one or two congee recipes from "Part 3: Seasonal Eating Recipes" to start your fun experiments.

Besides congee, foods that can nourish qi include potatoes, Chinese yam, sweet potatoes, beef, mushrooms, chives, sticky rice, pumpkins, coconut meat, chestnuts, carrots, hawthorn berries, spinach, walnuts, shrimp, eel, and loach; meanwhile, you can also consider these Chinese herbs: Chinese dates, longan, ginseng, astragalus, and lotus seeds.

Now, do you see why "Part 1: Season Eating Basic" is so important? I am constantly referring back to chapters in Part 1 to explain what to eat and why you should do things the way that's recommended. Once again, let's review Chapter 3 one more time on how TCM sees the difference between the lungs and the heart. I've again attached the familiar image below for you to look at as a reference while I explain details to you.

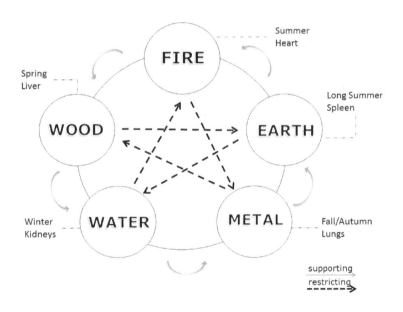

[Side note: if you cannot view it clearly, you could visit here for a larger version of this chart - http://bit.ly/5-elements-2.]

According to Chinese medicine, the heart belongs to the fire element, while the lungs belong to the metal element. As fire is believed to restrict metal, excess energy in the heart can, therefore, inhibit the functions of the lungs. As a result, managing the energy in the heart well helps to nourish the lungs in autumn.

Since bitter foods can lead to excess energy buildup in the heart, it is recommended that you should **moderate the intake of bitter foods,** to avoid excess energy in the heart, so that you can better take care of the lungs.

Example bitter foods are bitter melons, broccoli rabe (also known as Rapini), and lettuce. More bitter food options can be found in "Appendix B: Foods of Five Flavors".

Additionally, you know from the "Autumn Overall Health Guidelines" above that it is crucial to take care of the liver at this time as well. Here I've listed two quick tips to make sure the liver functions are well supported: **increase the intake of sour foods** (such as lemon, lime, and plums) to nourish the liver and **eat more dark leafy green vegetables** to help detoxify the liver. You can find more options for sour foods also in "Appendix B: Foods of Five Flavors".

Improving spleen and stomach functions

Specifically, there are four ways that I'd like to describe here to help you to improve your spleen and stomach functions in autumn.

First, **consume more sweet whole foods**. TCM sees that the spleen and the stomach have a love affair with sweet foods and believes that these foods help the two organs to perform their tasks better.

Note that sweet foods, according to Chinese medicine's standard, may be different from what you are thinking right now. Instead of refined sugar, artificial sweetener, pre-packaged vegetable or fruit juices, or desserts that you find at a bakery, what I recommend here are the original forms of sweet foods derived from nature such as pumpkins, butternut squash, sweet potatoes, whole grains, and potatoes.

Next, make yourself more congee. Do you still remember what I have said about the benefits of congee? Congee can help replenish qi and improve qi circulation. The benefits of congee do not just stop there. Congee has a myriad of healing properties which also include, in this case, strengthening the stomach and spleen functions.

This also explains why I love consuming congee so much: not only can it nourish and moisturize my skin, it can also deliver a series of health benefits for my body to enjoy.

Last but not least, make sure that you **consume foods that are easy to digest**. Eating too many hard-to-digest foods can cause a burden to both organs and decrease the efficiency of their work. A general rule of thumb for eating easy-to-digest foods is to eat a plant-based diet and have only moderate intakes of greasy, raw, cold, and sticky foods.

After learning the general characteristics about autumn, let's now turn to the next chapter to go deeper into this season to uncover how the six *jieqi* in autumn are different from one another, how they can affect your health, and how to eat accordingly based on the differences.

Chapter 10: Specific Eating Guidelines in Six *Jieqi* in Autumn

Once again, let's go over them together: arrival of autumn (*liqiu*), hot summer almost gone (*chushu*), dew starting to form (*bailu*), official autumn (*qiufen*), dew becoming colder (*hanlu*), and frost staring to appear (*shuangjiang*).

As you can see from the common pattern across all six *jieqi*, the key theme is that there are lower and lower temperatures and decreasing humidity day by day. While the key dietary principles are the same – to nourish the lungs and hydrate the whole body, you switch the priority in each *jieqi* as the level of humidity decreases and temperatures continue to drop.

Liqiu (Arrival of Autumn): Focus on Protecting and Nourishing the Lungs

Liqiu starts from around August 7 or 8 of every year (if you reside in the Southern hemisphere, it will be around February 7 or 8 of every year). The Chinese name this "the arrival of autumn" because usually you begin to feel temperatures start to drop and you find that the air is less stuffy than before.

Autumn is the season when you should pay the most attention to your lungs. As the temperatures drop and as you feel that nature is silently migrating from summer to autumn, it is time to switch your focus to these organs.

From thousands of years of observation, the ancient Chinese realized that, if you don't take care of the lungs in autumn, this can lead to a series of health issues related to the lungs (respiratory problems are often seen in this season). Because of this, starting from *liqiu* (arrival of autumn), a variety of lung-nourishing foods should be introduced.

Chushu (Summer Almost Gone): Focus on Expelling Heat and Calming the Mind

Chushu begins from around August 23 or 24 of each year (this will be around February 23 or 24 for people who reside in the Southern hemisphere).

As you can tell from the name, autumn hasn't officially arrived yet. While temperatures in the middle of the day can still stay high, temperatures in early morning, in the evening, and at night are lower than those in summertime. This means that there are larger temperature differences on the same day.

As summer heat still lingers on, consuming foods to avoid internal heat buildup and to expel internal heat is still one of the tasks that you should persist in doing. Also, it still helps to take care of the body by consuming foods that can calm the mind. That's why foods that have soothing properties are recommended particularly on this *jieqi*.

Bailu (Dew Starting to Form): Focus on Moisturizing the Skin and Body

From September 8 or 9 begins *bailu* (for people in the Southern hemisphere, *bailu* begins on around March 8 or 9). At this time, it is getting cooler and cooler and temperature differences on the same day become more distinct. This provides favorable conditions for dew to form. That's why dew is often seen around this time, hence the name of this *jieqi*, *bailu* (dew staring to form). Starting from *bailu*, there is lower humidity in the air and you may experience dryness of the skin.

Starting from this *jieqi*, one key characteristic of autumn becomes more distinct – low humidity in the air, which can lead to dry and itchy skin, as well as a series of lung problems triggered by this kind of weather. Therefore, it is important to switch your focus to moisturizing the skin and hydrating the body. That's why in Chapter 29, recipes for moistening and hydrating dishes are introduced for *bailu*.

Qiufen (Official Autumn): Focus on Keeping Internal Balance Inside the Body

Qiufen starts from around September 23 or 24 (this is around March 23 or 24 if you live in Southern hemisphere). On this day, the day and the night each last for 12 hours. After this day, the days slowly get shorter, the nights gradually get longer, the temperatures continue to drop, and the weather is still dry with low humidity in the air.

As you have already learned from *chunfen* (official spring), a *jieqi* from spring mentioned in Chapter 6, the fact that day and night hours each last for the same length of time suggests that it is time to pay more attention to your own body and to make more efforts in restoring the internal balance in the body, according to

TCM.

At the same time, Chinese Medicine sees that people start to develop more health issues related to the digestive system after *qiufen*. Keeping your body in balance is an effective way to prevent these diseases and to improve your overall immunity.

You can again refer to Chapter 6 to find out your own body type. Once you identify the constitution that your body belongs to, you can then visit the recipe section in Chapter 30 to find out what's especially good for your current body type in autumn, so that you can help your body to restore balance and to improve its immunity.

Hanlu (Dew Becoming Colder): Focus on Nourishing Yin Energy and Hydrating the Body

Hanlu arrives roughly on October 9 or 10 (around April 9 or 10 for people in the Southern hemisphere).

As it is getting closer and closer to winter, the temperatures continue to drop day by day. You can even feel the coldness of the dew on this *jieqi*, hence the name *hanlu* (dew becoming colder).

As it's getting colder, it becomes more important for you to harness the yin energy inside the body – which reflects TCM's belief that human beings should respect and follow the law of nature. This means that more attention should go to consuming foods that can enrich the yin energy within.

Shuangjiang (Frost Starting to Appear): Focus on Preventing Respiratory Diseases

Shuangjiang begins from around October 23 or 24 (or, April 23 or 24 in the Southern hemisphere).

Welcome to the last *jieqi* of autumn; and winter is almost here! This is a time when temperatures can drop below 0 °C (or 32 °F). You may see water that turns into frost or ice on the road, due to the low temperatures. Temperature differences between the day and the night become very large. Animals start to decrease the amount of activity and choose to stay inside their caves, getting ready for the winter.

Dry weather and low temperatures are still the major characteristics around this time. You should keep on consuming foods that hydrate the body and nourish internal yin energy.

Meanwhile, a lot of people tend to develop respiratory diseases at the end of autumn. It is particularly important to take whatever precautions you can to keep you away from these potential problems (as always, Traditional Chinese Medicine is all about disease prevention).

As a result, TCM recommends that you select and eat more foods that can moisten the throat and the lungs, hydrate the whole body, and nourish the kidneys and the lungs. You can find recipes ideas for *shuangjiang* in Chapter 32.

Part 2-3: Autumn Eating Details Summary

Autumn is a golden season with harvest and leaves changing colors. There is cooler and drier weather, less sunlight, less rain, and a decreasing number of animal activities on earth.

To maintain a strong and healthy body in autumn, choose to eat foods by following **three** guidelines:

Consume foods that can nourish your yin energy within, pay special attention to taking care of the lungs and the liver, and strengthen the spleen and stomach function to improve your digestion.

There are different priorities that you need to pay attention to in the six *jieqi*: in *liqiu* (arrival of autumn), focus on protecting and nourishing the lungs; in *chushu* (summer almost gone), place more emphasis on expelling heat and calming the mind; in *bailu* (dew starting to form), pay more attention to moisturizing the skin and the body; in *qiufen* (official autumn), focus on keeping the internal balance in the body; in *hanlu* (dew becoming colder), you should focus on nourishing yin energy and hydrating the body; and in the last *jieqi* in autumn – *shuangjiang* (frost starting to appear), you need to focus on preventing respiratory diseases.

By now you have learned all of the basic dietary principles in spring, summer, and autumn. It's time to jump to the last season of the year and learn how to take care of the body for optimal health in winter.

Part 2-4: Winter Eating Details

Now, we are in the last season of the year. Similar to what you've learned from the previous chapters in Part 2, you will learn atmospheric characteristics in this season, general health guidelines, and best practices in winter; additionally, we will look into each *jieqi* and learn all of the fundamental dietary suggestions for the 15 days after each *jieqi*.

Specifically, in Chapter 11, I will discuss the general winter eating principles and will describe the overall climate in this fourth and last season of the year as well as the overarching dietary suggestions based on Traditional Chinese Medicine.

Chapter 12 gets into the details of each of the six *jieqi* in winter including the different dietary priorities in each *jieqi* and the days that follow.

Chapter 11: General Eating Guidelines in Winter

Winter Characteristics

I live in Boston. It seems to me that people are more likely to talk about the troubles rather than to share the joys that winter gives them.

I totally understand that: snow can fill the street when a storm hits; roads are often slippery, wet, and dirty; snow and ice on the floor can reflect sunlight which directly goes into your eyes, making you feel uncomfortable; for drivers, snowy days suggest that they need to spend time clearing their doorway every day (on the day after a snow storm, they may have to spend up to three hours digging their cars out of the ocean of snow).

I think that I may belong to the minority of the population who actually enjoy winter in Boston (each time when I tell people I actually like winter, I receive shocked looks from them).

But, think about this, on every morning when I pull up the curtain, all I can see is everything covered under a blanket of whiteness; birds are too cold to sing early in the morning, so they decide to sleep late; all I can hear is nothing but silence itself, with occasional sounds of engines from cars that swing by. Particularly, the colder it is, the more grateful I am for the shelter that I have to keep me away from the coldness.

You see, winter is a time for me to remind myself that I am blessed.

Human beings are emotional creatures and we tend to wrap our feelings around objective things. Whatever emotions you are feeling in winter, objective things stay the same: lower temperatures, cold winds, dry weather, fewer outdoor activities, withering flowers and trees, animals hibernating, and lots of snow (if you are living at a place that snows in winter). Usually, this is the common pattern that you see in the season.

According to Traditional Chinese Medicine, the energy moves inwards during winter, a way that helps the body sustain enough energy for you to live through the winter.

Winter Overall Health Guidelines

Specifically, there are **five** major principles to follow in this season:

First, you should consume more warm and nourishing foods to help your body build up and store enough energy. Remember the word "warm" does not apply to the physical temperature of foods, but to the kind of energy that a particular type of food can give you. Specifically speaking, nourishing qi and yang energy is the key in winter. You should choose foods that can enrich qi, improve qi circulation, and nourish and replenish the yang energy inside your body.

Next, you will need to take care of the organs that share the same element with winter. Since both winter and the kidneys belong to the same element, water, TCM sees that the kidneys are the organs that you should focus on in this season.

But that's not enough. You should also nourish the organ belonging to the element that water restricts – fire. That's because the process of nourishing the kidneys (water elements) can lead to a weakening of the heart (a fire element). Chinese medicine believes that if there is excess energy in the kidneys (water elements), it can inhibit the functions of the heart (a fire element). Thus, in essence, winter is the time when you should especially take good care of both the kidneys and the heart.

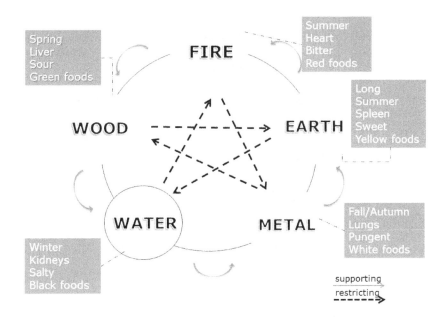

[Side note: if you cannot view it clearly, you could visit here for a larger version of this chart - http://bit.ly/5-elements-3.]

Besides the kidneys and the heart, other organs that you should pay attention to are the lungs. As you can tell from the chart above, metal strengthens water. In other words, if the lungs (metal elements) are taken good care of, the kidneys (water elements) can be strengthened. Therefore, taking care of the lungs is an effective way to protect and nourish the kidneys as well, according to TCM's five element theory.

Here is another important thing to consider: as it is crucial to consume more warm foods to replenish energy in the body, consuming too many warm foods can create excess yang energy and heat buildup in the body, which leads to an internal heat imbalance. A common symptom that you experience in winter may be constipation. TCM sees nothing is good or bad permanently. In this case, even though consuming more warm foods is particularly beneficial for the body, it doesn't mean that you can enjoy them without control.

There should be a fine balance between eating whatever is good for the body and knowing when it is time to have a break. As a result, another good guideline to follow is to consume foods that can "cool down" the body and drive out internal heat in this season.

Once again, cooling down does not mean bringing down the body temperature; rather, it means balancing out excess energy caused by you consuming too many foods with warm energy.

In review, what are the five key health principles you've just learned? Here is a little recap for you: in winter, you should consume foods that can nourish your qi and yang energy, pay special attention to taking care of the kidneys, eat foods that nourish the heart, strengthen functions of the lungs, and, from time to time, enjoy foods with cooling properties to balance out excess warm energy from foods you consume on cold winter days.

In the section that follows, I am going to explain in detail specific health tips, guided by these five principles. Let's move on.

General Dietary Practices in Winter

Consuming foods that nourish qi and yang energy

One way to nourish qi and yang energy is to **consume foods with higher calories**. Note that when foods with high calories are recommended here this does not mean any processed or fast foods like fried potatoes chips, burgers, or French fries. All of the foods recommended in this book are whole foods.

Examples are lamb, walnuts, black sesame seeds, and chestnuts. These foods can give the body enough energy to perform daily activities in winter, give it warmth, and improve its immunity to protect you from colds, asthma, or other diseases.

Additionally, pungent foods can also provide yang energy to the body. As a result, you can choose to **consume a proper amount of pungent foods**, too. You can consider adding ingredients like red chili peppers, black peppers, ginger, scallions, and garlic into your dishes as your prepare your meals.

Next, choose to **eat foods and herbs that replenish qi and blood**. Example foods and herbs are red dates, Longan, American ginseng, astragalus, Chinese yam, mushrooms, shrimp, organic chicken breast, grass-fed beef, sticky rice, and red beans.

Taking care of the kidneys

In Chapter 3, we've talked about how salty foods can especially nourish the kidneys. While it is right that a proper amount of salty foods can strengthen kidney functions, too many of them can lead to excess energy buildup in the kidneys, leading to imbalances in these organs. As a result, it is recommended that you **moderate the intake of salty foods** (however, do not misinterpret this message as suggesting that you not consume salty foods at all).

Another way to seek foods that are particularly good for the kidneys is to look at the colors of the foods. If you look into nature, a lot of black foods have kidney-nourishing benefits. It is recommended that you **enjoy more foods with black or darkish colors**.

Examples are black rice, black beans, black sesame seeds, black dates, black fungus, dried mushrooms, and black sticky rice. Besides black foods, foods with darkish colors like dark green (such as kelp and roasted seaweed) also provide similar kidney-nourishing results.

Nourishing the heart

Mother Nature also leaves signals in the tastes of foods to tell you what foods can nourish your body. When it comes to nourishing the heart, there is a specific taste that is associated with this organ. Do you remember what it is?

The answer is saltiness. That's right. Your heart functions can be strengthened, if you **consume a proper amount of salty whole foods**. You could **consider bitter foods** like bitter melons, lettuce, broccoli rabe (also known as rapini), and turmeric. Or, you could add a few pinches of Himalayan salt into your dishes if they taste too bland to you. In Chapter 14, I will explain to you why I only use this type of salt for cooking.

What's more, TCM sees that the heart connects to the mind. It's actually not hard to connect them together: when you become anxious or overly excited, your heart beat goes faster and it is usually hard for your mind to stay calm in this situation. Therefore, to nourish your heart also means to nourish and calm your mind. Because of this, make sure you **eat mind-calming foods** in this season as well. You could consider rose, lily bulbs, red beans, millet, lotus roots, lotus seeds, and dates.

Winter is also a time when one can easily experience low mood or depression. A friend of mine, who lives in Maryland, told me that he would experience mild depression when winter comes. He also told me that he would have very low productivity whenever he experienced a mood swing. In fact, this happens to a lot of people.

There is a series of treatments to deal with low mood or depression, such as increasing the amount of physical activity, changing your attitude or thinking pattern on how you perceive the world, and doing positive affirmations; and consuming the right foods is definitely one of the ways that can help fight depression and cope with low mood in winter.

You could **consider eating mood-boosting foods and herbs** like cilantro, strawberries, tomatoes, red chili peppers, carrots, pumpkin, and peanut butter.

Strengthening the lungs

I recommend that you **enjoy lung-nourishing white foods** more often, such as lotus seeds, Chinese yam, white radishes, and water chestnuts. Other than that, **consuming whole foods that enrich and replenish qi** also helps. Examples are congee, potatoes, sweet potatoes, grass-fed beef, chives, hawthorn berries, ginseng, and astragalus.

Consuming foods with cooling properties from time to time

There are three ways to bring down the excess heat inside your body in winter. First, you can **consider eating foods with cool or cold energies**. Example foods are white radishes, mung bean soups, lotus seeds, and lotus roots. You can find out more about foods with cool or cold energies in "Appendix A: Foods with Five Energies".

Additionally, you could **enjoy some salads from time to time**. You can also **consider drinking boiled water**, which is believed to be able to bring down excess heat accumulated in the stomach.

Speaking of drinking boiled water, it is recommended you drink boiled water that is made on the same day; and it's *not* recommended you keep boiled water that is more than two days old, as bacteria may grow in boiled water that's kept for too long. When you drink this kind of boiled water, it may lead to a series of discomforts like headaches, nausea, and palpitations.

After learning the general characteristics and healthy eating guidelines for winter, let's now turn to the next chapter to go deeper into this season to uncover how the six *jieqi* in winter are different from one another, how they can affect your health, and what to eat accordingly based on the differences.

Chapter 12: Specific Eating Guidelines in Six *Jieqi* in Winter

Previously, you have learned the names of the six *jieqi* in winter, which are: arrival of winter (*lidong*), beginning to snow (*xiaoxue*), getting more snow (*daxue*), official winter (*dognzhi*), starting to get freezing cold (*xiaohan*), and the coldest time of the year (*dahan*).

In this chapter, I'm will describe to you what each *jieqi* in winter means, their characteristics, which explain why they are named this way, and the priorities to abide by in each particular *jieqi* and the 15 days that follow to keep the body in balance.

Lidong (Arrival of Winter): Focus on Harnessing Yang Energy and Protecting the Kidneys

Lidong starts from around November 7 of every year (if you reside in the Southern hemisphere, it will be around May 7 of every year).

Beginning from this *jieqi*, you may find that in some places, water starts to freeze and humidity levels drop dramatically around this time. What else can you see? Withering trees and flowers, fewer animal activities out here in nature, few or almost no fruit flies hovering over ripe bananas on the kitchen counter (which is based on what I observe) - these are all signs that winter has slowly arrived.

Winter is the season when you should pay the most attention to your kidneys, which, according to Traditional Chinese Medicine, are the primary source that distributes energy to the different organs inside the body. You especially want to activate the kidney functions in winter to give the body enough fuel and energy to live through the cold season.

That's why TCM sees that it is the top priority to nourish the kidneys, as well as to build up more yang energy inside, to help the body build a solid foundation and prepare for the coming of winter.

Xiaoxue (Beginning to Snow): Focus on Nourishing the Heart and Boosting the Mood

Xiaoxue begins from around November 22 of each year (this will be around May 22 for people who reside in the Southern hemisphere). At around this *jieqi*, temperatures continue to drop and, as you can tell from the name, snow starts to fall in some places already.

Dropping temperatures and shortened daylight hours can cause people to develop mood swings around this time. As a result, it is important to nourish the heart (as the heart and mind are connected) and to proactively consume more foods that can boost your mood.

In fact, this is not the only *jieqi* when you have to consume more of this kind of food. Instead, the coming of *xiaoxue* should only be a sign for you to *start* introducing mood-boosting foods; and I personally think that you should continue doing so throughout the winter. As you can imagine, after *xiaoxue* the days only get shorter and the weather gets colder and colder, it is very beneficial to keep consuming mood-boosting foods.

Daxue (Getting More Snow): Focus on Having a Balanced Diet and Do Not Overly Consume High-Calories Nourishing Foods

From December 7 begins *daxue* (for people in the Southern hemisphere, *daxue* begins on around June 7).

The name has already told you what you may expect at around this *jieqi*: heavier and heavier snow. The ancient Chinese believed that heavier snow is a good sign for a fruitful year to come, because the heavy snow can kill all of the bugs in the fields, which provides favorable conditions for the crop to grow in the following year.

With increasing appetite in colder winter days, some people may tend to consume a lot of high-calorie foods all day to keep the body warm. While your body really needs this kind of food particularly in freezing cold weather, there should be a fine balance between when to eat more foods with warm energies and when to pause to give your body a rest from time to time.

TCM believes that to achieve an optimal state of health is to keep the body in balance. If you blindly consume too many high-calorie foods, this may cause excess heat buildup inside the body and lead to health issues like constipation, bloating, and breakouts.

Therefore, starting from *daxue*, it is time to constantly remind yourself to eat light from time to time and consume foods with cooling properties, in order to balance out potential heat buildup inside the body and to give fewer burdens to your digestive system.

Dongzhi (Official Winter): Focus on Eating Foods of More Varieties

Dongzhi starts from around December 22 or 23 (this is around June 22 or 23 if you live in Southern hemisphere).

On this day, the daylight hours are the shortest, whereas the nighttime hours are the longest of the year. After this day, daylight hours slowly get longer day by day, while night hours get shorter and shorter.

Eating more lung-nourishing foods? Check. Consuming more mood-boosting foods? Check. Eating light and enjoying foods with cooling properties from time to time? Check.

Now what?

Winter can be a time when some people forget about consuming more fruits and vegetables as most of the attention is directed to eating more high-calorie foods such as lamb, beef, and other kinds of meat to give the body enough energy. This can lead to vitamin or mineral deficiencies as too few fruits and vegetables are consumed in this season.

Therefore, increasing food varieties means that you should incorporate more fruits and vegetables (especially dark leafy greens) into your diet in winter.

Xiaohan (Starting to Get Freezing Cold): Focus on Trying to Incorporate More Herbal Tea into Your Diets

Xiaohan arrives roughly on January 5 or 6 (around July 5 or 6 for people in the Southern hemisphere).

Some people believe that it is the coldest time of the year even though the next *jieqi* – *dahan* (which literally means "coldest time of the year") makes us believe that *xiaohan* is not yet the coldest time. Despite the lack of consistency in describing *xiaohan*, it is easy to cope with the myth: simply compare both *jieqi* to feel the temperature yourself and then you will get an answer!

As always, remember that the Traditional Chinese Medicine wisdom introduced throughout this book is for reference only. You should also take into consideration how you personally feel about nature.

Additionally, whether *xiaohan* is colder or *dahan* is colder is not that important. What's certain is that these two *jieqi*, along with *dongzhi* (official winter), are together considered to be the coldest time of the year.

This suggests that the ways needed to take care of the body around these three *jieqi* are actually similar. In other words, instead of treating each priority in each *jieqi* as the *only* focus you should attend to, you can consider each priority in each *jieqi* as one habit that you would want to build and collect all of the habits into your bucket as you move into the different phases in winter.

So, what is the habit that you want to build in *xiaohan*? As Chinese herbs have stronger healing benefits, make sure that you also incorporate some nourishing Chinese herbal tea into your life from time to time to help build up warm energies. In Chapter 37, I will be introducing different herbal tea options to help you start with your experiments in the kitchen.

Dahan (Coldest Time of the Year): Focus on Slightly Cutting Down High-Calories Nourishing Foods, Consuming More Pungent Foods, and Eating Foods that can Fight Colds

Dahan begins from around January 20 (or, July 20 in the Southern hemisphere). This is the last *jieqi* in winter and the last one of the year. Weather continues to be cold and dry.

As the season that immediately follows *dahan* is spring, TCM sees that *dahan* is a time to start preparing for spring. This means that you should start cutting down high-calories foods and consume more foods that have the same movements displayed in spring— upward (think about trees growing taller) and outward (imagine flowers blossoming) movements. Therefore, it's recommended that you try to introduce more pungent foods into your diet at around this time.

Meanwhile, the end of winter is also a time when most people may start catching a cold. This suggests you should also consume a proper amount of foods that can prevent or fight off colds and strengthen your immunity.

Part 2-4: Winter Eating Details Summary

Winter is usually a time with very few animal activities, cold or even freezing cold weather, and dryness; it's also a season when people can easily suffer from low mood and depression.

To help maintain a strong and healthy body and a balanced mind in winter, choose to eat foods by following **five** guidelines: consume foods that can nourish your qi and yang energy, pay special attention to taking care of the kidneys, eat foods that nourish the heart, strengthen functions of the lungs, and occasionally enjoy foods with cooling properties to balance out excess warm energy from foods you consume on cold winter days.

There are different priorities you need to pay attention to in six *jieqi*: in *lidong* (arrival of winter), focus on harnessing yang energy and protecting the kidneys; in *xiaoxue* (beginning to snow), place more emphasis on nourishing the heart and boosting the mood; in *daxue* (getting more snow), pay more attention to having a balanced diet and not overconsuming high-calories nourishing foods; in *dongzhi* (official winter), focus on eating foods of more varieties; in *xiaohan* (starting to get freezing cold), you should focus on trying to incorporate more herbal tea into your diets; and in the last *jieqi* in winter – *dahan* (coldest time of the year) you need to prioritize on starting to cut down high-calories nourishing foods, consuming more pungent foods, and eating foods that can fight colds.

Congratulations! You have learned all the basic dietary principles in all four seasons. Let's continue on the journey and discover how I can help you get started with different recipes and start your experiments in the kitchen immediately.

Part 3: Seasonal Eating Recipes

Chapter 13: How to Get Started

Welcome to the most flavorful part of this book.

Now that you know all of the fundamental dietary principles on how to eat for vibrant health in all four seasons, you can dive into the practice right away and try out some recipes that I've provided for you in Part 3.

There are over 240 recipes in total, to help you get started with your seasonal eating journey. I have included more than 60 recipes for each season.

Here is a quick action plan for you:

- The first thing to do is to figure out the season that you are in right now;
- Then, remind yourself of today's date and figure out what *jieqi* you are on (if today happens to fall on the same day as one of the 24 *jieqi*) or what the closest *jieqi* is before today's date;
- Third, visit "Part 2: Seasonal Eating Details" to review the priorities that you should pay attention to in this particular time of the year;
- Next, fast forward to the chapter in this part where I share recipes recommended for this particular *jieqi*, or around this time, and choose one or two recipes that you would like to experiment on;

- Now jot down the key ingredients;
- Then, off you go – visit the grocery stores or farmer's markets to get the ingredients that you need and start your fun experiments in the kitchen!

Now, sit back, relax, and welcome again to the world of recipes.

Chapter 14: General Guidelines and Healthy Eating Tips Before You Get Started

Before you officially get into the recipes, there are a few things that I would like to point out, so that you understand why I design recipes in a certain way.

I have also incorporated eight healthy living guidelines that I personally follow for your reference. These will help you maximize the therapeutic benefits of all of the dishes that I have suggested for you, as a healthier lifestyle can amplify the healing effects in food.

Here we go.

About the Instructions in Each Recipe

The majority of recipes each have eight key pieces of information provided: a name, the ingredients used to make the dish, serving size, total time used from start to finish, the amount of time that you need to prepare the ingredients before you officially start cooking, the amount of time that you need to cook before the final dish is ready to serve, detailed step-by-step instructions, and the therapeutic benefits that this dish gives you, according to Traditional Chinese Medicine.

Additionally, besides these eight key areas, if I feel that there is something else that you should pay attention to, or remarks that I want to bring to your attention, then I will add a few more words in the "Notes" section.

In the instructions, you will see the phrase "to taste" used many times. That means adding a certain ingredient to suit your own preferences. If you see an instruction such as "salt, to taste", I would suggest that you start from one pinch of salt – the amount of salt that can be held by using one thumb, index finger, and middle finger placed together; and then, increase by one pinch at a time if you think that the dish that you are preparing still tastes too bland.

Even though "salt, to taste" means adding sodium at your will, I'd recommend that you moderate your intake of salt, as consuming too much salt can lead to a series of health issues such as water retention (which is manifested as puffiness, bloating, and weight gain), hypertension, heart failure, kidney diseases, and headaches, just to name a few.

Usability of All Recipes

You will see that a lot of the recipes can be used not only on the *jieqi* for which the dishes are recommended, but can also be used on other *jieqi*, as long as these dishes meet the requirements for taking care of the body on other *jieqi*.

For example, in Chapter 19, I introduce one dish called "Fried Mushrooms and Chinese Cabbage" which can improve your immune system. Since both *jieqi* of *jingzhe* (awakening from hibernation) and *qingming* (freshness and clarity) require you to focus on consuming more foods that help strengthen the body, this immunity-strengthening dish – though listed as a recipe for *qingming* – can also be used for *jingzhe*.

As a result, in this book, you can get more than 10 recipes to choose from for each *jieqi* and the 15 days that follow!

A Few Words on Certain Ingredients

In this particular section, we will explore the right way to use oil for cooking. As well, I will share with you the ingredients – Himalayan pink salt, miso paste, and various types of whole grains – that I use on a regular basis and why I use them.

How to Cook with Different Oils

Different levels of heat can activate or destroy the nutrients in foods. That's why I recommend that you pay attention to the level of heat that you use to cook different foods or ingredients. In this case, let's talk about oil use.

Each type of oil has its own smoking point, the temperature at which visible gaseous vapor from the heating of oil becomes evident. The smoking point of a particular type of oil is traditionally used as a marker for when decomposition of the oil begins to take place. When decomposition takes place, or when a particular type of oil reaches its smoking point, a series of damaging effects occur subsequently:

It causes loss of available nutrients contained in the oils, including fat-soluble vitamin E; the heating oil can lead to the formation of free radicals, which causes cell damage, premature aging, and other health issues; and the formation of unpleasant aromatic substances (like polycyclic aromatic hydrocarbons, or PAHs) in the oil that can increase the risk of chronic health problems including cancer.

Therefore, it is important to cook foods at a certain level of heat below each particular type of oil's smoking point. In other words, you should know the temperature ranges for low, medium, and high heat and the different smoking points for different oils. That way, you will be able to adjust the temperature at which you cook, to make sure that the oils are properly used in a safe and healthy way.

Below is a chart that shows different heat levels and their temperatures:

Heat Level	Temperature °C	Temperature °F
High	232 - 343°C	450 - 650°F
Medium to High	190 - 232°C	375 - 449°F
Medium	162 - 190°C	325 - 374°F
Low to Medium	121 - 162°C	250 - 324°F
Low	107 - 121°C	225 - 249°F

Chart from Smart Kitchen

Below, you will find a chart to show you a sample of oils with different smoking points. I'm about to explain how to use some of these oils. For a longer list with more oils and their smoking points, you can visit Appendix G: Cooking Oils Smoking Points.

Cooking Oils / Fats	Smoke Point °C	Smoke Point °F
Unrefined flaxseed oil	107°C	225°F

121

Unrefined sunflower oil	107°C	225°F
Extra virgin olive oil	160°C	320°F
Unrefined peanut oil	160°C	320°F
Unrefined walnut oil	160°C	320°F
Hemp seed oil	165°C	330°F
Butter	177°C	350°F
Coconut oil	177°C	350°F
Unrefined sesame oil	177°C	350°F
Macadamia nut oil	199°C	390°F
Semi-refined walnut oil	204°C	400°F
High quality (low acidity) extra virgin olive oil	207°C	405°F
Sesame oil	210°C	410°F
Grapeseed oil	216°C	420°F
Virgin olive oil	216°C	420°F
Almond oil	216°C	420°F
Hazelnut oil	221°C	430°F
Peanut oil	227°C	440°F
Sunflower oil	227°C	440°F
Palm oil	232°C	450°F
Extra light olive oil	242°C	468°F

Rice Bran Oil	254°C	490°F
Avocado oil	271°C	520°F

Chart from Serious Eats

From these two charts, you can tell that unrefined flaxseed oil has a very low smoking point (107°C / 225°F). Even a low heat temperature (107 - 121°C / 225 - 249°F) can easily exceed its smoking point. Because of this, it is better to use unrefined flaxseed oil in salads or in cooked foods; and you should definitely *not* use this oil for cooking.

Though coconut oil and unrefined sesame oil both have relatively higher smoking points than unrefined flaxseed oil, the former two are still considered to have low smoking points (they both have the same smoking point of 177°C / 350°F). Therefore, you should not use higher than medium heat (162 - 190°C / 325 - 374°F) to cook with either coconut oil or unrefined sesame oil.

You will find in the recipes that I would always add coconut oil or sesame oil after I turn off the heat (most of the time) or when I cook with medium to low heat.

When it comes to high temperature cooking, I would always use avocado oil, which has a very high smoking point (271°C / 520°F). That's why you will see that, whenever I introduce fried dishes, I always use avocado oil for cooking.

The Kind of Salt That I Recommend

As you may have known already, adding a proper amount of sodium can bring up the flavor of the whole dish, so that it tastes better. But it is more than just the taste. You should also consider the nutritional values that come along with the salty taste.

In my daily life, I choose to add either one of these two types of sodium – Himalayan pink salt or miso paste – on a regular basis, whenever I feel like adding more salty flavor to a dish, because of the abundant nutritional values from both sources.

While I will introduce miso paste to you in the next section, let's talk about the benefits of Himalayan salt for now.

Compared to other types of salt (the ingredients of which can contain harmful chemicals or have been contaminated these days), Himalayan pink salt has more nutritional value and is healthier for the body, as it offers natural elements exactly identical to the elements in your body.

Its benefits include, but are not limited to, regulating water content throughout your body, promoting blood sugar health and helping to reduce the signs of aging, promoting bone strength, promoting healthy pH balance in your cells (particularly your brain cells), and regulating and promoting your sleep.

The more I know about the benefits of Himalayan pink salt and about the problems with conventional salts, the more I feel the need to stick with the pink salt for enhancing flavors (in moderation, of course). That's why you will see that I always mention "Himalayan salt" in the instructions when I think that a proper amount of salt can be added to a dish.

The Benefits of Miso

Another type of seasoning that I often use to add saltiness to a dish is miso paste, a traditional Japanese seasoning produced by fermenting soybeans with barley, rice, or other ingredients. This high-sodium food <u>is</u> a good source of protein and dietary fiber, and contains three important mineral antioxidants: manganese, copper, and zinc. According to my Chinese doctor, Fang-Tusey Lin, who has been practicing Traditional Chinese Medicine since 2001, miso can also effectively protect against radiation poisoning.

As for choosing a reliable miso, make sure that you select certified organic miso to lower your chance of exposure to unwanted contaminants in your miso. My Chinese doctor suggests choosing miso that is at least two years old.

There is one brand that she recommends called South River Organic Miso, which you can find in Whole Foods (if you live in the US). If you live outside of the US, you can still stick with the criteria for selecting the best miso possible for your own health.

Image from South River Miso Company's Website

The Nutritional Values of Whole Grains

According to Traditional Chinese Medicine, whole grains – such as oats, millet, brown rice, barley, and Chinese barley – act on the spleen and the stomach, which belong to the earth element (if you want, you can go back to Chapter 3 to revisit what you have learned about the Chinese five elements).

Earth, or soil, is considered to be the foundation for life – we need soil to grow crops, in order to get food supplies for sustenance; and we need to conduct most of our activities on earth.

Thus, it is crucial to take good care of your stomach and the spleen, organs connected to the earth element. Since TCM believes that whole grains nourish both organs, it becomes very important to consume enough whole grains for strengthening your stomach and spleen functions and for your overall health and well-being.

Additionally, whole grains are a good source of minerals, vitamins and dietary fiber, which promotes digestion and relieves constipation. They also have antioxidant properties. Studies show that consuming whole grains on a regular basis may reduce the risk of heart disease, help with weight management, and prevent stroke, cancer, and diabetes.

With all of the benefits listed above, I would recommend that you consume whole grains every day. My favorite way to consume whole grains is to make Chinese congee, which can be easily digested, has skin-beautifying benefits, and helps the body better absorb nutrients from the grains.

In the following recipe section, I have included a lot of recipes for different types of congee with different healing effects for you to choose from, so that you can start enjoying congee's therapeutic benefits.

General Guidelines for a Healthier Lifestyle

To help you to maximize the healing benefits that you can get from all of the recipes that follow, it is also important to keep up with some basic rules when you can. Meanwhile, also note that it is not about being perfect and trying to accomplish everything listed below all at once. Rather, it is about discovering areas in which you can improve the quality of your life and taking one small step at a time.

Specifically, below I have eight tips for you, which I personally follow in my daily life, with the first three being the most fundamental and the most important principles to abide by:

1. Live a plant-based lifestyle:

    A plant-based lifestyle helps to ensure that you have good digestion and keeps your body alkalized. Consuming a variety of vegetables allows you to enjoy different beautifying benefits and therapeutic properties from those foods, to help you look radiant, feel great, and heal the body and mind.

2. Stay hydrated:

    How much water do you drink per day?

    Most people do not have enough water each day. It is recommended that every day you drink between half an ounce and an ounce of water for each pound that you weigh. For example, if you weigh 110 pounds, then you would need between 55 and 110 ounces of water each day.

Of course, the amount of water consumption required also depends on the amount of physical activity that you perform, and the climate of the location where you are at the time. But at least it gives you a rough idea of how much water you need each day.

A "lazier" way to find out how much water you need is to check out the color of your urine after you visit the bathroom. If your urine is clear and very light yellow with little odor, it is a sign that you are well-hydrated. On the other hand, the darker and more aromatic your urine is, the more dehydrated you are.

In my daily life, I stick with my drinking goal – drinking at least 3 liters of water, or about 101 ounces, per day. And, I have a water bottle (with a volume of one liter, or about 34 ounces) with me, even when I am at home, to help me keep track of how much fluid I consume per day.

3. Eat whole foods:

Nothing beats eating whole foods.

While consuming whole foods may not guarantee that you reap all of the benefits from the foods (because it also depends on how you prepare and cook them), eating whole foods is definitely a better way to gain nutrients than consuming a large amount of packaged or canned foods, which may contain harmful chemicals. The process of making packaged or canned foods may cause loss of nutrients as well.

4. Avoid refined sugar or artificial sweeteners:

Refined sugar or artificial sweeteners may cause an increase in your sugar level and lead to mood swings, hormonal imbalance, and aging, as pointed out by David Wolfe, one of the world's leading authorities on nutrition and best-selling author of *Eating for Beauty*: http://bit.ly/eating-for-beauty.

Better alternatives include honey, royal jelly, and stevia.

5. Cut down on, or cut out completely, all canned or packaged goods
6. Avoid foods with preservatives or other artificial ingredients
7. Avoid packaged, pre-bottled fruit and vegetable juices:

The best time to drink fruit or vegetable juices is within 30 minutes after you make them to reap the most nutritional benefits from the natural juices.

Usually, I see the a lot of pre-bottled fruit and vegetable juices that contain artificial sweeteners or preservatives to prolong their shelf life, which may not be good for your overall health if you consume this kind of juice on a regular basis.

The best way to enjoy the benefits from juicing is to make your own juices and drink them immediately afterwards.

8. Avoid fried foods:

Now that you have learned that each type of oil has its own smoking point, can you guess what the potential dangers of fried foods are?

First, the heat that you use to fry a certain food may exceed the smoking point of the oil that you use. Then, high temperature cooking may well destroy most of the nutritional value of the foods. What's more, consuming fried foods on a regular basis can lead to weigh gain. If you have acne prone skin, I *highly* recommend that you avoid fried foods, as consuming fried foods is one of the primary causes of more breakouts.

Resources to Learn More about Chinese Herbs

Consuming Chinese herbal tea is one of the major TCM dietary traditions. In the recipe section, I've included several Chinese herbal teas with different healing benefits, so that you can have a taste of what kinds of herbal tea you can make and enjoy on a particular *jieqi* of the year.

If you want to learn more about Chinese herbs, you can check out my other book to understand Chinese herbs on a deeper level, including more basics about TCM, how Chinese herbal therapy is tied into TCM, and how to select the right herbs that fit your own body type.

Click here to check out my book on Chinese herbs: http://bit.ly/chinese-herbs.

At this point, you have almost come to the end of this chapter: you have better understood why I use different oils in different ways and why I repeatedly use Himalayan salt, miso, and whole grains. In addition, you have been introduced to eight fundamental and important principles that will guide you as you transition to a healthier lifestyle.

At the same time, also remember that this is not about being perfect, but about becoming more aware of what you can do to improve your health. So, don't stretch yourself too much and try to incorporate everything all at once. Instead, take baby steps by incorporating one new habit at a time.

Now, go ahead to turn to the next page and start exploring the fun of therapeutic healing through food.

Part 3-1: Spring Eating Recipes

Chapter 15: Recipes for *Lichun* (Arrival of Spring)

It is recommended to have more pungent and sweet foods and foods with more energy on this *jieqi*. I am a big fan of Chinese congee and have incorporated several congee recipes here.

Oatmeal congee

Ingredients:

- Rolled oats, 1/2 cup
- Goji berries, 30 pieces
- Black sesame seeds, 2 tbsp
- Almonds, 14 pieces
- Clean water, 2 cups
- Cilantro, chopped, 1/3 cup (optional but highly recommended)

Serving size:

- 2

Total cooking time (estimated):

- 25 minutes

Preparation time (estimated):

- 5 minutes

Cooking time (estimated):

- 20 minutes

Instructions:

- Mix rolled oats, goji berries, black sesame seeds, and almonds with water, and bring the mixture to boil (with the lid on top of the pot)
- Simmer for 15 minutes
- Turn off heat
- Mix cilantro into oatmeal
- Serve

This dish is especially good for:

- Improving digestion
- Improving vision
- Nourishing the liver, the spleen, and the kidneys

Notes:

- I start with this recipe because this is one of my favorite breakfast ideas. I make this almost every day because it is quick, easy, and full of nutrients such as fiber and protein.

  The smell of black sesame seeds mix very well with cooked rolled oats, whereas the refreshing cilantro immediately wakes me up right on the spot as soon as I chop it into small pieces. I highly recommend you try this *first*.
- If you are allergic to gluten like me, try gluten-free rolled oats.

Goji Congee

Ingredients:

- Goji berries, about 30 pieces
- Brown rice, about 1/4 cup
- Clean water, 2 cups

Serving size:

- 2

Total cooking time (estimated):

- 55 minutes

Preparation time (estimated):

- 2 minutes

Cooking time (estimated):

- 53 minutes

Instructions:

- Wash brown rice and place it to a pot
- Add in 2 cups of water to brown rice and bring the mixture to boil (with the lid on top of the pot)
- Bring it to simmer and cook for about 40 minutes (with the lid on top of the pot)
- Add goji berries to brown rice and cook for another 2-3 minutes (with the lid on top of the pot)
- Turn off heat and serve

This dish is especially good for:

- Improving vision
- Nourishing the liver and the kidneys

Chrysanthemum Congee

Ingredients:

- Brown rice, 1/4 cup
- Dry chrysanthemum flowers, 1/3 cup
- Clean water, 2 cups

Serving size:

- 2

Total cooking time (estimated):

- 67 minutes

Preparation time (estimated):

- 2 minutes

Cooking time (estimated):

- 65 minutes

Instructions:

- Wash chrysanthemum flowers
- Place them into a pot, add in 2 cups of water, and bring the mixture to boil (with the lid on top of the pot)
- Simmer the mixture for 15 minutes (with the lid on top of the pot)
- Remove the flowers and keep the juice
- Add brown rice to the juice and bring it to boil again (with the lid on top of the pot)
- Simmer the mixture for 40 minutes (with the lid on top of the pot)
- Turn off heat and serve

This dish is especially good for:

- Detoxifying the liver
- Improving vision

Stirred Fried Broad Beans

Ingredients:

- Broad beans, 1 cup
- Garlic, chopped, 2 cloves
- Scallions, chopped, 1/4 cup
- Avocado oil, 1 tbsp
- Clean water, 1/3 cup
- Himalayan salt, to taste

Serving size:

- 2

Total cooking time (estimated):

- 20 minutes

Preparation time (estimated):

- 5 minutes

Cooking time (estimated):

- 15 minutes

Instructions:

- Add avocado oil to the pot and heat up the oil using medium heat
- Add the chopped garlic into the oil and stir fry until you can smell the flavor
- Add in broad beans and continue to stir fry until the beans turn dark green
- Add in clean water and simmer with the lid on top of the pot for 5 minutes (or until the beans become soft)

- Add in salt and scallions, mix well, and continue to simmer for another 2 minutes
- Turn off heat and serve

This dish is especially good for:

- Bowel movements
- Healing internal organs altogether
- Detoxifying the body (as scallions and garlic have anti-bacterial properties)
- Improving your immunity

Notes:

- I choose to use avocado oil for cooking instead of other kinds of oil because avocado oil has a very high smoke point, making it ideal for higher temperature cooking.
- I use Himalayan salt because it is full of traces of minerals and with lots of health benefits like supporting thyroid and adrenal functions, aiding overall hormonal balance, and helping produce adequate stomach acid.

Ginger Spinach

Ingredients:

- Baby spinach, 10 cups
- Fresh ginger, juiced, 25 grams
- Sesame oil, 1 tsp
- Himalayan salt, to taste
- Clean water, 4 cup

Serving size:

- 2

Total cooking time (estimated):

- 7 minutes

Preparation time (estimated):

- 2 minutes

Cooking time (estimated):

- 5 minutes

Instructions:

- Add water to pot and bring it boil
- Add in spinach and cook it with low to medium heat for 2 minutes (with lid on top of the pot)
- Drain the spinach and mix it with ginger juice, sesame oil, and a pinch of salt (you can add more salt to further enhance the flavor)
- Serve when it cools down

This dish is especially good for:

- Moistening your mouth and throat
- Improving blood circulation
- Stimulating bowel movements
- Treating a hangover
- Relieving constipation
- High blood pressure

Notes:

- Ginger is a very popular herb deeply loved and widely used by Chinese population. This herb has a myriad of benefits including, not limited to, expelling heat out of the body, bringing down the level of inflammation, preventing and treating nausea, preventing heart problems, improving qi circulation and blood flow, promoting stamina, relieving insomnia, improving digestion, and fighting off bacteria.

In my book, *CHINESE HERBS: Your 101 Guide To Top 10 Chinese Herbs That Clear Up Your Skin And Restore Natural Glow* (http://bit.ly/chinese-herbs), there is a section that specifically talks about ginger. If interested, you could download the book to learn more about this herb, how to eat it, more recipes featuring ginger, and whether your specific body type allows you to have ginger on a continuous basis (because, even though ginger in general is beneficial, the amount and frequency of ginger consumption depends on your body type).

Honey Radish

Ingredients:

- Raw honey, 2 tbsp
- White radish, chopped to sizes of sugar cubes, 4 cups
- Clean water, 4 cups

Serving size:

- 1-2

Total cooking time (estimated):

- 63 minutes

Preparation time (estimated):

- 3 minutes

Cooking time (estimated):

- 60 minutes

Instructions:

- Bring the water to boil
- Add in chopped radish and honey and simmer the mixture for one hour
- Serve

This dish is especially good for:

- Clearing up your throat
- Improving digestion
- Hydrating the skin and the body
- Removing the heat
- Detoxifying the body
- Relieving constipation
- Relieving sore throats, fever, and cold

Brown Rice Peanut Butter

Ingredients:

- Brown rice, 1/4 cup
- Ginger, chopped, 1 tbsp
- Peanut butter, 1 tbsp
- Clean water, 1/2 cup
- Cilantro, chopped, 1/4 cup

Serving size:

- 2

Total cooking time (estimated):

- 49 minutes

Preparation time (estimated):

- 4 minutes

Cooking time (estimated):

- 45 minutes

Instructions:

- Wash brown rice, mix it with water, and bring the mixture to boil
- Add in chopped ginger and simmer for 40 minutes
- Turn off heat, add in peanut butter, and mix well
- Mix in cilantro
- Serve

This dish is especially good for:

- Nourishing the spleen
- Fighting the winds and coldness in the season
- Improving digestion

Pineapple Ginger Smoothie

Ingredients:

- Ginger, about 30 grams and with skin peeled off
- Pineapple, chopped, 2 cups
- Spinach, 1 cup
- Clean water, 1 cup

Serving size:

- 1

Total cooking time (estimated):

- 10 minutes

Preparation time (estimated):

- 10 minutes (considering if you need to cut a small piece out of the entire pineapple)

Cooking time (estimated):

- 20 seconds

Instructions:

- Throw everything into the blender and blend away
- Serve

This dish is especially good for:

- Nourishing the skin
- Improving immunity
- Improving appetite
- Improving digestion

Notes:

- The smell of ginger blends very well with pineapple. According to TCM, the mixture of raw vegetables and fruits can introduce too much cold energy (or yin energy) into the body. Considering good health means to maintain the balance of yin and yang inside the body, it helps when you introduce ginger into the smoothie to balance out the cold energy.
- Additionally, if you have a body type that causes you suffer from cold digits easily in the winter or in the air-conditioned room in the summer, consider consuming smoothies at noon or around noontime (yang energy peaks during the day, which helps balance out the cold energy introduced by smoothies).

Stir-Fried Shrimp with Chives

Ingredients:

- Shrimps, peeled, 1.5 cups
- Chives, cut into 1-inch pieces, 4 cups
- Organic egg, 1
- Avocado oil, 1 tbsp
- Sesame oil, 1 tsp
- Himalayan salt, to taste

Serving size:

- 2-3

Total cooking time (estimated):

- 30-35 minutes

Preparation time (estimated):

- 5 minutes

Cooking time (estimated):

- 30 minutes (actual cooking is just about 10 minutes)

Instructions:

- Wash the shrimps and immerse them in clean water for 20 minutes (you can chop the chives and perform the second step while waiting)
- Crack open the egg, place the egg white, egg yolk, and sesame oil into a bowl, mix up everything into a paste
- Add avocado oil into the pot, heat it up with medium to high heat, add in shrimps, and stir fry till shrimps turn red
- Lower the heat to low to medium and add in egg paste
- When the paste starts to become solid, stir fry for 30 to 60 seconds

- Add chopped chives into the mix and stir fry for 3-4 minutes
- Turn off heat, add about two pinches of salt, and mix well
- Serve

This dish is especially good for:

- Improving bowel movements
- Relieving constipation
- Nourishing the liver and the kidneys

White Radish Congee

- Ingredients:
- Brown rice, 1/3 cup
- Goji berries, 30 pieces
- White radish, chopped, 1.5 cups
- Ginger, 4 slices
- Cilantro, chopped, 1 cup
- Clean water, 1 cup
- Coconut oil, 1 tbsp
- Himalayan salt, 1 pinch

Serving size:

- 2

Total cooking time (estimated):

- 45 minutes

Preparation time (estimated):

- 2 minutes

Cooking time (estimated):

- 42 minutes

Instructions:

- Wash brown rice, mix it with chopped white radish, goji berries, ginger, and clean water into a pot, and bring it to boil
- Simmer for 40 minutes (with the lid on the top of the pot)
- Turn off heat, add in chopped cilantro, coconut oil, and salt, and mix well
- Serve

This dish is especially good for:

- Improving digestion
- Improving appetite
- Fighting off coldness
- Improving qi circulation
- Detoxifying the body
- Reducing or removing phlegm
- Moisturizing the skin
- Nourishing the liver, the spleen and the stomach

Notes:

- White radish goes *very* well with cilantro; and the whole dish is very nourishing. Back in China, my parents had been making this dish for me since I was little. For this dish, I also added a little bit of coconut oil; it makes tasting this dish a more enjoyable experience because it smells good, too.

Chapter 16: Recipes for *Yushui* (Increase of Rains)

On this *jieqi*, the priority goes to eating right to take care of the spleen. Key practices are increasing the amount of sweet foods while reducing the intake of sour foods and moderating the consumption of hard, sticky, raw, cold, and oily foods.

Spinach Congee

Ingredients:

- Baby spinach, 4 cups
- Brown rice, 1/3 cups
- Clean water, 2 cups

Serving size:

- 2

Total cooking time (estimated):

- 52 minutes

Preparation time (estimated)

- 2 minutes

Cooking time (estimated):

- 50 minutes

Instructions:

- Wash brown rice, add brown rice and water into a pot, and bring the water to boil
- Simmer for 40 minutes (with the lid on the top of the pot)
- Add in spinach, mix well with brown rice, and simmer for

about 3-4 minutes (with the lid on the top of the pot)
- Serve

This dish is especially good for:

- Nourishing the blood
- Hydrating the body and the skin
- Relieving constipation
- People with high blood pressure
- Improving urinary flow

White Fungus Congee

Ingredients:

- White fungus, dried, 1 piece
- Chinese dates, pitted, 8 pieces
- Brown rice, 1/3 cup
- Clean water, 3cups

Serving size:

- 2

Total cooking time (estimated):

- 115 minutes

Preparation time (estimated):

- 65 minutes (for soaking the white fungus and cutting it into small pieces)

Cooking time (estimated):

- 50 minutes

Instructions:

- Soak white fungus in water in a bowl until it fully expands and softens (this usually takes about one hour)
- Rinse white fungus, drain it, and cut it into small pieces
- Wash brown rice and Chinese dates, add brown rice, dates, pieces of white fungus, and water into a pot, and bring the water to boil
- Simmer for 45 minutes (with the lid on the top of the pot)
- Serve

This dish is especially good for:

- Hydrating the skin and body
- Nourishing the kidneys
- Nourishing the blood
- Relieving heart palpitation

Notes:

- If you have read my book on Chinese herbs (http://bit.ly/chinese-herbs), you will know that white fungus is a type of fungus that grows on trees.

  It can hold water equivalent of nearly 500 times its weight. This water holding capacity is more than that of hyaluronic acid, a carbohydrate that occurs naturally in various parts of human body that helps retain the skin's natural moisture to keep the skin nourished.

  One piece of white fungus can be as big as the size you can hold with one palm. You can find white fungus at a Chinese super market. Usually, you will find dried and packaged white fungus there.

Roasted Nuts

Ingredients:

- Almonds, 7 pieces
- Clean water, 1/4 cup

Serving size:

- 1

Total cooking time (estimated):

- 6 minutes

Preparation time (estimated):

- 1 minute

Cooking time (estimated):

- 5 minutes

Instructions:

- Place water and nuts into a small frying pan and bring the water to boil with medium heat
- Simmer without the lid on the top of the pan until water totally evaporates
- Serve

Notes:

- This is a simple instruction to show you how I prepare nuts every day.
- Cooked nuts can be digested more easily by the stomach; and you can replace almonds with other kinds of nuts such as walnuts and hazelnuts.
- Pay attention to the amount of nuts you consume, as overeating nuts can cause breakouts to some people. I

would control the amount of nuts to fewer than 10 pieces each day.

Celeries with Red Dates Soup

Ingredients:

- Celeries, 9 stalks
- Red dates, pitted, 12 pieces
- Scallions, chopped, 1/2 cup
- Avocado oil, 2 tbsp
- Miso paste, 1 tbsp
- Clean water, 6 cups

Serving size:

- 3

Total cooking time (estimated):

- 18 minutes

Preparation time (estimated):

- 5 minutes

Cooking time (estimated):

- 13 minutes

Instructions:

- Wash celeries, drain them, and cut them into small chunks
- Heat up the frying pan with medium heat, add oil into it, and heat up the oils until your hand can feel the heat by hovering over the oil
- Add in scallions and stir fry until you can smell the flavor
- Add in water, red dates, chopped celeries, and miso paste

and mix well
- Lower the heat to low to medium and simmer for 10 minutes (with the lid on top of the pot)
- Serve

This dish is especially good for:

- Nourishing the liver and keeping it in balance
- People who suffer from high blood pressure, heart disease, and high hyperlipidemia
- Improving digestion
- Nourishing the blood

Black and White Fungus

Ingredients:

- White fungus, dried, 1 piece
- Black fungus, dried, 2/3 cup
- Clean water, 6 cups (for soaking fungus)
- Clean water, 5 cups (for boiling water)
- Himalayan salt, to taste
- Black pepper, to taste
- Sesame oil, 1 tbsp

Serving size:

- 2-3

Total cooking time (estimated):

- 75 minutes

Preparation time (estimated):

- 65 minutes

Cooking time (estimated):

- 10 minutes

Instructions:

- Soak both white and black fungus in the water in a container for about 60 minutes
- Wash fungus in running water and make sure they are clean
- Drain the fungus
- Cut white fungus into small pieces
- Add 5 cups of water into a pot and bring it to boil
- Add in black fungus and small pieces of white fungus and cook them for 4-5 minutes with medium heat
- Drain both types of fungus and place them in a container
- Add in sesame oil, salt, and black pepper and mix well

Serve

- This dish is especially good for:
- Fighting aging process
- Nourishing qi flow inside the body
- Nourishing the kidneys
- Improving immunity
- Hydrating the body and the skin
- Nourishing blood flow
- People with diabetes, heart diseases, and high blood pressure

Notes:

- You can buy both dried white fungus and black fungus at a Chinese supermarket. Both types of fungus, if soaked for one hour, can expand to three to four times the size of dried fungus. Therefore, make sure you add enough water which allows the dried fungus to fully expand to their original sizes. In this case, I would recommend using 6 cups of water to soak both types of fungus.

Chinese Yam Red Date Congee

Ingredients:

- Chinese yam, peeled and cut in pieces, 1/2 cup
- Brown rice, 1/3 cup
- Red Dates, pitted and cut into pieces, 12 pieces
- Clean water, 3 cups

Serving size:

- 2

Total cooking time (estimated):

- 47 minutes

Preparation time (estimated):

- 2 minutes

Cooking time (estimated):

- 45 minutes

Instructions:

- Wash brown rice, add brown rice and water into the pot, and bring the water to boil
- Add in pieces of Chinese yam and red dates, mix well, and simmer for 40 minutes
- Serve

This dish is especially good for:

- Nourishing the stomach and the spleen
- Calming the mind
- Hydrating the body
- Relieving fatigue
- Improving digestion

Moistening the lungs

Red Dates with Millet

Ingredients:

- Red dates, pitted and cut into pieces, 10 pieces
- Millet, 1/2 cup
- Clean water, 4 cups

Serving size:

- 2

Total cooking time (estimated):

- 48 minutes

Preparation time (estimated):

- 3 minutes

Cooking time (estimated):

- 45 minutes

Instructions:

- Wash millet, mix it with water, and bring the water to boil
- Add in pieces of red dates, mix well, and simmer for 40 minutes
- Serve

This dish is especially good for:

- Nourishing the liver, the stomach, and the spleen
- Improving appetite
- Improving digestion

Notes:

- Millet is especially good at driving out dampness inside the body, according to Traditional Chinese Medicine. If you have acne prone skin, chances are you may have a heat-dampness body type (you can learn more details from Bonus Chapter for different body types: http://bit.ly/sign-up-for-bonus-chapter). In that case, consuming millet on a regular basis is good for driving out excess dampness inside the body, which can help with your skin conditions.

Baby Creamy Bok Choy with Garlic

Ingredients:

- Baby creamy bok choy, peeled into pieces, 8 cups
- Garlic, chopped, 5 cloves
- Avocado oil, 2 tbsp
- Clean water, 1/2 cup
- Salt, to taste
- Black pepper, to taste

Serving size:

- 2

Total cooking time (estimated):

- 14 minutes

Preparation time (estimated):

- 7 minutes

Cooking time (estimated):

- 7 minutes

Instructions:

- Wash baby creamy bok choy, rinse the vegetables for a few times, and drain them
- Heat up a big frying pan with medium to high heat and add avocado oil
- Wait until your hand feels heat by hovering your hand over the oil, add in chopped garlic, and stir fry with medium heat until garlic starts to turn brownish
- Add baby creamy bok choy and water, cover the pan with a lid, and simmer with low to medium heat for about 4 minutes
- Remove the lid, continue to stir the vegetables until heat and oil are evenly distributed
- Turn off heat, add one or two pinches of salt and pepper, and mix well
- Serve

This dish is especially good for:

- Improving digestion
- Cleansing the liver

Notes:

- The word "creamy" can be misleading, as it has nothing to do with cream, unless you put whip cream on top of the dish. "Creamy" only refers to the color of the lower part of the tiny vegetables (each baby bok choy is only about as tall as your little finger or even shorter).

I personally prefer the taste of baby creamy bok choy as it tastes more crunchy, juicy, and sweet than regular creamy bok choy. With a little bit of garlic and salt, the smell and flavor of the whole dish is enhanced. You should definitely give it a try.

Carrot Pumpkin Paste

Ingredients:

- Baby carrots, 1 cup
- Pumpkin, chopped into small pieces, 1 cup
- Brown rice, 1/2 cup
- Clean water, 5 cups
- Coconut oil, 1 tbsp
- Salt, to taste
- Black pepper, to taste

Serving size:

- 2

Total cooking time (estimated):

- 48 minutes

Preparation time (estimated):

- 3 minutes

Cooking time (estimated):

- 45 minutes

Instructions:

- Add baby carrots, pumpkin, brown rice, and water into a

pot and bring the water to boil
- Simmer for 40 minutes (with the lid on the top of the pot)
- Transport everything in the pot to a blender and blend away
- Pour the paste into a container, add in coconut oil, salt, and pepper， mix well
- Serve

This dish is especially good for:

- Nourishing and brightening up the skin
- Hydrating the body
- Nourishing the spleen
- Improving digestion

Notes:

- I love this dish very much. Blending all ingredients into a paste helps your stomach to digest this dish more easily. I've made this for my family for a few times and they all loved it. I highly recommend this one to you, too.

White Chrysanthemum Goji Tea

Ingredients:

- White chrysanthemum, dried, 3 tbsp
- Goji berries, 15 pieces
- Green tea, 2 tsp
- Hot water

Serving size:

- You can serve as many people as you want by refilling the teapot, until the tea is tasteless

Total cooking time (estimated):

- 11 minutes

Preparation time (estimated):

- 1 minute

Cooking time (estimated):

- 10 minutes

Instructions:

- Boil water
- Place white chrysanthemum, goji berries, and green tea in a teapot
- Add the boiled water into the teapot, cover the lid, and wait for 10 minutes
- Pour the juice from teapot into a cup
- If the flavor is too strong for you, add more hot water, and enjoy the tea after it is cooled down

This dish is especially good for:

- Nourishing the liver, the stomach, and the spleen
- Improving vision
- Driving out excess heat inside the liver to keep the organ in balance

Notes:

- If you don't have a teapot, you could simply add all ingredients into a 500ml cup that can hold burning hot water. Then, you pour the hot water in and wait for about 10 minutes before drinking this herbal tea. You can use a spoon to keep the ingredients from floating into your mouth when you drink the tea.

Chapter 17: Recipes for *Jingzhe* (Awakening from Hibernation)

This is the time when animals start to get more and more active and spend more time outside. That's when different organisms (including bacteria) start to reproduce and grow, potentially making you feel sick. Improving your immunity by eating right and participating physical exercises is important to keep good health on this *jieqi*.

Three key issues when it comes to improving your immune systems by eating right: eating a variety of foods, eating light meals, and consuming more foods that can strengthen your body. The following recipes are designed to meet one or more of these requirements to keep you strong.

Home-made Sauerkrauts

Ingredients:

- Cabbage, enough to fill one 25-ounce Mason jars
- Ginger, chopped, 1 tbsp
- Clean water, 1/3 cup
- Total cooking time (estimated):
- 12 minutes (disregarding the time it needs for fermentation)
- Preparation time (estimated):
- 2 minutes
- Cooking time (estimated):
- 10 minutes (disregarding the time it needs for fermentation)

Instructions:

- Keep 2-3 outer leaves of the cabbage for later use
- Add 1 tbsp of chopped ginger into the Mason jar
- Peel off layers of cabbage, cut them into small pieces, pack the jar with pieces of cabbage as tight as possible, but leave out 1-inch space between the top of the jar and the cabbage
- Add water into the jar
- Roll up 2 cabbage leaves, and pack them on the top of the pieces of cabbage
- Cover the jar with a lid and make sure the jar is air-tight
- Leave the jar at a dark, cool, and dry place for 3-5 days
- When it's done (check out "notes" below to see how to tell when it is ready to be served), twist off the lid and discard the two rolls of cabbage leaves
- Place the jar in the fridge to keep it fresh
- This dish is especially good for:
- Improving digestion
- Nourishing the skin
- Promoting overall health due to its amount of vitamins, minerals, and enzymes

Notes:

- Fun fact: I actually learned about making sauerkraut from nutritionist Kimberly Snyder in her book *The Beauty Detox Solutions: http://bit.ly/beauty-detox-solutions.* ;)

  You can make this throughout the year and consume it regularly. Depending on which season you prepare sauerkraut, the time it takes for making the sauerkraut varies. According to my experience, it takes about 2-3 days in summer and about 4-5 days in winter before the sauerkraut is ready to be served.

Usually, the time when you can tell it's ready to serve is when you see the size of pieces of cabbage start to shrink, leaving extra space inside the jar.

When the sauerkraut is ready, it is normal to see air bubbles starting to appear and hear sizzling sounds as you twist off the lid. So, don't have to freak out.

Lemon Water

Ingredients:

- Half of a lemon, or one lemon, peeled
- Warm to hot water, 500ml

Serving size:

- 1

Total cooking time (estimated):

- 8 minutes

Preparation time (estimated):

- 7 minutes (for boiling the water and cutting lemon)

Cooking time (estimated):

- 1 minute or less (for juicing the lemon, preparing warm water, and adding lemon juice into the warm water)

Instructions:

- Boil water

- Cut the lemon into halves and place pieces into the juicer
- Mix drinking water with room temperature with boiling hot water to make the temperature between warm and hot
- Pour the juice into the warm water (the warmer, the better)
- Serve

This dish is especially good for:

- Improving your immunity
- Alkalizing and hydrating the body
- Cleansing the liver
- Stimulating bowel movements
- Brightening up the skin

Notes:

- Now that we are on the *jieqi* that focuses on improving your immunity, nothing comes more easily than consuming lemon water as the first thing in the morning.

  Lemon water is full of vitamin C and contains anti-bacterial properties. I have been drinking lemon water as soon as I wake up for a long time and have been enjoying benefits it gives me. I would highly recommend you do the same, too.

  Besides drinking warm lemon juices, I also would add slices of fresh lemon into my water bottle, so that I can continue to enjoy lemon water throughout the day.

Ginger Congee with Dates

Ingredients:

- Ginger, chopped, 2 tbsp
- Brown rice, 1/3 cup
- Red dates, pitted and cut into pieces, 8 pieces
- Clean water, 2 cups

Serving size:

- 2

Total cooking time (estimated):

- 45 minutes

Preparation time (estimated):

- 5 minutes

Cooking time (estimated):

- 40 minutes

Instructions:

- Add brown rice, ginger, and red dates into a pot, mix them with water, and bring the water to boil
- Simmer for another 40 minutes (with the lid on the top of the pot)
- Serve

This dish is especially good for:

- Nourishing the stomach, the spleen, the heart, and the lungs
- Expelling the coldness out of the body and keeping the body warm
- Treating digestive issues that cause nausea, vomiting and

diarrhea
- People who suffer from hyperglycemia and heart diseases
- Preventing you from cancer
- Treating health issues related with the respiratory system such as asthma and phlegm in the lungs

Notes:

- Traditionally, ginger and red dates have been used together for deep healing benefits. You could also try mixing both to make yourself Chinese herbal tea to gain similar benefits mentioned above.

Fried Mushrooms with Celeries

Ingredients:

- Dried mushrooms, 1/2 cup
- Celeries, chopped into small chunks, 10 stalks
- Himalayan salt, to taste
- Avocado oil, 2 tbsp
- Sesame oil, 1 tsp

Serving size:

- 3

Total cooking time (estimated):

- 11 minutes + 1 night for soaking the dried mushrooms

Preparation time (estimated):

- 5 minutes + 1 night for soaking the dried mushrooms

Cooking time (estimated):

- 6 minutes

Instructions:

- Soak dried mushrooms in water overnight (about 6 to 10 hours)
- Wash the mushrooms in running water, rinse them, and drain them
- Cut mushrooms into thin slices
- Heat the pan with medium to high heat and add avocado oil
- When your hand can feel the heat by hovering over the oil, add in slices of mushrooms and chopped celeries, stir fry with medium heat for about 5 minutes
- Sprinkle one to two pinches of salt and mix well (add more if need be)
- Turn off heat, wait till the dish cools down a little, add sesame oil and mix well
- Serve

This dish is especially good for:

- Driving heat in the liver to bring this organ back to balance
- Relieving high blood pressure, heart diseases, and hyperlipidemia
- Improving immune system
- Fighting cancer
- Fight radiation
- Slowing down aging process
- Nourishing the skin, the liver, the kidneys, the stomach, and the spleen
- Improving qi and blood flow in the body

Broccoli with Garlic

Ingredients:

- Broccoli, 1 head broccoli
- Garlic, chopped, 5 cloves
- Avocado oil, 2 tbsp
- Himalayan salt, to taste
- Clean water, 1/2 cup (for cooking the broccoli stem)
- Clean water, 1/2 cup (for cooking the florets added later on)

Serving size:

- 2-3

Total cooking time (estimated):

- 10 minutes

Preparation time (estimated):

- 5 minutes

Cooking time (estimated):

- 5 minutes

Instructions:

- Trim off the florets, cut off the "trunk" of each floret to make bite-sized pieces, and place florets in a bowl (Bowl A)
- Trim and slice the stem and place the pieces in a separate bowl (Bowl B)
- Heat up the frying pan with avocado oil with medium to high heat
- Add chopped garlic into the pan and stir fry until garlic starts to turn brownish
- Lower the heat to medium to low, add in ingredients in

Bowl B and 1/4 cup of clean water, cover up the pan with a lid, and cook for 1 – 1.5 minute
- Add in ingredients in Bowl A and 1/4 cup of clean water, cover up the pan again, and cook for 1.5 - 2 minutes
- Remove the lid, add in one or two pinches of salt, and mix well
- Serve

This dish is especially good for:

- Improving your immune system because studies show that broccoli has antibacterial and antioxidant properties and because garlic alone also has antibacterial properties as well

Notes:

- This is a good example that shows how a simple and easy-to-make dish can contain loads of nutritional benefits to help you become stronger and healthier. As soon as you remove the lid, you will immediately be attracted by the smell of this dish. Additionally, it not only smells good, but tastes very good as well.

Chinese Barley with Red Dates and Longan

Ingredients:

- Chinese barley, 1/4 cup
- Red dates, 8 pieces
- Longan, 15 – 20 pieces
- Clean water, 2 cups

Serving size:

- 1

Total cooking time (estimated):

- 41 minutes

Preparation time (estimated):

- 1 minute

Cooking time (estimated):

- 40 minutes

Instructions:

- Mix everything together into a pot and bring the water to boil
- Simmer for 40 minutes (with a lid on the top of the top)
- Serve

This dish is especially good for:

- Improving your immunity
- Preventing you from cancer
- Nourishing and brightening up the skin
- Nourishing the blood and qi
- Calming the mind
- Nourishing the heart and the spleen
- Treating anemia, forgetfulness, palpitation, and insomnia

Notes:

- This is one of my favorite Chinese herbal tea, which I make for myself from time to time.

  As a side note, if you consume Chinese barley on a regular basis, you will gradually experience glow on the skin. If you have acne prone skin, Chinese barley can be an effective healing herb to heal your skin (TCM believes that Chinese barley can drive out dampness and heat inside the body, both of which are the major reasons for breaking out often).

Millet Black Bean Congee

Ingredients:

- Millet, 1/4 cup
- Black beans, 1/4 cup
- Goji berries, 30 pieces
- Clean water, 4 cups
- Cilantro, chopped, 1/2 cup

Serving size:

- 2

Total cooking time (estimated):

- 57 minutes

Preparation time (estimated):

- 2 minutes

Cooking time (estimated):

- 55 minutes

Instructions:

- Mix millet, black beans, goji berries, and clean water into a pot and bring the water to boil
- Add in goji berries and simmer for 50 minutes (with a lid on the top of the pot)
- Turn off heat, add cilantro into the pot, and mix well

- Serve

This dish is especially good for:

- Improving your immune system because of the benefits from nutrient-dense millet, which is especially good for those who have a weak body type
- Nourishing the liver, the spleen and the kidneys
- Improving vision
- Treating anemia and constipation
- Women's reproductive system

Pear with White Fungus

Ingredients:

- Pears, 2
- White fungus, dried, 2 pieces
- Goji berries, 30 pieces
- Clean water, 8 cups

Serving size:

- 5-6 servings

Total cooking time (estimated):

- 120 minutes

Preparation time (estimated):

- 65 minutes

Cooking time (estimated):

- 55 minutes

Instructions:

- Soak dried white fungus in water for 60 minutes
- Run white fungus under water till it is clean and drain it
- Cut white fungus into small pieces
- Wash pears, cut them into small pieces and take out seeds
- Add pieces of white fungus into water and bring the water to boil
- Add in goji berries and chunks of pears and simmer for 50 minutes
- Serve

This dish is especially good for:

- Nourishing the spleen, the kidneys, the liver, and the lungs
- Clearing phlegm in the lungs
- Moistening the lungs
- Hydrating the skin and the body
- Preventing bronchitis in spring

Carrot, Sweet Potato, Squash Paste

Ingredients:

- Baby carrots, 1 cup
- Sweet potatoes, peeled and chopped into bitable pieces, 1 cup
- Butternut squash, peeled and chopped into bitable pieces, 1 cup
- Baby spinach, 2 cups
- Ginger, chopped, 2 tbsp
- Clean water, 7 cups
- Coconut oil, 1 tbsp
- Himalayan salt, to taste

Serving size:

- 2

Total cooking time (estimated):

- 47 minutes

Preparation time (estimated):

- 12 minutes

Cooking time (estimated):

- 35 minutes

Instructions:

- Put baby carrots, chopped sweet potatoes, butternut squash, and water into a pot and bring the water to boil
- Simmer for 30 minutes (with the lid on the top of the pot)
- Transport everything inside the pot to the blender, add spinach and ginger, and blend away
- Pour the paste into a container, add coconut oil and one or two pinches of salt, and mix well
- Serve

This dish is especially good for:

- Nourishing the spleen, the stomach, and the skin
- Protecting the upper respiratory tract
- Enhancing the functions of the respiratory system

Sweet Potato Congee

Ingredients:

- Sweet potatoes, peeled and chopped into bitable pieces, 1 cup

- Brown rice, 1/3 cup
- Ginger, chopped, 2 tbsp
- Cilantro, cut into small pieces, 1/2 cup
- Coconut oil, 1 tbsp
- Clean water, 3 cups

Serving size:

- 2

Total cooking time (estimated):

- 50 minutes

Preparation time (estimated):

- 5 minutes

Cooking time (estimated):

- 45 minutes

Instructions:

- Wash brown rice, place brown rice and sweet potatoes into the water, and bring the water to boil
- Add in ginger and simmer for 40 minutes
- Turn off heat, add in cilantro and coconut oil, and mix well
- Serve

This dish is especially good for:

- Nourishing the spleen and the stomach
- Improving digestion
- Improving bowel movements
- Protecting joints
- Nourishing the respiratory system

Notes:

- I personally add cilantro and coconut oil into the congee because they both contain antioxidant properties, which help you improve your immunity. Additionally, they both add refreshing and pleasant flavors to the dish, too.

Mustard Greens Soup with Egg

Ingredients:

- Mustard greens, chopped, 2-3 cups
- Organic egg, 1
- Clean water, 2 cups
- Ginger, chopped, 1 tbsp
- Miso paste, 1 tsp

Serving size:

- 1

Total cooking time (estimated):

- 13 minutes

Preparation time (estimated):

- 5 minutes

Cooking time (estimated):

- 8 minutes

Instructions:

- Bring the water to boil
- Lower the heat to medium to low, add miso paste into the water, and stir well
- Add in chopped mustard greens and chopped ginger, and cook for about 2 minutes (add water if needed)

- Turn off heat, break the egg into the soup, and stir well
- Serve

This dish is especially good for:

- Improving your immune system
- Improving digestion
- Improving vision
- Stimulating bowel movements
- Relieving constipation
- Detoxifying and bringing down inflammation
- Helping you heal wounds faster

Chapter 18: Recipes for *Chunfen* (Official Spring)

On March 21 (or September 21, if you reside in the southern hemisphere), the night and day hours each last for 12 hours. TCM believes that it is a time to seek balance internally. In other words, it is time to pay more attention to what your body needs and give it what it needs. Prof. Qi Wang has summarized nine body types to help you identify your own body type, so that you can find more targeted solutions accordingly.

Before you get into the recipes, make sure you identify your body types first. Then you can dive into the sections that describe your specific body type and find out what's recommended for you on this *jieqi*. You can have a quick reference regarding which body type in Appendix G: Foods for Nine Body Type.

For the recipes below, I've included two recipes for each body type to help you get started to bring your body back to a balanced state, a very key step to radiant skin, vibrant health, and longevity.

Qi Deficiency
Symptoms: You constantly feel weak and tired and easily get sick.

Recipe 1: Chinese Yam Millet

Ingredients:

- Millet, 1/4 cup
- Chinese Yam, sliced, 1 cup
- Clean water, 3 cups

Serving size:

- 1

Total cooking time (estimated):

- 48 minutes

Preparation time (estimated):

- 3 minutes

Cooking time (estimated):

- 45 minutes

Instructions:

- Wash millet, add millet, Chinese yam slices, and water into a pot, and bring the water to boil
- Simmer for 40 minutes (with a lid on top of the pot)
- Serve

Notes:

- It is recommended you consume this at dinner time every day.

Recipe 2: Astragalus Spring Chicken Soup

Ingredients:

- Boneless, skinless spring chicken thighs, 250g

- Astragalus, 5g
- Ginger, chopped, 2 tbsp
- Scallions, chopped into small pieces, 1/2 cup
- Himalayan salt, to taste
- Black pepper, grinded, to taste
- Cooking wine, 1/4 cup
- Clean water, 1/3 cup (for frying ginger, scallions, and chicken thighs)
- Clean water, 2 cups

Serving size:

- 2

Total cooking time (estimated):

- 47 minutes

Preparation time (estimated):

- 7 minutes

Cooking time (estimated):

- 40 minutes

Instructions:

- Wrap up astragalus in a cheesecloth and use a string to tie up the cloth, so that astragalus won't fall out into the soup
- Add ginger, scallions, chicken thighs, and 1/3 cup of water into a pot and fry with medium heat until chicken is slightly colored
- Add astragalus and 2 cups of water into a pot and bring it to boil
- Simmer for 30 minutes (with a lid on the top of the pot)
- Take out astragalus wrapped in a cheesecloth, add one or two pinches of salt, black pepper, one or two pinches of

grinded black pepper, and cooking wine, and sauté for 2 minutes
- Serve

Notes:

- Astragalus is one of the popular Chinese herbs. It is good for improving qi circulation inside the body. For details of this herb regarding healing benefits and more recipes, you can check out my book about Chinese herbs (http://bit.ly/chinese-herbs), where there are also nine other herbs are described for different healing benefits.

Yang Deficiency

Symptoms: You tend to have cold hands and feet.

Recipe 1: Ginger Lamb Carrot Soup

Ingredients:

- Ginger, sliced, 15g
- Lamb, 250g
- Baby carrots, 1 cup
- Cooking wine, 1/4 cup
- Clean water, 2 cups
- Clean water, 2 cups
- Himalayan salt, to taste

Serving size:

- 2

Total cooking time (estimated):

- 190 minutes

Preparation time (estimated):

- 7 minutes

Cooking time (estimated):

- 180 minutes

Instructions:

- Bring 2 cups of clean water to boil, add lamb into the boiling water, cook it for 30 seconds, and run lamb under tap water for about 10-15 seconds
- Put ginger, lamb, carrots, and 2 cups of clean water into a pot and bring the water to boil
- Add cooking wine into the mixture and simmer for about 3 hours (with the lid on the top of the pot)
- Add one or two pinches of salt (add more if needed)
- Serve

Recipe 2: Chives with Walnut

Ingredients:

- Chives, chopped, 1 cup
- Walnuts, 1/4 cup
- Sesame oil, 1tsp
- Himalayan salt, to taste
- Clean water, 1/4 cup

Serving size:

- 1

Total cooking time (estimated):

- 7 minutes

Preparation time (estimated):

- 2 minutes

Cooking time (estimated):

- 5 minutes

Instructions:

- Add water and walnuts into a pan and bring the water to boil with medium heat
- Lower the heat to medium to low and simmer for 1 minutes (with the lid on the top of the pot)
- Add in chives and sauté until they turn darker green and become soft
- Turn off heat, add salt and sesame oil, and mix well
- Serve

Yin Deficiency

Symptoms: It is likely that you have dry skin, warm hands and feet, a red face, dry eyes, and dry stool. You easily get thirsty.

Recipe 1: Lotus Seeds Lily Bulbs Herbal Tea

Ingredients:

- Dried lotus seeds, all embryos taken out of the seeds, 1/4

cup
- Dried lily bulbs, 1/4 cup
- Longan, 15 pieces
- Clean water, 2 cups

Serving size:

- 1

Total cooking time (estimated):

- 85 - 145 minutes

Preparation time (estimated):

- 60 - 120 minutes

Cooking time (estimated):

- 25 minutes

Instructions:

- Soak dried lotus seeds and dried lily bulbs in water for about 1-2 hours until lotus seeds and lily bulbs become soft
- Place lotus seeds, lily bulbs, longan, and clean water into a pot and bring the water to boil
- Simmer for 20 minutes (with a lid on the top of the pot)
- Serve

Recipe 2: Black Bean Black Sesame Paste

- Ingredients:
- Black rice, 1/4 cup
- Black beans, 1/4 cup

- Black sesame seeds, 2 tbsp
- Clean water, 2 cups

Serving size:

- 2

Total cooking time (estimated):

- 47 minutes

Preparation time (estimated):

- 2 minutes

Cooking time (estimated):

- 45 minutes

Instructions:

- Wash black rice and black beans
- Add black rice, black beans, and clean water to a pot and bring the water to boil
- Add black sesame seeds into the mix and simmer for 40 minutes (with a lid on the top of the pot)
- Turn off heat, transport the mixture from a pot to a blender, and blender away
- Pour the paste into a bowl
- Serve

Blood Stasis

Symptoms: You easily get dark eye circles, and easily get bruises even you are only mildly hurt.

Recipe 1: Black Rice Black Bean with Hawthorn Berries

Ingredients:

-   Black rice, 1/4 cup
-   Black beans, 1/4 cup
-   Hawthorn berries, pitted and cut them into thin slices, 1/3 cup
-   Clean water, 2 cups

Serving size:

-   2

Total cooking time (estimated):

-   48 minutes

Preparation time (estimated):

-   3 minutes

Cooking time (estimated):

-   45 minutes

Instructions:

-   Wash black rice
-   Mix black rice and black beans into a pot, add water, and bring the water to boil
-   Add in hawthorn berries, simmer for 40 minutes
-   Serve

Recipe 2: Soybean Radish Seaweed Soup

Ingredients:

- Soybeans, 1/2 cup
- White radishes, chopped, 1 cup
- Roasted seaweed, 25g
- Clean water, 2 cups
- Organic eggs, 2
- Himalayan salt, to taste

Serving size:

- 2

Total cooking time (estimated):

- 63 minutes

Preparation time (estimated):

- 3 minutes

Cooking time (estimated):

- 60 minutes

Instructions:

- Wash soybeans and white radishes, mix them with water into a pot, and bring the water to boil
- Simmer for 50 minutes (with a lid on the top of the pot)
- Add roasted seaweed to the soup and stir for 2 minutes
- Turn off heat, break the eggs into the soup, and stir well
- Add one or two pinches of salt (add more if needed)
- Serve

Dampness Heat

Symptoms: You have acne-prone skin and may have bad breaths from time to time.

Recipe 1: Bitter Melon Barley Soup

Ingredients:

- Bitter melon, chopped into bitable pieces, 1 cup
- Chinese barley, 1/2 cup
- Clean water, 2 cups
- Himalayan salt, to taste

Serving size:

- 2

Total cooking time (estimated):

- 68 minutes

Preparation time (estimated):

- 3 minutes

Cooking time (estimated):

- 65 minutes

Instructions:

- Wash and drain Chinese barley
- Put barley and water into a pot and bring the water to boil
- Simmer for 50 minutes (with a lid on the top of the pot)
- Put pieces of bitter melon into the pot and continue to cook for 10 minutes
- Turn off heat and add one pinch of salt (add more if needed)
- Serve

Recipe 2: Mung Bean Chinese Barley

Ingredients:

- Mung beans, 1/4 cup
- Chinese barley, 1/4 cup
- Clean water, 2 cups

Serving size:

- 2

Total cooking time (estimated):

- 56 minutes

Preparation time (estimated):

- 1 minute

Cooking time (estimated):

- 55 minutes

Instructions:

- Wash mung beans and Chinese barley
- Put mung beans, Chinese barley, and clean water into a pot and bring the water to boil
- Simmer for 50 minutes (with a lid on the top of the pot)
- Turn off heat and serve

Qi Depression

Symptoms: You often feel depressed and suffer from insomnia.

Recipe 1: Chinese Yam Winter Melon Soup

Ingredients:

- Chinese yam, chopped into bitable pieces, 1/4 cup
- Winter melon, chopped into bitable pieces, ¾ cup
- Clean water,
- Himalayan salt, to taste

Serving size:

- 1

Total cooking time (estimated):

- 40 minutes

Preparation time (estimated):

- 5 minutes

Cooking time (estimated):

- 35 minutes

Instructions:

- Add Chinese yam, winter melon and water into a pot and bring the water to boil
- Simmer for 30 minutes (with a lid on the top of the pot)
- Turn off heat and add a pinch of salt (add more if needed)
- Serve

Recipe 2: Chicken Liver Soup with Chrysanthemums

Ingredients:

- Fried white fungus, 1/4 cup
- Dried chrysanthemum flowers, 24 pieces
- Chicken livers, 1/4 cup
- Ginger, 20g
- Himalayan salt, to taste
- Cooking wine, 1/4 cup
- Clean water, 1 cup
- Clean water, 2 cups

Serving size:

- 2

Total cooking time (estimated):

- 155 minutes

Preparation time (estimated):

- 130 minutes

Cooking time (estimated):

- 25 minutes

Instructions:

- Soak dried white fungus in water for about 2 hours
- Wash white fungus, rise it, drain it
- Cut white fungus into small pieces and set them aside
- Peel off ginger skin, place the ginger into a juicer, save ginger juice in a container, and set it aside
- Clean the livers by trimming and discarding any visible fat or membrane, cut chicken livers into slices, and set them aside
- Boil 1 cup of clean water, place chicken liver slices in

boiling water for 30-60 seconds, take them out, and run them under tap water
- Wash the pot and use it to boil 2 cups of clean water
- Add chicken liver slices, cooking wine, ginger juice, and white fungus to boiling water and continue to cook with medium heat for 10 minutes
- Add in chrysanthemum flowers and cook for 2-3 minutes
- Turn off heat and add 1-2 pinches of salt (add more if needed)
- Serve

Phlegm Dampness

Symptoms: You might be overweight and feel heavy in four limbs.

Recipe 1: Chinese Yam Winter Melon Soup with Chinese Barley

Ingredients:

- Chinese yam, cut into pieces, 1/4 cup
- Chinese barley, 1/4 cup
- Winter melon, cut into bitable chunks, 1 cup
- Clean water, 4 cups
- Himalayan salt, to taste

Serving size:

- 2

Total cooking time (estimated):

- 60 minutes

Preparation time (estimated):

- 5 minutes

Cooking time (estimated):

- 55 minutes

Instructions:

- Put Chinese yam, Chinese barley, and winter melon into water and bring the water to boil
- Cook with medium to low heat for 50 minutes (with lid on top of the pot)
- Turn off heat and add 1-2 pinches of salt
- Serve

Recipe 2: Radish Miso Soup

Ingredients:

- White radish, chopped into bitable chunks, 2 cups
- Scallions, chopped into small pieces, 1/3 cup
- Garlic, peeled and chopped, 3 cloves
- Clean water, 4 cups
- Miso paste, 1 tbsp
- Avocado oil, 1 tbsp

Serving size:

- 4

Total cooking time (estimated):

- 35 minutes

Preparation time (estimated):

- 10 minutes

Cooking time (estimated):

- 25 minutes

Instructions:

- Heat up the pot with medium heat, add in chopped garlic, and cook it until you can smell garlic
- Add in chunks of white radish and sauté for 5 minute
- Add in water and miso paste and cook with medium to low heat for 20 minutes (with lid on top of the pot)
- Add in scallions and stir well
- Turn off heat
- Serve

Special Diathesis

Symptoms: You easily get allergy and are sensitive to environmental changes.

Recipe 1: Scallion Lily Bulb Congee

Ingredients:

- Brown rice, 1/2 cup
- Dried lily bulbs, 1/4 cup
- Mint leaves, 5
- buckwheat, 1/4 cup
- Scallions, chopped, 1/3 cup

- Clean water, 4 cups

Serving size:

- 4

Total cooking time (estimated):

- 53 minutes

Preparation time (estimated):

- 3 minutes

Cooking time (estimated):

- 50 minutes

Instructions:

- Add brown rice, dried lily bulbs, buckwheat, and water to a pot and bring the water to boil
- Simmer for 45 minutes (with a lid on the top of the pot)
- Add chopped scallions and mint leaves and mix well
- Turn off heat and add 1-2 pinches of salt (add more if needed) and stir well
- Serve

Recipe 2: Celery Congee with Mixed Beans

Ingredients:

- Celeries, chopped into small pieces, 4 stalks
- Red beans, 1/4 cup
- Black beans, 1/4 cup
- Millet, 1/2 cup
- Clean water, 4 cups

- Miso paste, 1 tbsp

Serving size:

- 2

Total cooking time (estimated):

- 55 minutes

Preparation time (estimated):

- 5 minutes

Cooking time (estimated):

- 50 minutes

Instructions:

- Wash red beans and black beans, place beans and millet into a pot, and add in water
- Bring the water to boil, add in celeries, and simmer for 45 minutes (with lid on top of the pot)
- Add in miso paste, stir well, and turn off heat
- Serve

Gentleness

If your body type belongs to "gentleness", congratulations! That means you are currently having a healthy and balanced body. All you need to do is to pay attention to all the key dietary principles in spring outlined in Chapter 5, incorporate them into your life, and stick with a balanced lifestyle. Below I've incorporated two types of Chinese herbal tea that nourish the liver and moisturize the skin, two key activities you should do in this season.

Recipe 1: Goji Chrysanthemum Green Tea

Ingredients:

- Goji berries, 10 pieces
- Chrysanthemum flowers, 1/4 cup
- Green tea, 2 tsp
- Boiling hot water, 1-2 cups

Serving size:

- 1

Total cooking time (estimated):

- 6 minutes

Preparation time (estimated):

- 1 minute

Cooking time (estimated):

- 5 minutes

Instructions:

- Place goji berries, chrysanthemum flowers, and green tea into a cup that can hold hot water
- Pour in a little bit of hot water just enough to cover the mixture, rinse the mixture, and discard the juice (the key is to clean goji berries, chrysanthemum flowers, and green tea leaves)
- Pour in hot water, cover the cup with a lid, and wait for 3-5 minutes
- Serve

Notes:

- The steps above describe how I usually prepare this tea. I would use a spoon to press goji berries, chrysanthemum flowers, and tea leaves to the bottom of the cup and to keep them from floating to the top.

If you think it is too much work for you, you can alternatively use a cheese-cloth to wrap up all ingredients, tie up the cloth so that ingredients stay inside the cloth, place the cloth at the bottom of the cup, pour in water, and wait for 3-5 minutes before you enjoy the tea.

Recipe 2: Rose Honey Lemon Tea

Ingredients:

- Rose petals, 2 tsp
- Black tea, 2 tsp
- Honey, 2 tsp
- Lemon, slices, 1-2 slices
- Boiling hot water, 1-2 cups

Serving size:

- 1

Total cooking time (estimated):

- 16 minutes

Preparation time (estimated):

- 1 minute

Cooking time (estimated):

- 15 minutes (assuming we wait for 10 minutes for the water the cool down a little bit)

Instructions:

- Place rose petals and black tea into a cup that can hold hot water
- Pour in a little bit of hot water just enough to cover the mixture, rinse the mixture, and discard the juice (the key is to clean rose petals and black tea leaves)
- Put lemon slices and pour in hot water
- Add in honey when water starts to cool down
- Mix well and serve
- This tea, if consumed on a regular basis, is especially good for:
- Improving metabolism
- Stimulating blood and qi circulation
- Nourishing the skin
- Improving functions of the liver, the stomach, and the spleen

Chapter 19: Recipes for Qingming (Freshness and Clarity)

This is the time when weathers continue to be warmer, grass and trees continue to grow, and flowers blossom. It is important to continue to make sure your keep yourself warm and continue to focus on strengthening your immune system.

White Button Mushrooms with Napa Cabbage

Ingredients:

- Napa cabbage, cut into 2-inch strips, 4 cups
- White button mushrooms, cut into thin slices, 1 cup
- Avocado oil, 1 tbsp
- Sesame oil, 1 tsp
- Himalayan salt, to taste
- Black pepper, to taste
- Clean water, 1/3 cup (to cook napa cabbage)

Serving size:

- 2

Total cooking time (estimated):

- 18 minutes

Preparation time (estimated):

- 10 minutes

Cooking time (estimated):

- 8 minutes

Instructions:

- Add oil to pot and heat oil with medium to high heat
- Turn the heat to medium, add in strips of napa cabbage to pot and 1/3 cup of water, and cook till cabbage become soft and about 70% cooked
- Add in slices of mushrooms and sauté until mushrooms are cooked
- Turn off heat, add 1-2 pinches of salt, 1-2 pinches of grinded black pepper, and sesame oil into the pot, and mix well
- Serve
- This dish is especially good for:
- Nourishing the stomach
- Lowering the lipid levels in the blood
- People with heart disease and high blood pressure

Fried Mushrooms and Chinese Cabbage

Ingredients:

- Dried mushrooms, 8 pieces
- Chinese cabbage, sliced, 4 cups
- Ginger, minced, 1 tsp
- Scallion, chopped into small pieces, 1/3 cup
- Clean water, enough to soak 8 pieces of mushrooms
- Avocado oil, 1 tbsp
- Sesame oil, 1 tsp
- Himalayan salt, to taste

Serving size:

- 2

Total cooking time (estimated):

- 25 minutes (plus 6-8 hours for soaking the dried mushrooms)

Preparation time (estimated):

- 10 minutes (plus 6-8 hours for soaking the dried mushrooms)

Cooking time (estimated):

- 15 minutes

Instructions:

- Wash mushrooms till they are clean
- Soak mushrooms overnight (about 6-8 hours, the amount of water just enough to cover the mushrooms)
- Remove the stems, cut mushrooms into slices, and place them aside (save the water used to soak mushrooms)
- Add avocado oil into the pan and heat the oil with medium heat
- Add in ginger and slices of mushrooms and sauté for 5 minutes
- Add in sliced cabbage and sauté with medium to low heat for 3 minutes
- Pour the water used to soak mushrooms into the pot and continue to cook for 3-4 minutes (with lid on top of the pot)
- Add 2 pinches of salt, chopped scallions, and sesame oil into the pot and mix well (add more salt if needed)
- Turn off heat and serve

This dish is especially good for:

- Replenishing qi and improving qi circulation inside the body
- Lowering blood lipid levels
- Lowering blood sugar levels
- Improving immunity

Potato Chinese Yam Congee

Ingredients:

- Potatoes, peeled and chopped into small pieces, 1/2 cup
- Chinese yam, peeled and sliced, 1/2 cup
- Brown rice, 1/2 cup
- Clean water, 5 cups
- Himalayan salt, to taste
- Black pepper, grinded, to taste
- Cilantro, chopped, 1/4 cup
- Coconut oil, 2 tbsp

Serving size:

- 3-4

Total cooking time (estimated):

- 65 minutes

Preparation time (estimated):

- 10 minutes

Cooking time (estimated):

- 55 minutes

Instructions:

- Wash brown rice, place chopped potato pieces, sliced Chinese yam, brown rice and water into a pot, and bring the water to boil
- Simmer for 50 minutes
- Turn off heat and add in coconut oil, cilantro, grinded black pepper, and 2-3 pinches of salt
- Mix well and serve

This dish is especially good for:

- Strengthening the spleen and the stomach functions

Peanut White Fungus Congee

Ingredients:

- Raw peanuts, 1/2 cup
- Brown rice, 1/2 cup
- Dried white fungus, 1
- Clean water, 5 cups
- Honey, 1 tbsp

Serving size:

- 4

Total cooking time (estimated):

- 60 minutes (plus 2 hours for soaking white fungus)

Preparation time (estimated):

- 5 minutes (plus 2 hours for soaking white fungus)

Cooking time (estimated):

- 55 minutes

Instructions:

- Soak white fungus for 2 hours or till it is soft
- Cut white fungus into small pieces and rinse them under running water
- Wash brown rice, put peanut, pieces of white fungus, and brown rice into water in a pot, and bring the water to boil
- Simmer for 50 minutes (with lid on top of the pot)
- Turn off heat, add honey into the mix, and stir well
- Serve

This dish is especially good for:

- Moisturizing the skin
- Anti-aging
- Improving memory
- Improving brain functions
- Treating heart diseases and high blood pressure
- Improving qi circulation
- Nourishing the spleen, the stomach, and the lungs

Black Rice with Chinese Red Dates

Ingredients:

- Black rice, 1 cup
- Chinese red dates, pitted, 20 pieces
- Longan, 20 pieces
- Goji berries, 20 pieces
- Clean water, 2 cups

Serving size:

- 4

Total cooking time (estimated):

- 60 minutes

Preparation time (estimated):

- 5 minutes

Cooking time (estimated):

- 55 minutes

Instructions:

- Wash Chinese red dates and Longan and soak them in warm water for 5 minutes
- When dates and Longan become soft, cut them into small pieces and keep the water used for soaking red dates and longan
- Add cups of water and black rice into a pot and bring the water the boil
- Mix in pieces of red dates, Longan, water used for soaking both ingredients, and goji berries into the pot, stir well, and simmer for 40 minutes
- Turn off heat and serve

This dish is especially good for:

- Improving liver functions and vision
- Nourishing the kidneys, the spleen, and the stomach
- Improving qi and blood circulation
- Strengthening the body and improving immunity
- Nourishing the heart

Fried Chives with Sprouts

Ingredients:

- Soybean sprouts, 2 cups
- Chives, chopped into 2-inch strips, 1 cup
- Avocado oil, 1 tbsp
- Scallions, cut into small pieces, 1/4 cup
- Himalayan salt, to taste
- Sesame oil, 1 tsp

Serving size:

- 2

Total cooking time (estimated):

- 15 minutes

Preparation time (estimated):

- 5 minutes

Cooking time (estimated):

- 10 minutes

Instructions:

- Add avocado oil into a pot and heat the oil with medium to high heat
- Lower the heat to medium to low, add in scallions, and cook for 1-2 minutes
- Add soybean sprouts into the pot and cook for 1-2 minutes
- Add chives into the pot and cook for 3-4 minutes
- Mix in 1-2 pinches of salt and sesame oil and stir well
- Turn off heat and serve

This dish is especially good for:

- Relieving constipation
- Nourishing the liver
- Improving immunity
- Detoxifying the body
- Strengthening spleen and stomach functions

Fried Eggs with Chives

Ingredients:

- Organic eggs, 2
- Chives, cut into 2-inch strips, 2 cups
- Avocado oil, 2 tbsp
- Sesame oil, 1 tsp
- Himalayan salt, to taste

Serving size:

- 2

Total cooking time (estimated):

- 15 minutes

Preparation time (estimated):

- 5 minutes

Cooking time (estimated):

- 10 minutes

Instructions:

- Crack the eggs into a bowl and stir well until they form a

yellow paste inside the bowl
- Add 1 tbsp of avocado oil into the pot and heat oil with medium to high heat, add in the yellow paste, lower the heat to medium to low, cook the paste until it just becomes solid, and cut it into small pieces right inside the pot (the whole process should only take about 2-3 minutes)
- Transfer small pieces into a bowl
- Add in 1 tbsp of avocado oil into the pot and heat oil with medium to high heat
- Lower the heat to medium to low, add in chives, and cook for about 3 minutes
- Mix the egg pieces into the pot to cook with chives and sauté for 1-2 minutes
- Add in 1-2 pinches of salt and sesame oil and mix well
- Turn off heat and serve

This dish is especially good for:

- Improving digestion
- Strengthening the stomach and the kidneys
- Refreshing the mind

Celery with Fried Cashew

Ingredients:

- Celeries cut into 2-inch chunks, 2 cups
- Cashews, 15 pieces
- Fresh lily bulbs, 1/2 cup
- Onion, chopped into small pieces, 1/4 cup
- Clean water, 2 cups

- Himalayan salt, to taste
- Avocado oil, 1 tbsp (for cooking cashews)
- Avocado oil, 1 tbsp (for cooking onions pieces and celeries)

Serving size:

- 2

Total cooking time (estimated):

- 20 minutes plus 6-8 hours (for soaking lily bulb petals overnight)

Preparation time (estimated):

- 6-8 hours (for soaking the lily bulb petals overnight)

Cooking time (estimated):

- 20 minutes

Instructions:

- Peel off the lily bulb petals, clean them, and soak them overnight (about 6-8 hours)
- Cut off dark spots on white petals, rinse them under running water, and set them aside
- Add 2 cups of water to a pot and bring the water to boil
- Add in chopped celeries in boiling water and cook them for about 1 minute
- Discard water and use a container to hold slightly cooked celeries
- Add in 1 tbsp of avocado oil and cashews, cook the nuts with medium to low heat until they turn slightly brown, and use another container to hold cooked cashews
- Add 1 tbsp of avocado oil into the pan and heat up oil with medium heat
- Add in onion pieces and cook them until you can smell the

onion
- Add in celeries and petals and sauté for 4-5 minutes
- Add in cashews and continue to sauté for another 1-2 minutes
- Add 1-2 pinches of salt (add more if needed) and mix well
- Turn off heat and serve

This dish is especially good for:

- Improving digestion
- Nourishing the skin
- Preventing cancer
- Improving immune system
- Calming the mind
- Nourishing the lungs
- Cough relief

Bamboo Shoots Chicken Soup

Ingredients:

- Bamboo shoots, chopped into small chunks, 2 cups
- Dried mushrooms, 15 pieces
- Organic chicken breast, cut into small strips, 1 cup
- Himalayan salt, to taste
- Scallions, chopped into small pieces, 1/3 cup
- Clean water, 2 cups (for soaking dried mushrooms)
- Clean water, 2 cups (for boiling bamboo shoots)
- Clean water, 2 cups (for boiling chicken)

Serving size:

- 4

Total cooking time (estimated):

- 80 minutes plus 6-8 hours for soaking dried mushrooms overnight

Preparation time (estimated):

- 10 minutes plus 6-8 hours for soaking dried mushrooms overnight

Cooking time (estimated):

- 70 minutes

Instructions:

- Wash dried mushrooms
- Soak dried mushrooms overnight (about 6-8 hours, water just enough to cover mushrooms) and keep both mushrooms and water for later use
- Bring 2 cups of clean water to boil, place bamboo shoots to boiling water, cook for 3 minutes, and discard water
- Add chicken strips and 2 cups of clean water into a pot and bring the water to boil
- Add mushrooms and water used to soak mushrooms into the pot and bring the water the boil
- Simmer for 30 minutes
- Add bamboo shoots into the pot and cook for 20 minutes
- Add 3-4 pinches of salt (add more if needed) and chopped scallions and mix well
- Turn off heat and serve

This dish is especially good for:

- Improving digestion
- Relieving constipation
- Removing phlegm

- Improving stomach functions
- Improving qi circulation
- Moisturizing the body

Pear Chrysanthemum Tea

Ingredients:

- Pear, peeled and chopped into bitable chunks, 1
- Goji berries, 20 pieces
- Chrysanthemum flowers, 1/4 cup
- Honey, 1 tbsp
- Clean water, 2 cups

Serving size:

- 1-2

Total cooking time (estimated):

- 20 minutes

Preparation time (estimated):

- 5 minutes

Cooking time (estimated):

- 15 minutes

Instructions:

- Add pear chunks and water into a pot and bring the water to boil
- Add in goji berries and chrysanthemum flowers and simmer for 5 minutes
- Turn off heat and, when the tea starts to cool down (in

about 5 minutes), add honey, and mix well
- Serve

This dish is especially good for:

- Supporting and improving liver functions
- Improving vision
- Bringing down internal heat inside the body
- Nourishing the kidneys
- People with high blood pressure
- Moisturizing and nourishing the skin
- Treating insomnia

Chapter 20: Recipes for *Guyu* (More Rains and Benefiting for Growing Crops)

This is a time when more rains are expected, which benefits crop growing. On the flip side, an increased level of humidity in the air can lead to an increased amount of dampness inside the body, according to TCM. More dampness inside the body suggests potential joint pains, heaviness in the head and the whole body, sore muscles, and other symptoms. Therefore, driving out dampness inside the body becomes the priority on this *jieqi* and the 15 days that follow. Below are ten recipes believed to be able to effectively drive dampness out of the body.

Goji Egg Paste Stew

Ingredients:

- Organic egg, 2
- Goji berries, 10 pieces
- Clean water, 2 tbsp (for diluting the egg paste)
- Clean water, 2-3 cups (for boiling to steam the egg paste)
- Himalayan salt, to taste

Serving size:

- 1-2

Total cooking time (estimated):

- 16 minutes

Preparation time (estimated):

- 1 minute

Cooking time (estimated):

- 15 minutes

Instructions:

- Add 2-3 cups of water to the bottom of a steamer and bring it to boil
- (While boiling the water) Break eggs into a bowl, add in clean water, and quickly stir them into a paste
- (While boiling the water) Add goji berries into the paste and stir well
- (When the water is boiled) Place the bowl into a steamer and cook for 8-10 minutes
- Turn off heat and serve

This dish is especially good for:

- Nourishing and brightening up the skin
- Improving vision
- Strengthening liver functions
- Improving the kidneys
- Potentially relieving waist pain and knee pain

Bok Choy Chinese Barley Congee

Ingredients:

- Bok choy, chopped into small pieces, 2 cups
- Brown rice, 1/2 cup
- Chinese barley, 1/2 cup
- Clean water, 4 cups

- Himalayan salt, to taste

Serving size:

- 4

Total cooking time (estimated):

- 63 minutes

Preparation time (estimated):

- 3 minutes

Cooking time (estimated):

- 60 minutes

Instructions:

- Wash Chinese barley and brown rice
- Add Chinese barley, brown rice, and clean water to a pot and bring the water to boil
- Simmer for 50 minutes
- Add chopped bok choy to the congee, mix well, and continue to cook for 2-3 minutes
- Add 2-3 pinches of salt (add more if needed), mix well, and turn off heat
- Serve

This dish is especially good for:

- People with acne-prone skin
- Brightening up and smoothening the skin
- Bringing down internal heat
- Driving out dampness inside
- Strengthening the spleen functions
- Improving urinary flow
- Improving the kidneys

Pea Congee with Ginger

Ingredients:

- Peas, 1/3 cup
- Brown rice, 1/2 cup
- Ginger, sliced, 4-5 slices
- Himalayan salt, to taste
- Clean water, 4 cups
- Coconut oil, 2 tbsp

Serving size:

- 3-4

Total cooking time (estimated):

- 47 minutes

Preparation time (estimated):

- 2 minutes

Cooking time (estimated):

- 45 minutes

Instructions:

- Wash brown rice
- Add brown rice and water into a pot and bring the water to boil
- Add ginger slices and peas into the pot and simmer for 40 minutes
- Turn off heat, add 2-3 pinches of salt (add more if needed) and coconut oil, and stir well

- Serve

This dish is especially good for:

- Driving out dampness
- Warming up the body
- Improving immunity
- Improving the spleen functions

Winter Melon Chinese Barley Soup

Ingredients:

- Winter melon, peeled and chopped into bitable chunks, 1 cup
- Chinese barley, 1/2 cup
- Clean water, 4 cups
- Himalayan salt, to taste

Serving size:

- 2

Total cooking time (estimated):

- 65 minutes

Preparation time (estimated):

- 5 minutes

Cooking time (estimated):

- 60 minutes

Instructions:

- Add Chinese barley and water into a pot and bring the

water to boil
- Simmer for 50 minutes
- Add winter melon into the soup and cook for 3-5 minutes
- Add 2-3 pinches of salt, turn off heat, and serve

This dish is especially good for:

- Weight loss
- Relieving coughs
- Improving urinary flow
- People with high blood pressure and kidney diseases
- Nourishing the lungs
- Improving digestion
- Detoxifying the body
- Brightening up and healing the skin
- Relieving hangover

Black Fungus with Chinese Yam

Ingredients:

- Dried black fungus, 1/3 cup
- Chinese yam, chopped into pieces, 1/3 cup
- Cilantro, chopped, 1/4 cup
- Garlic, chopped, 2-3 cloves
- Clean water, 3/4 cup
- Coconut oil, 2 tbsp

Serving size:

- 2

Total cooking time (estimated):

- 22 minutes plus 3-4 hours for soaking dried black fungus

Preparation time (estimated):

- 5 minutes plus 3-4 hours for soaking dried black fungus

Cooking time (estimated):

- 17 minutes

Instructions:

- Soak dried black fungus in water for 3-4 hours
- Discard the water and rinse black fungus under running water
- Add coconut oil into a pot and cook with medium to low heat for 20-30 seconds
- Add chopped garlic into the pot and cook until you can smell garlic
- Add Chinese yam pieces into the pot, sauté for 2-3 minutes, and stew for another 5 minutes
- Add black fungus and water into the pot and stew the mixture for 4-5 minutes
- Add cilantro into the pot and continue to sauté for 1-2 minutes
- Turn off heat and add 1-2 pinches of salt (add more if needed)
- Serve

This dish is especially good for:

- Improving digestion
- Nourishing the stomach and the spleen
- Improving kidney functions
- Lowering blood sugar levels
- Improving longevity

- People with heart diseases
- Improving blood flow and circulation
- Improving immunity

Winter Melon with Fried Dried Shrimp

Ingredients:

- Winter melon, chopped into bitable slices, 1 cup
- Dried shrimp, 8-10 pieces
- Scallions, chopped, 2 tbsp
- Avocado oil, 1 tbsp
- Clean water, ¾ cup

Serving size:

- 2

Total cooking time (estimated):

- 20 minutes

Preparation time (estimated):

- 5 minutes

Cooking time (estimated):

- 15 minutes

Instructions:

- Add oil to pot and heat up the oil
- Wash dried shrimps, add them into pot, sauté for 3-4 minutes with medium to high heat
- Add in winter melon slices and sauté with medium heat for 2-3 minutes

- Add water into pot and stew for another 8 minutes with medium to low heat
- Add in scallions and 1-2 pinches of salt (add more if needed) and mix well
- Turn off heat and serve

This dish is especially good for:

- Weight loss
- Relieving coughs
- Improving urinary flow
- People with high blood pressure and kidney diseases
- Nourishing the lungs
- Improving digestion
- Detoxifying the body
- Brightening up and healing the skin
- Relieving hangover

Lotus Root Soup

Ingredients:

- Lotus roots, chopped into small chunks, 2 cups
- Raw peanuts, 1/2 cup
- Dried lotus seeds, embryos taken out of the seeds, 1/2 cup
- Lily bulbs with petals peeled off, 1/2 cup
- Honey dates, 1
- Chinese red dates, 5 pieces
- Dried mushrooms, 1/2 cup
- Cilantro, chopped, 1/2 cup
- Scallions, 1/3 cup

- Clean water, 6 cups
- Coconut oil, 3 tbsp
- Himalayan salt, to taste

Serving size:

- 4

Total cooking time (estimated):

- 95-125 minutes plus 6-8 hours for soaking dried mushrooms overnight and 2 hours for soaking dried lotus seeds

Preparation time (estimated):

- 5 minutes plus 6-8 hours for soaking dried mushrooms overnight and 2 hours for soaking dried lotus seeds

Cooking time (estimated):

- 90-120 minutes

Instructions:

- Wash dried mushrooms and soak them overnight for about 6-8 hours (add just enough water to cover the mushrooms; do not discard water and keep both mushrooms and water used for soaking mushrooms for later use)
- Soak dried lotus seeds for 2 hours
- Discard the water used for soaking lotus seeds and rinse seeds under running water
- Add mushrooms, water used for soaking mushrooms, raw peanuts, lotus seeds, lily bulb petals, honey dates, Chinese red dates, lotus roots, and clean water into a pot and bring it to boil
- Simmer for 1.5-2 hours

- Add in cilantro, scallions, 3-4 pinches of salt (add more if needed), and coconut oil and stir well
- Turn off heat and serve

This dish is especially good for:

- Improving digestion
- Improving appetite
- Strengthening the stomach and the spleen functions
- Relieving diarrhea
- Improving immunity
- Bringing down internal heat
- Nourishing the lungs
- Relieving coughs

Soybean Sprouts with Kelp

Ingredients:

- Soybean sprouts, 1 cup
- Kelp, cut into 2-inch strips, 1 cup
- Dried tofu, cut into 2-inch strips, 1 cup
- Scallions, chopped into small pieces, 1/3 cup
- Cooking wine, 1 tbsp
- Avocado oil, 2 tbsp
- Sesame oil, 1 tsp
- Himalayan salt, to taste
- Black pepper, grinded, to taste
- Clean water, 2 cups (for briefly boiling kelp trips)
- Clean water, 1/2 cup (for cooking)

Serving size:

- 4

Total cooking time (estimated):

- 22 minutes

Preparation time (estimated):

- 5 minutes

Cooking time (estimated):

- 17 minutes

Instructions:

- Bring the 2 cups of clean water to boil, add kelp strips into boiling water, quickly cook for 1-2 minutes, and discard the water
- Heat up avocado oil in a pan with medium to high heat
- Add in tofu strips and cook until strips turn brownish
- Add in kelp strips and stir fry for 2-3 minutes
- Lower the heat to medium, add in soybean sprouts, and sauté for 1-2 minutes
- Add in scallions, cooking wine, 1/2 cup of water, cooking wine, and 2-3 pinches of salt and stew with medium to low heat for 1-2 minutes
- Turn off heat, add in sesame oil and 2-3 pinches of grinded black pepper
- Serve

This dish is especially good for:

- Bringing down internal heat
- Driving out dampness
- Lowering blood lipid levels
- Detoxifying the body
- Improving urinary flow

- Removing phlegm
- Losing weight
- Relieving swelling
- Relieving coughs
- Treating heart disease
- Nourishing the skin

Sardine Soybean Sprout Zucchini Soup

Ingredients:

- Sardine fish, sliced with bones removed, 2 fish
- Soybean sprouts, 1 cup
- Ginger, sliced, 2-3 slices
- Zucchini, chopped into bitable chunks, 1 cup
- Clean water, 4 cups
- Avocado oil, 1 tbsp

Serving size:

- 2

Total cooking time (estimated):

- 73 minutes

Preparation time (estimated):

- 5 minutes

Cooking time (estimated):

- 68 minutes

Instructions:

- Heat up oil in a pan with medium to high heat

- Add in ginger slices
- Add in sardine fish and cook until fish turns brownish
- Add in 4 cups of water and zucchini chunks into the pan and bring the water to boil
- Add soybean sprouts into the mix and simmer for 1 hour (with lid on top of the pan)
- Add 1-2 pinches of salt (add more if needed)
- Turn off heat and serve
- This dish is especially good for:
- Strengthening the spleen functions
- Bringing down internal heat
- Driving out dampness
- Lowering blood lipid levels
- Detoxifying the body
- Improving urinary flow
- Removing phlegm
- Losing weight
- Relieving swelling
- Relieving coughs
- Treating heart disease
- Nourishing the skin

Mixed Vegetable Stew (Carrots, Straw Mushrooms, Bamboo Shoots, and Lettuce)

Ingredients:

- Baby carrots, cut into slices, 1 cup
- Straw mushrooms, 1 cup
- Bamboo shoots, cut into 2-inch strips, 1 cup

- Roman lettuce, sliced, 4 cups
- Black pepper, grinded, to taste
- Himalayan salt, to taste
- Chicken broth, 6 cups

Serving size:

- 4

Total cooking time (estimated):

- 32 minutes

Preparation time (estimated):

- 5 minutes

Cooking time (estimated):

- 27 minutes

Instructions:

- Add chicken broth to a pot and bring it to boil
- Add baby carrots, straw mushrooms, and bamboo shoots into boiling water and stew for 20 minutes with medium to low heat
- Add in lettuce and continue to cook for 1-2 minutes
- Add in 2-3 pinches of salt (add more if needed) and 2-3 pinches of grinded black pepper and mix well
- Turn off heat and serve

This dish is especially good for:

- Improving digestion
- Nourishing the skin
- Improving vision
- Lowering blood lipid levels
- Relieving constipation

- Driving out dampness and improving urinary flow
- Relieving swelling
- Losing weight

Part 3-2: Summer Eating Recipes

Chapter 21: Recipes for *Lixia* (Arrival of Summer)

As a reminder, you have learned from Chapter 6 already: it is recommended to protect the heart on this *jieqi*. Below are a series of heart-nourishing recipes for your reference.

Oatmeal Congee with Red Dates

Ingredients:

- Rolled oats, 1/2 cup
- Chinese red dates, pitted, 6 pieces
- Clean water, 2 cups
- Raisins, 2 tsp
- Himalayan salt, to taste

Serving size:

- 1-2

Total cooking time (estimated):

- 22 minutes

Preparation time (estimated):

- 2 minutes

Cooking time (estimated):

- 20 minutes

Instructions:

- Add rolled oats into water and bring the mixture to boil (with the lid on top of the pot)
- Add in Chinese red dates and simmer for 15 minutes
- Turn off heat
- Add in 1-2 pinches of salt (add more if needed) and raisins
- serve

This dish is especially good for:

- Improving digestion
- Preventing heart problems
- Nourishing the skin
- Enriching and replenishing
- Bringing down blood pressure

Seaweed with Egg Soup

Ingredients:

- Roasted seaweed, 15 g
- Organic egg, 1
- Clean water, 2 cups
- Himalayan salt, to taste

Serving size:

- 1

Total cooking time (estimated):

- 9 minutes

Preparation time (estimated):

- 1 minutes

Cooking time (estimated):

- 8 minutes

Instructions:

- Bring the water to boil
- Turn the heat down to medium to low heat, add in roasted seaweed, and stir well until seaweed becomes soft (the process should be only about 2 minutes)
- Turn off heat, break the egg into the pot, stir well in circular motion until the egg is cooked
- Add in 1 pinch of salt
- Serve

This dish is especially good for:

- Nourishing the heart and body
- Expel summer heat
- Preventing heart problems and high blood pressure (if you consume seaweed on a regular basis)
- Improving immunity
- Preventing you from cancer
- Improving memory
- Improving urinary flow
- Removing phlegm

Notes:

- I suggest only 1 pinch of salt because seaweed already tastes a little salty. As a result, you actually don't need that much sodium into your soup.

Pear with Red Dates

Ingredients:

- Pear, peeled and chopped to small pieces, 3
- Red dates, pitted, 15 pieces
- Goji berries, 30
- Clean water, 5 cups
- Honey, 3 tsp (optional, I personally would skip this)

Serving size:

- 3

Total cooking time (estimated):

- 30 minutes

Preparation time (estimated):

- 10 minutes

Cooking time (estimated):

- 20 minutes

Instructions:

- Bring the water to boil
- Add in chunks of pear, red dates, and goji berries and simmer for 15 minutes
- Turn off heat
- Serve

This dish is especially good for:

- Nourishing and moistening the lungs and the throat
- Hydrating the body
- Bringing down internal heat

Tomato with Fried Egg

Ingredients:

- Tomatoes, cut into small pieces, 6
- Organic eggs, 4
- Garlic, chopped, 2 cloves
- Celery stalks, chopped into small pieces, 2
- Himalayan salt, to taste
- Clean water, 1 cup
- Avocado oil, 2 tbsp
- Sesame oil, 2 tsp

Serving size:

- 3

Total cooking time (estimated):

- 20 minutes

Preparation time (estimated):

- 5 minutes

Cooking time (estimated):

- 15 minutes

Instructions:

- Crack the eggs into a bowl, mix them up until a yellow paste is formed, set the bowl aside for later use
- Heat the pan with 1 tbsp of avocado oil using medium to high heat
- Add in the egg paste, turn the heat to medium to low, and let it sit without stirring until the bottom of the egg paste becomes solid and forms a thin slice of an egg pancake
- Turn the egg pancake over with the turner and cook the other side for about 15-30 seconds (it doesn't matter if you break the cooked egg paste into pieces, because you are going to break the pancake into small pieces later on anyway)
- Use the edge of the turner to cut the cooked egg pancake into small bitable pieces right in the frying pan
- Place egg pancake pieces into a bowl and set the pieces aside for later use
- Add 1 tbsp of avocado oil into the pan and heat it up with medium to high heat
- Lower the heat to medium, add in garlic and cook until garlic starts to turn brown-ish and you can smell it
- Add in tomato pieces and sauté for 2-3 minutes
- Add 1 cup of water into tomato pieces and stew with medium to low heat for 5 minutes
- Use the turner to press the tomato pieces so that tomato juices come out into the soup
- Add egg pancake pieces and chopped celeries into tomato soup and stew with medium to low heat for 2-3 minutes (this step help egg pancake pieces absorb as many tomato juice as possible)
- Turn off heat and add in 2-3 pinches of salt and sesame oil
- Serve

This dish is especially good for:

- Improving immunity
- Nourishing the skin
- Lowering blood pressure
- Strengthening the stomach
- Improving appetite and digestion
- Driving out internal heat
- Detoxifying the body
- Nourishing the liver
- Preventing heart problems

Purple Cabbage Salad with White Sesame Seeds

Ingredients:

- Purple cabbage, sliced, 2 cups
- Scallions, chopped, 1/4 cup
- Sesame oil, 2 tsp
- Cilantro, cut into small pieces, 1/3 cup
- White sesame seeds, 1-2 tbsp
- Red chili oil, to taste (optional)
- Himalayan salt, to taste

Serving size:

- 2

Total cooking time (estimated):

- 5 minutes

Preparation time (estimated):

- 2 minutes

Cooking time (estimated):

- 3 minutes

Instructions:

- Wash and drain white sesame seeds and cook them on a pan with medium to low heat until they are dry and become brown-ish
- Mix slices of purple cabbage, scallions, sesame oil, cooked white sesame seeds, and cilantro together into a bowl
- Add 2 pinches of salt into the mixture (add more if needed)
- Add 1-2 tsp of red chili oil into the mixture (add more if needed)
- Stir well and serve

This dish is especially good for:

- Nourishing the skin
- Treating various kinds of skin issues such as itchiness and eczema
- Anti-aging
- Losing weight
- Improving immunity
- Preventing you from catching a cold
- Relieving joint pains
- Bringing down inflammation
- Improving digestion and alleviate constipation

Notes:

- If you have sensitive and acne-prone skin like mine, then red chili oil is not recommended. As TCM believes that red chili oil can bring up internal heat inside your body which already has excess heat (if you have acne-prone skin). Therefore, consuming red chili oil may lead to breakouts.

Chinese Barley Red Bean Soup

Ingredients:

- Red beans, 1 cup
- Chinese barley, 1/2 cup
- Clean water, 5 cups

Serving size:

- 3

Total cooking time (estimated):

- 56 minutes

Preparation time (estimated):

- 1 minutes

Cooking time (estimated):

- 55 minutes

Instructions:

- Add red beans and Chinese barley into the water and bring the water to boil
- Simmer for 50 minutes (with a lid on top of the pot)
- Turn off heat and serve

This dish is especially good for:

- Improving metabolism
- Driving out dampness out of the body
- Strengthening kidney functions
- Nourishing the skin
- Nourishing the heart
- Bringing down internal heat
- Calming the mind
- Reducing swelling
- Bringing down blood sugar level

Lotus Seeds Congee

Ingredients:

- Dried lotus seeds, with embryos removed, 1/2 cup
- Brown rice, 1/2 cup
- Clean water, 4 cups

Serving size:

- 2

Total cooking time (estimated):

- 49 minutes

Preparation time (estimated):

- 4 minutes

Cooking time (estimated):

- 45 minutes

Instructions:

- Soak dried lotus seeds for 3-4 hours, drain them, and wash them under running water, and drain them again
- Put lotus seeds and brown rice into the water and bring the water to boil
- Simmer for 50 minutes (with lid on top of the top)
- Turn off heat and serve

This dish is especially good for:

- Calming the mind
- Treating insomnia
- Alleviating agitation
- Improving vision
- Nourishing the spleen and the stomach
- Treating diarrhea

Millet Longan Congee

Ingredients:

- Millet, 1/2 cup
- Goji berries, 20 pieces
- Longan, 15 pieces
- Clean water, 3 cups

Serving size:

- 2

Total cooking time (estimated):

- 41 minutes

Preparation time (estimated):

- 1 minutes

Cooking time (estimated):

- 40 minutes

Instructions:

- Add millet into the water and bring the water to boil
- Simmer for 25 minutes
- Add goji berries and longan into the congee and continue to simmer for 10 minutes
- Turn off heat and serve

This dish is especially good for:

- Nourishing the spleen
- Nourishing the heart
- Calming the mind
- Enriching and replenishing the blood

Pumpkin Millet Congee

Ingredients:

- Millet, 1 cup
- Pumpkin, peeled and cut into bitable chunks, 4 cups
- Clean water, 7 cups

Serving size:

- 4

Total cooking time (estimated):

- 50 minutes

Preparation time (estimated):

- 5 minutes

Cooking time (estimated):

- 45 minutes (actual cooking is just about 10 minutes)

Instructions:

- Wash millet, add it to water 3 cups of water, and bring the water to boil
- Simmer for 25 minutes
- (While cooking millet), add pumpkin chunks and 4 cups of water into a blender, blend the mixture into a paste, and pour the paste into a bowl for later use
- (After simmering for 25 minutes) add pumpkin paste into the congee, stir well, and continue to simmer for another 15 minutes
- Turn off heat and serve

This dish is especially good for:

- Nourishing the skin
- Improving digestion
- Fighting wrinkles
- Lowering blood sugar level
- Preventing cancer
- Calming the mind

Rose Brown Rice Congee

Ingredients:

- Brown rice, 1/2 cup
- Rose petals, 1/4 cup
- Clean water, 3 cups

Serving size:

- 2

Total cooking time (estimated):

- 45 minutes

Preparation time (estimated):

- 2 minutes

Cooking time (estimated):

- 42 minutes

Instructions:

- Wash brown rice, add it to the water, and bring the water to boil
- Simmer for 35 minutes (with lid on top of the pot)
- (While cooking brown rice) wash rose petals under running water, drain them, and set them aside for later use
- (After simmering for 35 minutes) Add in rose petals, mix well, and continue to simmer for 5 minutes
- Turn off heat and serve

This dish is especially good for:

- Preventing heart problems
- Calming the mind
- Improving the stomach and the spleen functions
- Nourishing the skin

Chapter 22: Recipes for *Xiaoman* (Crops Almost Mature but not Fully Ripe)

In this *jieqi*, there is more rain, lots of sunlight, and warmer and warmer weather. This type of climate characteristics can trigger a series of health issues such as in joints and in your skin. The priority, therefore, should go to preventing disease. Key practices are eating a plant-based diet and enjoying foods that can expel heat and drive out dampness due to higher humidity.

Steamed Bitter Melon Slices

Ingredients:
- Bitter melons, with seeds removed and cut it into thin slices, 2 cups
- Clean water, 4 cups
- Himalayan salt, to taste
- Sesame oil, 4 tsp

Serving size:
- 4

Total cooking time (estimated):
- 15 minutes

Preparation time (estimated):
- 5 minutes

Cooking time (estimated):
- 10 minutes

Instructions:
- Place water at the bottom of the steamer and bring it to boil
- Place bitter melon slices onto the rack and make sure slices are evenly spread out
- Steam for 3-5 minutes

- Take bitter melon slices out into a bowl
- Mix with 1- 2 pinches of salt and sesame oil and stir well
- Serve

This dish is especially good for:
- Bringing down internal heat
- Driving out dampness
- Activating skin cells and brightening the skin
- Improving vision
- Cleansing your liver
- Detoxifying your body
- Treating acne breakouts
- Bringing down blood sugar level
- Losing weight

Notes:
- You could add more salt if you want. But make sure you don't add too much. The point of adding salt here is to just slightly enhance the flavor. Too much salt can make the dish tastes too heavy and too much of saltiness does not blend well with bitterness. And, it is not good for your health either by making the dish too salty.

Mung Bean Soup

Ingredients:
- Mung beans, 1 cup
- clean water, 5 cup

Serving size:
- 4

Total cooking time (estimated):
- 41 minutes

Preparation time (estimated):
- 1 minute

Cooking time (estimated):
- 40 minutes

Instructions:
- Wash mung beans and add them to water
- Bring the water to boil
- Simmer for 35 minutes (with lid on top of the pot)
- Serve

This dish is especially good for:
- Improving immunity
- Effectively preventing different skin problems such inflammation, eczema, and acne breakouts
- Bringing down internal heat
- Treating food poisoning
- Treating and preventing high level of blood lipid

Notes:
- In China, a lot of people would like to make this soup into a desert by adding sugar into it. While I do not recommend adding refined sugar into the soup, you would add a little bit of honey to make the soup taste better. Personally, I would just enjoy this mung bean soup without adding anything else.

Broad Bean Congee

Ingredients:
- Broad beans, 1/2 cup
- Brown rice, 1/2 cup
- Clean water, 4 cup
- Himalayan salt, to taste

Serving size:
- 2

Total cooking time (estimated):
- 51 minutes

Preparation time (estimated):
- 1 minutes

Cooking time (estimated):

- 50 minutes

Instructions:
- Wash brown rice, add brown rice into water, and bring the water to boil
- (While boil the water) wash broad beans
- When water is boiled, add in broad beans and simmer for 45 minutes (with lid on top of the pot)
- Turn off heat and add 1-2 pinches of salt
- Serve

This dish is especially good for:
- Supporting and strengthening spleen functions
- Driving out dampness
- Nourishing different organs
- Reducing swelling
- Improving digestion

Celery Tofu Mix

Ingredients:
- Celery stalks, cut into small 2-inch pieces, 2 cups
- Dried tofu, cut into small bitable pieces, 1 cup
- Clean water, 3 cups
- Himalayan salt, to taste
- Sesame oil, 3-4 tsp

Serving size:
- 3-4

Total cooking time (estimated):
- 18 minutes

Preparation time (estimated):
- 5 minutes

Cooking time (estimated):
- 13 minutes

Instructions:
- Bring the water to boil

- Lower the heat to medium, add celery chunks and pieces of tofu into the water, and cook for 5 minutes
- Take cooked celery and tofu pieces out of the water, rinse them under clean water with room temperature, drain them, and place them in a bowl
- Mix in 3-4 pinches of salt and sesame oil and stir well
- Serve

This dish is especially good for:
- Nourishing the liver
- Bringing down internal heat
- Detoxifying the body
- Driving out dampness
- Stimulating bowel movements
- Improving digestion

Water Chestnut Lotus Root Mix

Ingredients:
- Water chestnuts, peeled and cut into bitable pieces, 1 cup
- Lotus roots, cleaned, peeled, and cut into bitable pieces, 1 cup
- Clean water, 2 cups
- Himalayan salt, to taste

Serving size:
- 2-3

Total cooking time (estimated):
- 35 minutes

Preparation time (estimated):
- 10 minutes

Cooking time (estimated):
- 25 minutes

Instructions:
- Bring the water to boil

- Add in water chestnut and lotus root pieces and simmer for 20 minutes
- Turn off heat, add 1-2 pinches of salt, and mix well
- Serve

This dish is especially good for:
- Nourishing the spleen and the stomach
- Expelling heat and dampness
- Treating diarrhea

Mung Bean Brown Rice Congee

Ingredients:
- Mung beans, 1/2 cup
- Brown rice, 1 cup
- Clean water, 4 cups

Serving size:
- 4

Total cooking time (estimated):
- 46 minutes

Preparation time (estimated):
- 1 minute

Cooking time (estimated):
- 45 minutes

Instructions:
- Wash mung beans and brown rice, add them into clean water, and bring the water to boil
- Simmer for 40 minutes (with lid on top of the pot)
- Turn off heat and serve

This dish is especially good for:
- Detoxifying the body
- Relieving thirst
- Reducing swelling
- Driving out internal heat
- Calming the mind

Bitter Melon Chrysanthemum Congee

Ingredients:
- Bitter melons, cut into small pieces, 1 cup
- Chrysanthemum flowers, 1/3 cup
- Brown rice, 1/2 cup
- Clean water, 4 cups
- (If you want to make savory congee) Himalayan salt, to taste
- (If you want to make the congee sweet) Honey, 2 tsp

Serving size:
- 2

Total cooking time (estimated):
- 53-63 minutes

Preparation time (estimated):
- 3 minutes

Cooking time (estimated):
- 50-60 minutes

Instructions:
- Wash brown rice, add it into water, and bring the water to boil
- Simmer for 40 minutes
- Add bitter melons and chrysanthemum flowers into congee and continue to simmer for another 5 minutes
- Turn off heat
- (If you want to make savory congee) add 1-2 pinches of salt and mix well
- (If you want to make sweet congee) wait until the congee is not burning hot before you add honey and mix well
- Serve

This dish is especially good for:
- Expel summer heat
- Treating heatstroke in summer

- Detoxifying the body
- Brightening up the skin
- Calming the mind

Watermelon Skin Congee (Yes, even watermelon skin is useful!)

Ingredients:
- Watermelon skin, with the green coating peeled off, cut into bitable chunks, 2 cups
- Brown rice, 1 cup
- Himalayan salt, to taste
- Clean water, 6 cups

Serving size:
- 4

Total cooking time (estimated):
- 50 minutes

Preparation time (estimated):
- 5 minutes

Cooking time (estimated):
- 45 minutes

Instructions:
- Wash brown rice, add brown rice and small chunks of water melon skin into water, and bring the water to boil
- Simmer for 40 minutes (with lid on top of the pot)
- Turn off heat, add 3-4 pinches of salt (add more if needed), and mix well
- Serve

This dish is especially good for:
- Improving unitary flow
- Reducing swelling
- Expelling heat
- Treating heatstroke

Notes:

- If you are wondering whether you can actually eat watermelon skin, the answer is yes. You can eat the whitish green portion of the skin. It's recommended that you skip the outer layer – the green part. That's why, in this recipe, the instruction asks you to peel off the green skin on the outside of the watermelon skin.

Chinese Barley Red Bean Congee

Ingredients:
- Chinese barley, 1/4 cup
- Red beans,1/4 cup
- Brown rice, 1/2 cup
- Clean water, 4 cups

Serving size:
- 2

Total cooking time (estimated):
- 56 minutes

Preparation time (estimated):
- 1 minutes

Cooking time (estimated):
- 55 minutes

Instructions:
- Wash Chinese barley, red beans, and brown rice, add them into clean water, and bring the water to boil
- Simmer for 50 minutes (with lid on top of the pot)
- Turn off heat and serve

This dish is especially good for:
- Nourishing and strengthening the spleen
- Removing dampness out of the body
- Detoxifying the body
- Expelling summer heat

Black Fungus with Celery

Ingredients:
- Dried black fungus, 1/2 cup
- Celery stalks, cut into 2-inch pieces, 1 cup
- Scallions, chopped into small pieces, 1/4 cup
- Clean water, 2 cups (for soaking dried black fungus)
- Clean water, 4 cups (for cooking black fungus and celery)
- Olive oil,
- Sesame oil
- Himalayan salt, to taste

Serving size:
- 3-4

Total cooking time (estimated):
- 13 minutes plus 3-4 hours for soaking black fungus

Preparation time (estimated):
- 3-4 hours (for soaking black fungus)

Cooking time (estimated):
- 13 minutes

Instructions:
- Soak dried black fungus in 2 cups of water for 3-4 hours
- Rinse black fungus under running water, drain fungus, and place them in a bowl for later use
- Bring 4 cups of water to boil
- Lower the heat to medium, add black fungus and celery pieces into water, and cook for 5 minutes
- Drain both black fungus and celery pieces and place them in a bowl
- Add scallions into the bowl and mix well
- Add 3-4 pinches of salt, olive oil and sesame oil and mix well

This dish is especially good for:
- Enriching the blood
- Nourishing the stomach, the kidneys, and the heart

- Preventing heart problems
- Detoxifying the body
- Improving digestion

Chapter 23: Recipes for *Mangzhong* (Grains Becoming Mature)

From *xiaoman* (crops almost mature but not fully ripe) to *mangzhong*, there is a continual increase in temperature and humidity. In addition to paying attention to strengthening your immune system, you should also focus on sun protection and moisture prevention. When you peel off the outer layers of these three phrases – "sun protection", "moisture prevention", and "improving immunity", you will find that these two *jieqi* are, in essence, basically advocating the same key health principles to maintain and improve health in summer: expelling heat and removing dampness out of the body.

Therefore, below are 10 recipes that also help you reduce summer heat and dampness. Enjoy!

Lotus Root Egg Paste

Ingredients:
- Lotus roots, peeled and cut into small chunks, 1 cup
- Organic eggs, 2
- Clean water, 1.5 cups (for blending lotus root chunks)
- Clean water, 2 cups (for steaming lotus root egg paste)
- Sesame oil, 2 tsp
- Himalayan salt, to taste

Serving size:
- 2

Total cooking time (estimated):
- 20 minutes

Preparation time (estimated):

- 5

Cooking time (estimated):
- 15 minutes

Instructions:
- Add 2 cups of clean water into the bottom of a steamer and bring it to boil
- (While boiling the water) place lotus root chunks and 1.5 cups of clean water into a blender, make it into a lotus root paste, and pour it into a bowl
- (While boiling the water) crack 2 eggs into another bowl, stir well, and make eggs into a paste
- (While boiling the water) pour the egg paste into lotus root paste and mix well
- After the water is boiled, place the bowl of lotus root egg paste on the rack and steam for 10 minutes with medium to high heat
- Turn off heat, take lotus root egg paste out of the steamer, add sesame oil, and sprinkle 2 pinches of salt on the top
- Serve

This dish is especially good for:
- Nourishing the spleen and the stomach
- Enriching the blood
- Improving blood circulation
- Relieving agitation due to hot weathers

Lotus Root Lily Paste

Ingredients:
- Lotus roots, peeled and chopped into small chunks, 1 cup
- Fresh lily bulbs, cleaned and peeled into small petals, 1/3 cup
- Honey, 2 tsp
- Clean water, 1.5 cups

Serving size:
- 2

Total cooking time (estimated):
- 25 minutes

Preparation time (estimated):
- 5 minutes

Cooking time (estimated):
- 20 minutes

Instructions:
- Add lotus root chunks and clean water into a blender and blend away until the mixture becomes a paste
- Pour the paste into a pot, add lily petals, and mix well
- Cook the mixture with medium heat for 10-15 minutes
- Turn off heat and add honey when lotus root lily paste cools down (which means that the paste is not burning hot)
- Serve

This dish is especially good for:
- Moistening the lungs and the throat
- Cough relief
- Calm the mind
- Reducing swelling
- Relieving insomnia

Sweet Sour Yellow-fin Tuna

Ingredients:
- Yellow-fin tuna fillets, 17 ounce
- Green peppers, chopped into bitable pieces, 1/3 cup
- Avocado oil, 2 tbsp
- Honey, 1 tbsp
- Vinegar, 1 tbsp
- Cooking wine, 2 tbsp
- Ginger, chopped into small pieces, 2 tbsp
- Scallions, chopped into small pieces, 1/4 cup

- Clean water, 1/2 cup
- Himalayan salt, to taste

Serving size:
- 2

Total cooking time (estimated):
- 17 minutes

Preparation time (estimated):
- 5 minutes

Cooking time (estimated):
- 12 minutes

Instructions:
- Heat up the frying pan with avocado oil
- Place tuna fillets on the pan and fry with medium to high heat for 2 minutes
- Flip the fish fillets over and cook the other side with medium to high heat again for 2 minutes
- Add 1/2 cup of water into the pan, lower the heat to medium, and stew for 4-5 minutes
- Place the fish fillets onto a plate and set aside
- Place green pepper pieces onto the same frying pan and sauté with medium to low heat for 1-2 minutes
- Turn the heat to medium to low, add in scallion pieces, ginger pieces, vinegar, honey, cooking wine, and 2 pinches of salt, and mix well
- Turn off heat and spread the seasoning evenly onto the fillets
- Serve

This dish is especially good for:
- Anti-aging
- Preventing cancer
- Fighting free radicals
- People with anemia
- Replenishing qi
- Improving qi flow
- Treating insomnia

Winter Melon Stew

Ingredients:
- Winter melons, peeled and chopped into bitable chunks, 1 cup
- Dried mushrooms, 8 pieces
- Ginger, chopped into small pieces, 2 tbsp
- Scallions, chopped into small pieces, 1/4 cup
- Clean water, 1 cup (for soaking dried mushrooms)
- Clean water, 1 cup
- Sesame oil, 2 tsp
- Himalayan salt, to taste

Serving size:
- 2

Total cooking time (estimated):
- 22 minutes

Preparation time (estimated):
- 5 minutes plus 6-8 hours for soaking dried mushrooms overnight

Cooking time (estimated):
- 17 minutes

Instructions:
- Wash dried mushrooms and soak fried mushrooms overnight (about 6-8 hours) in 1 cup of water
- Cut mushrooms into small pieces
- Place pieces of mushrooms, water used to soak mushrooms overnight, winter melon chunks, and 1 more cup of water into a pot
- Bring the water to boil and simmer for 10 minutes
- Add ginger, scallions, and 2 pinches of salt into the stew and continue to simmer for another 2 minutes
- Turns off heat, add in sesame oil, and mix well
- Serve

This dish is especially good for:
- Bringing down summer heat
- Improving immunity
- Driving out dampness
- Weight loss
- Nourishing the lungs
- Reducing swelling
- Stimulate bowel movements
- Preventing cancer
- Lowering blood sugar level

Steamed Lotus Roots Stuffed with Black Rice

Ingredients:
- Lotus root, peeled, 1 (about 6 inches long)
- Black rice, 1/2 cup
- Honey, 1 tbsp
- Clean water, 4 cups (for boiling the lotus root)

Serving size:
- 2

Total cooking time (estimated):
- 39 minutes (disregarding the time needed to cool down the stuffed lotus roots and to cut it into thin slices)

Preparation time (estimated):
- 1 minutes plus 3-4 hours for soaking black rice

Cooking time (estimated):
- 38 minutes (disregarding the time needed to cool down the stuffed lotus roots and to cut it into thin slices)

Instructions:
- Wash black rice and soak it for 3-4 hours
- Cut off one end of the lotus root
- Stuff soaked black rice into the holes

- Place the piece of lotus root that has been cut off back to its original spot to seal the holes and prevent black rice from dropping out (you can use 2 or 3 toothpicks to hold two parts together – the part that has been cut off and the rest of the lotus root)
- Put 4 cups of water into a pot and bring it to boil
- Place stuffed lotus into the pot and steam with medium heat for 30 minutes
- Turn off heat, take stuffed lotus root out of the pot, and let it sit until the temperature cools down
- Cut the stuffed lotus root into thin slices (an image is attached below for your reference)
- Dip slices of stuffed lotus root into honey and serve

This dish is especially good for:
- Nourishing and moistening the lungs
- Clearing summer heat
- Nourishing the spleen and the stomach
- Treating diarrhea
- Reducing agitation due to hot weathers
- Improving blood circulation
- Improving appetite
- Enriching, replenishing, and nourishing the blood
- Fighting free radicals
- Improving immunity

Notes:

- Below is an image of lotus root slices.

Chicken Breast Strips with Black Fungus, Cucumbers, and Eggs

Ingredients:
- Chicken breast, cut into 2-inch long thin strips, 1 cup
- Organic eggs, 4
- Dried black fungus, 1/3 cup
- Cucumbers, cut into small bitable pieces, 1 cup
- Ginger, chopped into small pieces, 2 tbsp
- Cooking wine, 2 tbsp
- Clean water, 2 cups (for soaking dried black fungus)
- Clean water, 2 cups (for boiling soaked black fungus)
- Avocado oil, 1 tbsp
- Himalayan salt, to taste

Serving size:
- 3-4

Total cooking time (estimated):
- 34 minutes plus 3-4 hours for soaking dried black fungus

Preparation time (estimated):
- 5 minutes plus 3-4 hours for soaking dried black fungus

Cooking time (estimated):
- 29 minutes

Instructions:
- Wash dried black fungus and soak them in 2 cups of water for 3-4 hours
- Boil 2 cups of water
- (While boiling the water) drain black fungus, rinse them under running water, drain them again, place them in a bowl for later use
- (After the water is boiled) place black fungus into boiling water and cook them with medium to lower heat for 20 minutes
- (While cooking black fungus) break eggs into a bowl and stir them into an egg paste
- (While cooking black fungus) heat up a pan with avocado oil, add egg paste into the pan, fry eggs with medium to low heat, place fried egg paste into a bowl for later use
- (While cooking black fungus) add chicken breast strips into the same frying pan and cook with medium to high heat until chicken starts to turn brown-ish
- (While cooking black fungus) Lower the heat to medium to low, add in cucumbers, and sauté for 1-2 minutes
- (While cooking black fungus) place fried chicken breast with cucumbers onto a plate for later use
- (After black fungus have been cooked for 20 minutes) add fried chicken breast with cucumbers, fried egg paste, and black fungus into the same frying pan and sauté with medium to low heat with 2 minutes

- Add ginger, cooking wine, and 3- pinches of salt, and continue to sauté with medium to low heat for 1-2 minutes
- Turn off heat and serve

This dish is especially good for:
- Preventing heart disease
- Nourishing qi and blood
- Improving qi and blood flow
- Lowering blood lipid level
- Detoxifying the body
- Nourishing the spleen, the stomach, and the kidneys
- Reducing swelling
- Calming the mind
- Treating insomnia
- Bringing down internal heat

Purple Yam Honey Soup with Lily Petals and White Fungus

Ingredients:
- Dried white fungus, 1
- Purple yam, peeled and cut into small pieces, 1 cup
- Fresh lily bulbs, peeled into petals, 1/3 cup
- Clean water, 2 cups (for soaking white fungus)
- Clean water, 4 cups (for making the soup)
- Honey

Serving size:
- 2

Total cooking time (estimated):
- 110 minutes plus 3-4 hours for soaking white fungus (disregarding the time needed to cool down the soup before adding honey)

Preparation time (estimated):
- 5 minutes plus 3-4 hours for soaking white fungus

Cooking time (estimated):
- 105 minutes (disregarding the time needed to cool down the soup before adding honey)

Instructions:
- Soak dried white fungus in 2 cups of water for 3-4 hours
- Cut soaked white fungus into small pieces, add pieces of white fungus into water, bring the water to boil, and simmer for 60 minutes
- Add pieces of purple yam and lily petals into white fungus and continue to simmer for 45 minutes
- Turn off heat, add honey when the soup cools down, and mix well
- Serve

This dish is especially good for:
- Strengthening liver functions
- Improving immunity
- Clearing internal heat
- Moisturizing and nourishing the body and the skin
- Losing weight
- Improving digestion
- Enriching and replenishing qi and blood
- Increasing energy and fighting fatigue
- Preventing cancer
- Nourishing the heart

Lotus Root Peanut Soup with Kelp

Ingredients:
- Lotus root, peeled and cut into small bitable chunks, 1 cup
- Peanut, 1/3 cup
- Kelp, cut into 2-inch long strips, 1 cup
- Ginger, cut into small pieces, 2 tbsp
- Clean water, 4 cups

- Himalayan salt, to taste

Serving size:
- 2

Total cooking time (estimated):
- 35 minutes

Preparation time (estimated):
- 10 minutes

Cooking time (estimated):
- 25 minutes

Instructions:
- Add peanuts into water and bring the water to boil
- Add lotus root chunks, ginger, and strips of kelp into the water and simmer for 20 minutes
- Turn off heat, add 1-2 pinches of salt, mix well
- Serve

This dish is especially good for:
- Bringing down internal heat
- Nourishing and moisturizing the skin
- Moistening and nourishing the lungs and the throat
- Nourishing and strengthening the spleen and the stomach
- Lowering blood pressure
- Lowering blood lipid level
- Preventing cancer
- Lowering blood sugar level
- Improving immunity
- Driving out dampness
- Reducing swelling
- Preventing heart problems

Chinese Yam with Goji Berries

Ingredients:

- Fresh Chinese yam, peeled and cut into 3-inch long strips, 1 cup
- Goji berries, 20 pieces
- Honey, 1 tbsp
- Apple cider vinegar, 1 tbsp
- Clean water, 3 cups

Serving size:
- 2

Total cooking time (estimated):
- 15 minutes

Preparation time (estimated):
- 3 minutes

Cooking time (estimated):
- 12 minutes

Instructions:
- Bring the water the boil
- Add Chinese yam into the water and cook with medium to high heat for 5 minutes
- Lower the heat to medium to low, add in goji berries, honey, and vinegar, and continue to cook for 2 minutes
- Turn off heat and serve

This dish is especially good for:
- Bringing down internal
- Improving vision
- Brightening up the skin
- Nourishing and moisturizing the skin

Notes:
- There are three ways you can enjoy this dish: first, you can immediately enjoy it when it's made; or, you can let it sit for 1 hour so that the sweet and sour flavors can sink into Chinese yam; for the third option, you can store it into the fridge after it cools down.

Coconut Lily Chinese Yam Milk

Ingredients:
- Fresh lily bulbs, peeled into lily petals, 1/3 cup
- Chinese yam, peeled and cut into 3-inch thin strips, 1 cup
- Clean water, 2 cups
- Young coconut, 1

Serving size:
- 2

Total cooking time (estimated):
- 15 minutes

Preparation time (estimated):
- 5 minutes

Cooking time (estimated):
- 10 minutes

Instructions:
- Bring the water to boil
- Place Chinese yam into the water and cook with medium to high heat for 5 minutes
- (While cooking Chinese yam) crack the young coconut, pour fresh coconut juice and coconut meat into a blender, and blend away
- (After cooking Chinese yam for 5 minutes) lower the heat to medium to low, add lily petals into Chinese yam, and continue to cook for 3-4 minutes
- Pour coconut milk into the pot, stir well, and cook for 1 minute
- Turn off heat and serve

This dish is especially good for:
- Moisturizing, nourishing, and brightening up the skin
- Moistening the lungs and throat
- Nourishing the spleen and the stomach
- Clearing internal heat
- Calming the mind

Notes:

- For tips on how to crack a coconut, you can go check this video on YouTube: http://bit.ly/crack-a-coconut.

Chapter 24: Recipes for *Xiazhi* (Official Summer)

It's getting hotter and hotter!

That's why your top priority is to make sure you don't get heatstroke and to minimize the chances of you being affected by internal heat buildup. Consuming dishes that clear away excess heat internally becomes the key on this *jieqi*.

Additionally, allow me to nag about it one more time: I know that you are likely to consume cold drinks or foods more often in this hot season. Make sure you do so with discipline, as excess intake of cold foods can affect your long-term health. But, yes, occasionally, feel free to indulge yourself from time to time with a cold drink or two.

Honeysuckle Flower Congee

Ingredients:
- Dried honeysuckle flowers, 2 tbsp
- Brown rice, 1/2 cup
- Clean water, 2 cups

Serving size:
- 2

Total cooking time (estimated):
- 51 minutes

Preparation time (estimated):
- 1

Cooking time (estimated):
- 50 minutes

Instructions:

- Wash brown rice, add brown rice into water, and bring the water to boil
- Wash honeysuckle flowers into the congee and simmer for 45 minutes
- Turn off heat and serve

This dish is especially good for:
- Driving out internal heat
- Treating sore throat
- Detoxifying the body
- Nourishing the skin
- Bringing down inflammation
- Healing itchy skin
- Improving urinary flow

Notes:
- Honeysuckle flowers, also known as *jin yin hua* in Chinese, are very well-known for their powerful cooling properties. That's why they are often used to treat heat-inducing <u>symptoms</u> like sore throats, acne breakouts, headache, constipation, and swelling. Now that you know the benefits of this type of flowers, what follows is another great option with honeysuckle flowers for a hot summer.

Chrysanthemum Honeysuckle Flower Herbal Tea

Ingredients:
- Honeysuckle flowers, 2 tbsp
- Chrysanthemum flowers, 1/2 cup
- Goji berries, 20 pieces
- Clean water, 4 cups
- Honey, 2 tsp (optional)

Serving size:
- 2

Total cooking time (estimated):

- 21 minutes(disregarding the time for cooling down the herbal tea)

Preparation time (estimated):
- 1 minutes plus 6-8 hours for soaking dried mushrooms overnight

Cooking time (estimated):
- 20 minutes (disregarding the time for cooling down the herbal tea)

Instructions:
- Wash honeysuckle flowers and chrysanthemum flowers
- Add both kinds of flowers and water into a pot and bring the water to boil
- Add goji berries into the herbal tea and simmer for 15 minutes
- Add honey into the pot when the tea cools down

This dish is especially good for:
- Expelling internal heat
- Treating sore throat
- Improving vision

Chinese Yam Winter Melon Soup

Ingredients:
- Winter melon, peeled and cut into small bitable chunks, 1 cup
- Chinese barley, 1/2 cup
- Clean water, 3 cups
- Himalayan salt, to taste

Serving size:
- 2

Total cooking time (estimated):
- 90 minutes

Preparation time (estimated):

- 5 minutes

Cooking time (estimated):
- 85 minutes

Instructions:
- Wash Chinese barley, add them to 2 cup of water, and bring the water to boil
- (While boiling the water) add winter melon chunks and 1 cup of clean water into a blender and blend away
- After the water is boiled, simmer for 50 minutes
- Add winter melon paste into Chinese barley soup, mix well, and continue to simmer for 30 minutes
- Turn off heat, add 1-2 pinches of salt, and stir well
- Serve

This dish is especially good for:
- Bringing down internal heat
- Driving out dampness
- Nourishing and strengthening the spleen
- Improving urinary flow
- Healing skin problems like acne breakouts
- Detoxifying the body

Cucumber Egg Soup

Ingredients:
- Cucumbers, cut into small pieces, 2 cups
- Organic eggs, 2
- Ginger, chopped into small pieces, 2 tbsp
- Scallions, 1/4 cup
- Chrysanthemum flowers, 1/2 cup
- Avocado oil, 2 tbsp
- Clean water, 3 cups
- Himalayan salt, to taste

Serving size:
- 2

Total cooking time (estimated):
- 12 minutes

Preparation time (estimated):
- 5 minutes

Cooking time (estimated):
- 7 minutes

Instructions:
- Break 2 eggs into a big bowl (that has room to hold 2 cups of small pieces of cucumbers) and stir them into a paste
- Add cucumber pieces, ginger, scallions, and chrysanthemum flowers into the below, mix them well with egg paste, and set the mixture aside for later use
- Heat up the pan with avocado oil, add cucumber pieces mixed with egg paste into the pan with medium to low heat, and sauté for 1-2 minutes
- Add 3 cups of water and 1-2 pinches of salt (add more if needed) into the pan and stew with medium heat for 3 minutes
- Turn off heat and serve

This dish is especially good for:
- A sore throat caused by excess heat inside the body
- Calming the mind
- Moistening the throat
- Relieving thirst
- Reducing swelling
- Improving urinary flow
- Detoxifying the body

Stuffed Lotus Roots with Chinese Barley

Ingredients:
- Lotus root, peeled, 1 (about 6 inches long)
- Chinese barley, 1/2 cup

- Honey, 1 tbsp
- Clean water, 4 cups (for boiling the lotus root)

Serving size:
- 2

Total cooking time (estimated):
- 59 minutes (disregarding the time needed to cool down the stuffed lotus roots and to cut it into thin slices)

Preparation time (estimated):
- 1 minutes plus 3-4 hours for soaking Chinese barley

Cooking time (estimated):
- 58 minutes (disregarding the time needed to cool down the stuffed lotus roots and to cut it into thin slices)

Instructions:
- Wash Chinese barley and soak them for 3-4 hours
- Cut off one end of the lotus root
- Stuff soaked black rice into the holes
- Place the piece of lotus root that has been cut off back to its original spot to seal the holes and prevent black rice from dropping out (you can use 2 or 3 toothpicks to hold two parts together – the part that has been cut off and the rest of the lotus root)
- Put 4 cups of water into a pot and bring it to boil
- Place stuffed lotus into the pot and steam with medium heat for 50 minutes
- Turn off heat, take stuffed lotus root out of the pot, and let it sit until the temperature cools down
- Cut the stuffed lotus root into thin slices (an image is attached below for your reference)
- Dip slices of stuffed lotus root into honey and serve

This dish is especially good for:
- Nourishing and moistening the lungs
- Clearing summer heat
- Nourishing the spleen and the stomach
- Treating diarrhea
- Reducing agitation due to hot weathers
- Improving blood circulation

- Improving appetite
- Reducing swelling
- Driving out dampness in the body

Notes:

- You may have discovered this already – this recipe is almost exactly the same as the recipe for making "Steamed Lotus Roots Stuffed with Black Rice" introduced in *mangzhong* (grains becoming mature). I simply have changed black rice into Chinese barley. By replacing black rice with Chines barley, this new dish can enhance its heat expelling properties, which is really needed on this *jieqi*.

  As you see, you can stuff a lot of different kinds of ingredients into the holes of lotus roots. The key is to understand different healing properties of various ingredients and choose depending on the time of the year and your body's specific needs.

Lotus Seeds Congee

Ingredients:
- Lotus seeds, with embryos removed, 1/2 cup
- Brown rice, 1/2 cup
- Clean water, 4 cups

Serving size:
- 2

Total cooking time (estimated):
- 56 minutes

Preparation time (estimated):
- 1 minutes

Cooking time (estimated):
- 55 minutes

Instructions:
- Place lotus seeds and brown rice into water and bring the water to boil
- Simmer for 50 minutes
- Turn off heat and serve

This dish is especially good for:
- Clearing excess heat in the heart and the body
- Brightening up the skin
- Potentially removing wrinkles
- Calming the mind
- Replenishing and nourishing qi
- Preventing cancer
- Lowering blood pressure

Chrysanthemum Lotus Seed Mung Bean Soup

Ingredients:
- Chrysanthemum flowers, 1/2 cup
- Lotus seeds, with embryos removed, 1/4 cup
- Mung beans, 1/2 cup
- Clean water, 4 cups

Serving size:
- 2

Total cooking time (estimated):
- 56 minutes

Preparation time (estimated):
- 1 minute

Cooking time (estimated):
- 55 minutes

Instructions:

- Place lotus seeds and mung beans into water and bring the water to boil
- Simmer for 45 minutes
- Wash chrysanthemum flowers, place them into the soup, and continue to simmer for 5 minutes
- Turn off heat and serve

This dish is especially good for:
- Clearing excess heat in the heart and the body
- Brightening up the skin
- Potentially removing dark spots
- Calming the mind
- Replenishing and nourishing qi
- Preventing cancer
- Lowering blood pressure
- Driving out dampness
- Healing acne breakouts
- Improving immunity

Chrysanthemum Lotus Seed White Fungus Soup

Ingredients:
- Lotus seeds, with embryos removed, 1/2 cup
- Dried white fungus, 1
- Chrysanthemum flowers, 1/2 cup
- Clean water

Serving size:
- 2

Total cooking time (estimated):
- 73 minutes plus 3-4 hours for soaking white fungus

Preparation time (estimated):
- 1 minute plus 3-4 hours for soaking white fungus

Cooking time (estimated):
- 72 minutes

Instructions:
- Soak white fungus in water for 3-4 hours
- Cut white fungus into small pieces, rinse white fungus pieces under running water, and drain them
- Add lotus seeds and white fungus pieces into water and bring the water to boil
- Simmer for 1 hour
- Add in chrysanthemum flowers and continue to simmer for 5 minutes
- Turn off heat and serve

This dish is especially good for:
- Clearing excess heat in the heart and the body
- Brightening up the skin
- Potentially removing dark spots
- Calming the mind
- Replenishing and nourishing qi
- Preventing cancer
- Lowering blood pressure
- Lowering blood sugar level
- Improving digestion
- Improving immunity
- Nourishing the skin

Lotus Seed White Fungus Pear Soup

Ingredients:
- Lotus seeds, with embryos removed, 1/2 cup
- White fungus, 1
- Pear, peeled and chopped into small chunks, 1
- Red dates, pitted, 10 pieces
- Clean water, 4 cups

Serving size:
- 2

Total cooking time (estimated):

- 71 minutes plus 3-4 hours for soaking white fungus

Preparation time (estimated):
- 3 minutes plus 3-4 hours for soaking white fungus

Cooking time (estimated):
- 68 minutes

Instructions:
- Soak white fungus for 3-4 hours
- Cut white fungus into small pieces, rinse pieces of white fungus under running water, and drain them
- Add pear chunks, pieces of white fungus, lotus seeds, and red dates into water and bring the water to boil
- Simmer for 1 hour
- Turn off heat and serve

This dish is especially good for:
- Moistening and nourishing the lungs and throat
- Improving digestion
- Improving the spleen functions
- Clearing away internal heat
- Enriching and replenishing blood

Lotus Seed White Fungus Papaya Stew

Ingredients:
- Papaya, peeled and cut into small bitable chunks, 2 cups
- Lotus seeds, 1/2 cup
- White fungus, 1
- Red dates, 10 pieces
- Honey, 1 tbsp
- Clean water, 4 cups

Serving size:
- 2

Total cooking time (estimated):
- 71 minutes plus 3-4 hours for soaking white fungus

Preparation time (estimated):
- 3 minutes

Cooking time (estimated):
- 68 minutes plus 3-4 hours for soaking white fungus

Instructions:
- Soak white fungus for 3-4 hours
- Cut white fungus into small pieces, rinse pieces of white fungus under running water, and drain them
- Add pieces of white fungus, papaya chunks, lotus seeds, and red dates into water and bring the water to boil
- Simmer for 1 hour
- Turn off heat, add honey, and mix well
- Serve

This dish is especially good for:
- Moistening and nourishing the lungs and throat
- Improving digestion
- Improving the spleen functions
- Clearing away internal heat
- Enriching and replenishing blood
- Treating insomnia
- Improving stamina
- Calming the mind
- Brightening up the skin
- Replenishing and improving qi
- Treating palpitation

Chapter 25: Recipes for *Xiaoshu* (Weather Becoming Hotter)

As the temperature continues to increase, eating the right foods that can expel internal heat becomes more and more important. As well, keeping the body hydrated is also crucial. Therefore, in *xiaoshu*, I've included recipes for different types of congee, herbal tea, and soups, all of which are hydrating and nourishing for the body and skin. Choose you top three and start your experiments in the kitchen right away!

Lotus Leaves Congee

Ingredients:
- Lotus leaves, with edges cut off, 1.5 ounces
- Brown rice, 1 cup
- Clean water, 6 cups
- Himalayan salt, to taste

Serving size:
- 4

Total cooking time (estimated):
- 52 minutes

Preparation time (estimated):
- 2 minutes

Cooking time (estimated):
- 50 minutes

Instructions:
- Wash brown rice and place rice into water
- Place lotus leaves on the top of brown rice
- Bring the water to boil
- Simmer for 45 minutes

- Turn off heat and add 3-4 pinches of salt
- Serve

This dish is especially good for:
- Expelling summer heat
- Driving out dampness
- Reducing swelling
- Relieving dizziness
- Relieving diarrhea
- Nourishing the body and the skin

Black Rice Congee with Mixed Beans

Ingredients:
- Black rice, 1/2 cup
- Red beans, 1/4 cup
- Mung beans, 1/4 cup
- Chinese barley, 1/4 cup
- Lotus seeds, with embryos removed, 1/4 cup
- Fresh lily bulbs, peeled into lily petals, 1/4 cup
- Red dates, 10 pieces
- Longan, 10 pieces
- Clean water, 4 cups

Serving size:
- 2

Total cooking time (estimated):
- 56 minutes (plus 6-8 hours for soaking the dried mushrooms)

Preparation time (estimated):
- 1 minutes (plus 6-8 hours for soaking red beans, mung beans, Chinese barley, and lotus seeds)

Cooking time (estimated):
- 55 minutes

Instructions:

- Soak red beans, mung beans, Chinese barley, and lotus seeds overnight (about 6-8 hours)
- Rinse red beans, mung beans, Chinese barley, and lotus seeds under running water and drain them
- Wash black rice and add rice, red beans, mung beans, Chinese barley, lotus seeds, and red dates into clean water and bring the water to boil
- Simmer for 40 minutes
- Add longan into the congee and continue to simmer for 5 minutes
- Add lily pedals into the mix and continue to simmer for 5 minutes
- Turn off heat and serve

This dish is especially good for:
- Driving out internal heat and dampness
- Brightening up the skin
- Nourishing the skin and the body
- Improving immunity
- Calming the mind

Notes:
- This dish smells and tastes good. I especially enjoy the chewiness of red beans and Chinese barley and the unique smell of mung beans. One thing you should pay attention to is that make sure you don't eat more than one serving each day, because consuming too much of this dish can lead to constipation and bloating.

Pumpkin Taro Congee

Ingredients:
- Brown rice, 1/2 cup
- Taro, peeled and chopped into bitable chunks, 1 cup

- Pumpkin, peeled, pitted, and chopped into bitable chunks, 1 cup
- Clean water, 4 cups
- Himalayan salt, to taste

Serving size:
- 2

Total cooking time (estimated):
- 50 minutes

Preparation time (estimated):
- 10 minutes

Cooking time (estimated):
- 40 minutes

Instructions:
- Wash brown rice and place brown rice, taro chunks, and pumpkin chunks into water
- Bring the water to boil
- Simmer for 35 minutes
- Add 1-2 pinches of salt and mix well
- Turn off heat and serve

This dish is especially good for:
- Improving digestion
- Nourishing the skin and the body

Winter Melon Red Bean Soup

Ingredients:
- Winter melons, peeled and chopped into bitable chunks, 2 cups
- Red beans, 1/2 cup
- Clean water, 4 cups
- Himalayan salt, to taste

Serving size:
- 2

Total cooking time (estimated):
- 53 minutes

Preparation time (estimated):
- 3 minutes

Cooking time (estimated):
- 50 minutes

Instructions:
- Add winter melon chunks and red beans into water
- Bring the water to boil
- Simmer for 45 minutes
- Turn off heat and add 1-2 pinches of salt
- Serve

This dish is especially good for:
- Improving urinary flow
- Reducing swelling
- Clearing internal heat
- Relieve thirst
- Calming the mind
- Relieving agitation due to summer heat

Tomato Tofu Soup

Ingredients:
- Tomatoes, chopped into bitable chunks, 4
- Dried tofu, cut into bitable chunks, 1 cup
- Clean water, 3 cups
- Scallions, chopped, 1/3 cup
- Avocado oil, 1 tbsp
- Himalayan salt, to taste

Serving size:
- 2

Total cooking time (estimated):
- 14 minutes

Preparation time (estimated):
- 5 minutes

Cooking time (estimated):
- 9 minutes

Instructions:
- Heat up the frying pan with avocado oil
- Add tomato chunks and tofu chunks into the pan and sauté with medium heat for 2-3 minutes
- Add 3 cups of water and stew with medium to low heat for 5 minutes
- Add 1-2 pinches of salt and scallions into the soup and mix well
- Turn off heat and serve

This dish is especially good for:
- Improving immunity
- Hydrating and nourishing the skin
- Improving metabolism
- Bringing down internal heat
- Improving appetite

Tomato Egg Soup

Ingredients:
- Tomatoes, chopped into bitable chunks, 4
- Organic eggs, 2
- Sesame oil, 2 tsp
- Avocado oil, 1 tbsp
- Scallions, chopped, 1/4 cup
- Clean water, 3 cups
- Himalayan salt, to taste

Serving size:
- 2

Total cooking time (estimated):
- 9 minutes

Preparation time (estimated):
- 2 minutes

Cooking time (estimated):
- 7 minutes

Instructions:
- Break 2 eggs into a bowl and stir them into a paste
- Heat up with pan with avocado oil
- Add tomato chunks into the pan and sauté for 1 minute
- Add egg paste into the pan and cook until egg paste is cooked (which means it does not appear runny)
- Add 3 cups of water, 1-2 pinches of salt, and scallions and stew with medium to low heat for 2-3 minutes
- Turn off heat, add sesame oil into the soup, and mix well
- Serve

This dish is especially good for:
- Improving immunity
- Hydrating and nourishing the skin
- Improving metabolism
- Bringing down internal heat
- Improving appetite
- Improving vision
- People with high blood pressure

Pumpkin Mung Bean Soup

Ingredients:
- Mung beans, 1/2 cup
- Pumpkin, peeled, pitted, and cut into bitable chunks, 1 cup
- Clean water, 4 cups

Serving size:
- 2

Total cooking time (estimated):
- 55 minutes

Preparation time (estimated):
- 5 minutes

Cooking time (estimated):
- 50 minutes

Instructions:
- Wash mung beans, place beans and water into a pot, and bring it to boil
- Simmer for 30 minutes
- Add pumpkin chunks into mung bean soup and cook with medium heat for 15 minutes (or until pumpkin chunks become soft)
- Turn off heat and mix well
- Serve

This dish is especially good for:
- Clearing internal heat
- Driving out dampness
- Calming the mind
- Improving digestion
- Reducing swelling
- Improving urinary flow
- Healing acne breakouts and eczema

Lily Soup

Ingredients:
- Fresh lily bulbs, peeled into lily petals, 1/2 cup
- Winter melons, peeled and cut into small chunks, 1 cup
- Clean water, 2 cups
- Himalayan salt, to taste

Serving size:
- 2

Total cooking time (estimated):
- 30 minutes

Preparation time (estimated):
- 10 minutes

Cooking time (estimated):
- 20 minutes

Instructions:
- Add winter melon chunks into water and bring the water to boil
- Add lily petals into winter melon soup and stew with medium to low heat for 15 minutes
- Add 1-2 pinches of salt and mix well
- Turn off heat and serve

This dish is especially good for:
- Bringing down internal heat
- Refreshing the mind
- Relieving constipation
- Driving out dampness
- Brightening up the skin

Rose Lemon Tea

Ingredients:
- Dried rose buds, 5-10 pieces
- Fresh lemon slices, 1-2
- Hot water

Serving size:
- 1

Total cooking time (estimated):
- 11 minutes

Preparation time (estimated):
- 1 minute

Cooking time (estimated):
- 10 minutes

Instructions:

- Boil a pot of water
- Wash rose buds
- Put rose buds and fresh lemon slices into a cup that can hold boiling hot water
- Pour water into the cup
- Let it sit for 5 minutes
- Sip with caution (as it still be too hot)

This dish is especially good for:
- Nourishing and brightening up the skin
- Calming the mind

Notes:
- As I am writing this book, I am drinking rose lemon tea, which is one of my favorite kinds of tea of all time. If you like, you could also add 1 teaspoon of black tea leaves, or a black tea teabag, into the tea as well, which is what I often do, too.

Watermelon Skin Red Date Herbal Tea

Ingredients:
- Watermelon skin, 3.5 ounces
- Red dates, 10 pieces
- Clean water, 4 cups

Serving size:
- 2-3

Total cooking time (estimated):
- 41 minutes

Preparation time (estimated):
- 1 minute

Cooking time (estimated):
- 40 minutes

Instructions:
- Peel off the green layer on the outside of watermelon skin
- Cut water lemon skin into small pieces

- Wash red dates
- Add watermelon skin into water and bring the water to boil
- Add red dates into the water and continue to simmer for 30 minutes
- Turn off heat and serve

This dish is especially good for:
- Enriching and nourishing the blood
- Expelling summer heat
- Improving spleen functions
- Nourishing the stomach and the spleen
- Reducing swelling
- Treating cold sores

Chapter 26: Recipes for *Dashu* (Weather Becoming the Hottest)

The hottest time of the year has arrived – the most crucial *jieqi* of the year to clear away excessive heat buildup. As I am a big fan of congee, I've included a few more recipes for different congee options for your choice.

Additionally, remember what I mention at the beginning of Chapter 11? Though constant consumption of cold drinks and foods are not recommended, you can still indulge yourself from time to time with some cold dietary options.

That's why I've also included a few cool or cold drinks and cold desserts that not only help you cool down the body, but also bring you a myriad of nourishing and amazing therapeutic benefits (yes, even desserts can heal the body, too)!

Let's explore.

Mung Bean Millet Congee

Ingredients:
- Mung Beans, 1/2 cup
- Brown rice, 1/2 cup
- Clean water, 2 cups

Serving size:
- 2

Total cooking time (estimated):
- 36 minutes

Preparation time (estimated):
- 1 minutes

Cooking time (estimated):
- 35 minutes

Instructions:
- Wash mung beans and brown rice, add mung beans and brown rice into clean water, and bring the water to boil
- Simmer for 30 minutes
- Turn off heat and serve

This dish is especially good for:
- Nourishing and brightening up the skin
- Relieving thirst
- Reducing internal heat and dampness
- Nourishing the spleen
- Detoxifying the body
- Lowering down blood lipid

Chinese Barley Corn Congee

Ingredients:
- Organic corn, 1/2 cup
- Lotus seeds, with embryos removed, 1/2 cup
- Chinese barley, 1/2 cup
- Lettuce, cut into small pieces, 2 cups
- Brown rice, 1 cup
- Clean water, 6 cups
- Himalayan salt, to taste

Serving size:
- 4 - 5

Total cooking time (estimated):
- 50 minutes plus 6-8 hours for soaking lotus seeds and Chinese barley

Preparation time (estimated):
- 2 minutes plus 6-8 hours for soaking lotus seeds and Chinese barley

Cooking time (estimated):

- 48 minutes

Instructions:
- Soak lotus seeds and Chinese barley for overnight (6-8 hours)
- Rinse lotus seeds and Chinese barley under running water and drain them
- Wash brown rice and place rice, soaked lotus seeds, and soaked Chinese barley into 6 cups of clean water
- Bring the water to boil
- Simmer for 25 minutes
- Add corn into the congee and continue to simmer for 15 minutes
- Add lettuce into congee, stir well, and continue to cook for 2-3 minutes
- Turn off heat and add 4-5 pinches of salt
- Serve

This dish is especially good for:
- Clearing internal heat
- Calming the mind
- Detoxifying the liver
- Removing dampness

Chrysanthemum Bitter Melon Congee

Ingredients:
- Bitter melon, pitted and chopped into small pieces, 1 cup
- Brown rice, 1/2 cup
- Chrysanthemum flowers, 1/4 cup
- Clean water, 5-6 cups
- Honey, 2 – 4 tsp (optional)

Serving size:
- 2

Total cooking time (estimated):

- 53 minutes

Preparation time (estimated):
- 5 minutes

Cooking time (estimated):
- 48 minutes

Instructions:
- Wash brown rice, add rice into water, and bring the water the boil
- Simmer for 30 minutes
- Add bitter melon into congee and continue to simmer for 10 minutes
- Add Chrysanthemum flowers into congee, mix well, and continue to simmer for 2-3 minutes
- Turn off heat and serve
- (Optional) if you like, you could add honey after congee is made

This dish is especially good for:
- Bringing down internal heat
- Driving out excess dampness
- Brightening up the skin
- Healing acne breakouts
- Losing weight
- Detoxifying the body
- Calming the mind
- Relieving heatstroke

Lemon Mint Water

Ingredients:
- Lemons, 3
- Mint leaves, 1/3 cup
- Ice water, 4 cups
- Honey, 2 tbsp

Serving size:
- 4

Total cooking time (estimated):
- 6 minutes

Preparation time (estimated):
- 1 minutes

Cooking time (estimated):
- 5 minutes

Instructions:
- Juice 3 lemons and add lemon juice and mint leaves into ice water
- Mix well and serve

This dish is especially good for:
- Hydrating the body
- Brightening the skin
- Refreshing the mind
- Cooling down the body

Lemon Chinese Barley Water

Ingredients:
- Chinese barley, 1 cup
- Lemon, 1
- Honey, 1 tbsp
- Clean water, 4 cups

Serving size:
- 2 - 4

Total cooking time (estimated):
- 61 minutes (disregarding the time needed for cooling down Chinese barley water)

Preparation time (estimated):
- 1 minute

Cooking time (estimated):

- 60 minutes (disregarding the time needed for cooling down Chinese barley water)

Instructions:
- Wash Chinese barley, add barley into water, and bring the water the boil
- Simmer for 50 minutes
- Turn off heat and pour the Chinese barley water into a container
- Set it aside until the water cools down
- Juice 1 lemon and add lemon juice into Chinese barley water
- Add honey into lemon Chinese barley water and mix well
- Serve

This dish is especially good for:
- Brightening up the skin
- Improving urinary flow
- Reducing swelling
- Strengthening and supporting the spleen
- Driving out dampness
- Nourishing and hydrating the skin

Smoked Plum Tea

Ingredients:
- Smoked plums, 10 pieces
- Dried hawthorn berries, pitted, 1/4 cup
- Red dates, pitted, 5 pieces
- Honey, 2 tbsp
- Clean water, 4 cups

Serving size:
- 4-6

Total cooking time (estimated):
- 36 minutes

Preparation time (estimated):
- 1 minute

Cooking time (estimated):
- 35 minutes

Instructions:
- Wash smoked plums, pitted dried hawthorn berries, and pitted red dates
- Bring the 4 cups of water to boil
- Lower heat to medium to low, add plums, hawthorn berries, and red dates into water, and cook with medium to low heat for 30 minutes
- Turn off heat, add honey, and mix well
- Serve

This dish is especially good for:
- Alkalizing the body
- Refreshing the mind
- Detoxifying the liver
- Strengthening the spleen and the stomach
- Improving digestion
- Nourishing the throat
- Improving appetite

Notes:

- Dried hawthorn berries are very popular in China. This much-loved kind of berries contain lots of health benefits such as strengthening heart functions, lowering blood lipid levels and blood pressure, improving appetite, potentially relieving diarrhea, and fighting aging. In China, I consumed hawthorn berries on a constant basis and would highly recommend you try them to enjoy their benefits on you, too.

Tomato Apple Spinach Juice

Ingredients:
- Tomatoes, 4
- Apples, 2
- Baby spinach, 2 cups

Serving size:
- 2

Total cooking time (estimated):
- 6 minutes

Preparation time (estimated):
- 1 minute

Cooking time (estimated):
- 5 minutes

Instructions:
- Wash tomatoes and apples and cut them into small chunks for juicing
- Place chunks of tomatoes and apples and baby spinach into a juicer
- Pour juice into a container and stir well
- Enjoy

This dish is especially good for:
- Hydrating and nourishing the skin
- Detoxifying the body

Purple Yam Sweet Potato Delight

Ingredients:
- Purple yam, peeled and chopped into small bitable chunks, 1 cup
- Sweet potato, peeled and chopped into small bitable chunks, 1 cup

- Clean water, 4 cups
- Honey, 1 tbsp

Serving size:
- 2

Total cooking time (estimated):
- 45 minutes (disregarding the time needed for cooling down the dish or for placement in the fridge)

Preparation time (estimated):
- 10 minutes

Cooking time (estimated):
- 35 minutes (disregarding the time needed for cooling down the dish or for placement in the fridge)

Instructions:
- Bring purple yam and sweet potato chunks into 5 cups of water and bring the water to boil
- Simmer for 30 minutes
- Turn off heat, add honey, and mix well
- Set aside until the dish cools down and store it into the fridge for 1-2 hours
- Take it out of the fridge and enjoy

This dish is especially good for:
- Preventing cancer
- Fighting fatigue
- Fighting aging
- Enriching and replenishing the blood
- Nourishing and strengthening the liver
- Preventing heart disease and improving heart functions
- Improving digestion

Skin Nourishing and Brightening Chinese Yam Ginseng Dessert

Ingredients:

- Lotus seeds, 1/4 cup
- Chinese barley, 1/2 cup
- Fresh Chinese yam, peeled and sliced into thin pieces 1/2 cup
- American ginseng, sliced, 1/4 cup
- Goji berries, 20 pieces
- Lily bulbs, peeled into lily petals, 1/4 cup
- Clean water, 4 cups
- Honey, 1-1.5 tbsp

Serving size:
- 2 - 3

Total cooking time (estimated):
- 50 minutes (disregarding the time needed for cooling down the dish or for placement in the fridge)

Preparation time (estimated):
- 5 minutes plus 3-4 hours for soaking lotus seeds and Chinese barley

Cooking time (estimated):
- 45 minutes (disregarding the time needed for cooling down the dish or for placement in the fridge)

Instructions:
- Soak Chinese barley and lotus seeds for 3-4 hours
- Rinse Chinese barley and lotus seeds under running water and rinse them
- Place Chinese barley, lotus seeds, Chinese yam and American ginseng into 4 cups of water and bring the water to boil
- Simmer for 30 minutes
- Add goji berries and lily petals into the mix and continue to simmer for 5 – 10 minutes
- Turn off heat, add honey into the mix, and stir well
- Set aside until it cools down
- Transport it into the fridge and let it stay inside for 1-2 hours
- Take it out and enjoy

This dish is especially good for:

- Brightening up the skin
- Nourishing the skin and body
- Cooling down the body
- Driving out excess heat and dampness
- Improving vision
- Calming the mind
- Improving immunity

Papaya Taro Mix

Ingredients:
- Taro, peeled and chopped into small bitable pieces, 1 cup
- Papaya, peeled, with seeds removed, and chopped into small bitable pieces, 1 cup
- Clean water, 4 cups
- Honey, 1 tbsp

Serving size:
- 2-3

Total cooking time (estimated):
- 32 minutes (disregarding the time needed for cooling down the dish or for placement in the fridge)

Preparation time (estimated):
- 10 minutes

Cooking time (estimated):
- 25 minutes (disregarding the time needed for cooling down the dish or for placement in the fridge)

Instructions:
- Add taro chunks into water and bring the water to boil
- Add papaya chunks into the pot and simmer for 20 minutes
- Turn off heat, add honey, and mix well
- Let it sit until the soup cools down

- Transport soup into the fridge and place it inside for 1-2 hours
- Take it out and enjoy

This dish is especially good for:
- Improving immunity
- Adjusting pH and alkalizing the body
- Replenishing qi
- Nourishing the skin and hair
- Strengthening teeth

Part 3-3: Autumn Eating Recipes

Chapter 27: Recipes for *Liqiu* (Arrival of Autumn)

Consume more foods that can nourish the lungs and strengthen their functions.

Peanut Congee

Ingredients:

- Raw peanuts, 1/4 cup
- Brown rice, 1/2 cup
- Clean water, 3 cups

Serving size:

- 2

Total cooking time (estimated):

- 56 minutes

Preparation time (estimated):

- 1 minutes

Cooking time (estimated):

- 55 minutes

Instructions:

- Wash peanuts and brown rice
- Add peanuts and brown rice into water and bring the water to boil
- Simmer for 50 minutes
- Turn off heat and serve

This dish is especially good for:

- Relieving coughs
- Moistening the throat
- Nourishing the lungs
- Relieving thirst
- Reducing phlegm

Scallion Congee

Ingredients:

- Scallions, chopped into small pieces, 1/4 cup
- Brown rice, 1/2 cup
- Clean water, 3 cups
- Coconut oil, 1 tbsp
- Himalayan salt, to taste

Serving size:

- 2

Total cooking time (estimated):

- 56 minutes

Preparation time (estimated):

- 3 minutes

Cooking time (estimated):

- 53 minutes

Instructions:

- Wash brown rice, add rice into water, and bring the water to boil
- Simmer for 45 minutes
- Add scallions and 1-2 pinches of salt into congee, mix well, and continue to simmer for 3 minutes
- Turn off heat, add coconut oil into congee, and mix well
- Serve

This dish is especially good for:

- People who catch a cold in this season
- Expelling cold outside the body

Whitebait Tofu Stew

Ingredients:

- Dried whitebaits, 1/2 cup
- Fresh tofu, cut into small pieces, 2 cups
- Clean water, 3 cups
- Cooking wine, 2 tbsp
- Ginger, sliced, 3-4 pieces
- Sesame oil, 2 tsp
- Himalayan salt, to taste

Serving size:

- 2

Total cooking time (estimated):

- 18 minutes plus 30-60 minutes for soaking dried whitebaits

Preparation time (estimated):

- 3 minutes plus 30-60 minutes for soaking dried whitebaits

Cooking time (estimated):

- 15 minutes

Instructions:

- Soak dried whitebaits for 30 – 60 minutes
- Bring the water to boil
- (While boiling the water) wash tofu pieces and whitebaits
- Add tofu, whitebaits, ginger slices, and cooking wine into boiling water and stew for 10 minutes with medium heat
- Turn off heat, add sesame oil and 1-2 pinches of salt, and mix well
- Serve

This dish is especially good for:

- Nourishing yin energy
- Nourishing the stomach
- Replenishing qi
- Relieving coughs

Peanut Lotus Root Celery Mix

Ingredients:

- Raw peanuts, 1 cup
- Celeries, chopped into small bitable chunks, 1 cup
- Lotus roots, peeled and chopped into small chunks, 1 cup
- Tea bags with jasmine tea, 2
- Clean water, 2 cups (for soaking peanuts)
- Clean water, 3 cups (for cooking peanuts)
- Clean water, 1 cup (for cooking lotus roots and celeries)
- Sesame oil, 1 tbsp
- Cilantro, chopped into small pieces, 1/2 cup
- Himalayan salt, to taste

Serving size:

- 4

Total cooking time (estimated):

- 115 minutes plus 4 hours for soaking peanuts

Preparation time (estimated):

- 5 minutes plus 4 hours for soaking peanuts

Cooking time (estimated):

- 110 minutes

Instructions:

- Soak peanuts in clean water for 4 hours
- Drain peanuts and place soaked peanuts, 2 jasmine tea bags, 3 cups of water into a pot

- Bring the water to boil and simmer for 30 minutes
- Turn off heat, pour the water, peanuts, and teabags into a contains, and let the mixture sit for another 60 minutes
- Add 1 cup of clean water into a frying pan and bring the water to boil
- Lower the heat to medium high, add lotus and celery chunks, and sauté for 5 – 10 minutes
- Drain lotus root and celery chunks and place them in a bowl
- Drain peanuts and mix nuts into lotus root and celery chunks
- Add cilantro, 3-4 pinches of salt, and sesame oil and mix well
- Serve

This dish is especially good for:

- Nourishing the stomach and the spleen
- Nourishing the lungs
- Relieving phlegm
- Replenishing qi
- Moistening the throat
- Fighting aging
- Improving memory
- Nourishing the skin
- Reducing swelling

Fried Eggs with Black Fungus and Onions

Ingredients:

- Black fungus, 1/3 cup
- Onions, chopped into small pieces, 1 cup
- Organic eggs, 4
- Avocado oil, 2 tbsp
- Himalayan salt, to taste

Serving size:

- 2-3

Total cooking time (estimated):

- 16 minutes plus 4 hours for soaking black fungus

Preparation time (estimated):

- 5 minutes plus 4 hours for soaking black fungus

Cooking time (estimated):

- 11 minutes

Instructions:

- Soak black fungus for 4 hours
- Rinse black fungus under running water and drain fungus
- Break eggs into a bowl, stir well, and make them into a paste
- Add 1 tbsp of avocado oil into a frying pan and heat up the pan
- Lower the heat to medium to low, pour egg paste into the pan, and sauté for 1-2 minutes until egg paste becomes solid
- Use turner to cut cooked egg paste into pieces and place cooked egg pieces into a container

- Add 1 tbsp of avocado oil into a frying pan and heat up the pan
- Lower the heat to medium, add black fungus into the pan, and sauté for 2-3 minutes
- Add chopped onions into the pan and sauté onions and fungus for 2-3 minutes
- Add egg pieces and 2-3 pinches of salt into the pan and continue to sauté for 1-2 minutes
- Turn off heat and serve

This dish is especially good for:

- Improving immunity
- Nourishing the kidneys, the stomach, the spleen, and the lungs
- Enriching the blood and qi
- Lowering blood lipid level
- Prevent heart diseases
- Detoxifying the body
- Prevent cancer
- Slowing down aging process

White Radish Mushroom Soup

Ingredients:

- White radishes, peeled and cut into small bitable chunks, 2 cups
- Dried mushrooms, 10 pieces
- Ginger, sliced, 3-4 slices
- Cilantro, chopped into small pieces, 1/4 cup

- Sesame oil, 3 tsp
- Clean water, 4 cups
- Himalayan salt, to taste

Serving size:

- 3

Total cooking time (estimated):

- 30 minutes plus 6-8 hours for soaking mushrooms

Preparation time (estimated):

- 5 minutes plus 6-8 hours for soaking mushrooms

Cooking time (estimated):

- 25 minutes

Instructions:

- Wash mushrooms and soak them overnight in 2 cups of water (about 6-8 hours)
- Add mushrooms along with water used for soaking mushrooms, chunks of white radishes, and another 2 cups of water into a pot
- Bring the water to boil
- Add slices of ginger into the pot and simmer for 20 minutes
- Turn off heat, add 2-3 pinches of salt, sesame oil, and cilantro into the soup, and mix well
- Serve

This dish is especially good for:

- Improving immunity

- Nourishing and moistening the lungs
- Detoxifying the body
- Relieving constipation
- Improving urinary flow
- Improving digestion
- Reducing phlegm

Lotus Pear Juice

Ingredients:

- Pear, peeled, pitted, and sliced, 4
- Lotus root, peeled and sliced, 4 cups
- Clean water, 6 cups
- Honey, 2 tbsp

Serving size:

- 4

Total cooking time (estimated):

- 133 minutes

Preparation time (estimated):

- 5 minutes

Cooking time (estimated):

- 128 minutes

Instructions:

- Add pear and lotus root slices into water and bring the water to boil
- Pour pear and lotus root slices and water into slow cooker and cook with low heat for 2 hours
- Use a sifter to separate lotus root and pear slices and the juice and keep the juice
- Add honey into the juice and mix well
- Pour juice into glasses and enjoy

This dish is especially good for:

- Hydrating the skin
- Nourishing and moisturizing the lungs
- Brightening up the skin
- Clearing away internal heat
- Nourishing the stomach and the spleen
- Enriching and replenishing blood

Notes:

- It is better if you could finish all the juice on the same time. This can keep it fresh and best benefit the body.

Lily Pear Paste

Ingredients:

- Fresh lily bulbs, peeled into petals, 1/2 cup
- Brown rice, 1/2 cup
- Pear, peeled, pitted, and cut into small chunks, 1
- Clean water, 4 cups
- Honey, 2-4 tsp (optional)

Serving size:

- 2-3

Total cooking time (estimated):

- 57 minutes

Preparation time (estimated):

- 10 minutes

Cooking time (estimated):

- 47 minutes

Instructions:

- Wash brown rice and lily petals
- Add brown rice, pear chunks, and water into a pot and bring the water to boil
- Simmer for 35 minutes
- Add lily petals into congee and continue to simmer for 3-5 minutes
- Turn off heat, pour everything in the pot into a blender, and blend away
- Pour the paste into a big bowl
- (Optional) add honey and mix well
- Serve

This dish is especially good for:

- Nourishing the lungs
- Relieving coughs
- Calming the mind
- Enriching and replenishing blood and qi
- Strengthening spleen functions

- Improving appetite

Notes:

- I personally would not add honey into the congee, as this dish is sweet enough for me already. If you have a sweet tooth, you can indulge yourself by adding a little bit of honey.

Pumpkin Paste with White Fungus

Ingredients:

- Pumpkin, peeled, pitted, and chopped into small bitable chunks, 2 cups
- White fungus, 1
- Red dates, pitted, 6-8 pieces
- Goji berries, 20 pieces
- Honey, 1 tbsp (optional)
- Clean water, 2 cups (for soaking white fungus)
- Clean water, 3 cups

Serving size:

- 2-3

Total cooking time (estimated):

- 45 minutes (plus 3-4 hours for soaking white fungus)

Preparation time (estimated):

- 5 minutes

Cooking time (estimated):

- 40 minutes (plus 3-4 hours for soaking white fungus)

Instructions:

- Soak white fungus in 2 cups of water for 3-4 hours
- Rinse white fungus under running water, cut it into small pieces, and place pieces of white fungus in a pot
- Add 2 cups of water into the pot
- Bring the water to boil
- Add plus red dates and goji berries into the pot, mix well, and simmer for 30 minutes
- (While simmering) add 1 cup of water and pumpkin chunks into a pan and bring the water to boil
- (While simmering) simmer pumpkin chunks for 10-15 minutes
- (While simmering) pour pumpkin chunks and water inside the pot into a blender and blend away
- (While simmering) pour pumpkin paste into a bowl for later use
- (After simmering white fungus for 30 minutes) pour pumpkin paste into white fungus soup and mix well
- Turn off heat
- (Optional) add honey and mix well
- Serve

This dish is especially good for:

- Nourishing the spleen and the stomach
- Improving appetite
- Nourishing qi
- Calming the mind
- Treating insomnia
- Nourishing yin

- Expelling heat out of the body
- Nourishing the lungs
- Moisturizing the skin

Pear Syrup

Ingredients:

- Pears, peeled, pitted, and cut into small chunks, 6
- Red dates, pitted, 20 pieces,
- Ginger, slices, 5 thin slices
- Clean water,
- Honey, 3 tbsp

Serving size:

- n/a

Total cooking time (estimated):

- 120 minutes (disregarding the time for cooling down the pear syrup)

Preparation time (estimated):

- 5 minutes

Cooking time (estimated):

- 115 minutes (disregarding the time for cooling down the pear syrup)

Instructions:

- Add pear chunks and 3 cups of water into a blender and blend away
- Pour pear paste into a pot, add ginger into pear paste and mix well
- Bring the mixture to boil, add red dates, mix well, and simmer for 60 minutes
- Prepare a bowl big enough to carry all the pear paste and place a cheesecloth (big enough to cover the bowl) on top of the bowl
- Pour pear paste onto the cheesecloth, squeeze juice out of the cloth into the bowl, and keep the juice
- Pour the juice into a pot and cook with medium to low heat for 30-45 minutes (without a lid on top of the top)
- Turn off heat, add honey into pear syrup until the syrup cools down, and mix well
- Pour the pear syrup into a glass container with air-tight seal

This dish is especially good for:

- Relieving thirst
- Nourishing the lungs
- Calming the mind
- Moistening the throat
- Hydrating the body and skin

Notes:

- I leave the serving size with "n/a" here because it is hard to measure, because it depends on how much you want to use it.

How can you enjoy this syrup? You can consume this syrup

by mixing 1 tbsp of it with warm water and drink it in the morning and repeat the same steps in the evening.

Try enjoying this yourself to see if you like it first before you introduce it to your family or treat it to your friends and guests.

Chapter 28: Recipes for *Chushu* (Summer Almost Gone)

From the name, you can tell that summer heat still lingers while it is getting cooler and cooler. Make sure you consume the right foods to avoid internal heat buildup.

At the same time, eating foods that can calm the mind helps nourish the body around this time as well.

As a result, I've included 5 recipes that are good for driving out internal heat to help the body stay in balance; I've also incorporated 5 recipes especially for calming the mind.

Enjoy!

Sesame Spinach

- Ingredients:
- Baby spinach, 8 cups
- White sesame seeds, 2 tbsp
- Clean water, 4 cups
- Himalayan salt, to taste
- Sesame oil, 2 tsp

Serving size:

- 2

Total cooking time (estimated):

- 10 minutes

Preparation time (estimated):

- 1 minute

Cooking time (estimated):

- 9 minutes

Instructions:

- Heat up white sesame seeds on the pan and sauté until sesame seeds turn brown-ish
- Turn off heat, place sesame seeds on a plate, and set the plate aside for later use
- Bring the water to boil, place spinach into the pot, lower the heat to medium to low, and cook till spinach becomes soft
- Drain spinach and place spinach on a plate
- Mix in white sesame seeds, 1-2 pinches of salt, and sesame oil and stir well
- Serve

This dish is especially good for:

- Improving digestion
- Improving immunity
- Improving metabolism
- Slowing down aging process
- Moisturizing the body
- Nourishing yin energy inside the body
- Enriching and replenishing blood
- Calming the mind
- Bringing down internal heat

Green Pepper Tofu Mix

Ingredients:

- Dried tofu, chopped into small bitable pieces, 1 cup
- Green peppers, with seeds removed and sliced, 2 cups
- Cilantro, chopped, 1/4 cup
- Clean water, 4 cups
- Sesame oil, 2 tsp
- Himalayan salt, to taste

Serving size:

- 2-3

Total cooking time (estimated):

- 15 minutes

Preparation time (estimated):

- 5 minute

Cooking time (estimated):

- 10 minutes

Instructions:

- Bring the water to boil
- Place tofu chunks into boiling water, cook for 1-2 minutes, and drain tofu chunks
- Place green pepper slices into boiling water, cook for 1 minute, and drain green pepper slices
- Place tofu chunks and green pepper slices into a bowl, add in 1-2 pinches of salt, sesame oil, and cilantro, and mix well
- Serve

This dish is especially good for:

- Nourishing qi

- Moisturizing the body
- Expelling internal heat
- Detoxifying the body
- Improving digestion
- Improving appetite

Pear Congee

Ingredients:

- Pears, peeled, pitted, and cut into small pieces, 2
- Brown rice, 1 cup
- Goji berries, 30 pieces
- Clean water, 4 cups

Serving size:

- 4

Total cooking time (estimated):

- 50 minutes

Preparation time (estimated):

- 5 minutes

Cooking time (estimated):

- 45 minutes

Instructions:

- Wash brown rice, add pear chunks, brown rice, and water into a pot, and bring the water to boil
- Simmer for 35 minutes
- Add in goji berries and continue to simmer for 5 minutes
- Turn off heat and serve

This dish is especially good for:

- Moistening the throat and the lungs
- Relieving coughs
- Nourishing the stomach and the intestines
- Driving out internal heat

White Cabbage with Fried Eggs and Mixed Seeds

Ingredients:

- Napa cabbage, sliced, 4 cups
- Organic eggs, 2
- Mixed seeds (I choose pumpkin seeds and sunflower seeds), 2 tbsp
- Himalayan salt, to taste
- Avocado oil, 2 tbsp

Serving size:

- 3-4

Total cooking time (estimated):

- 14 minutes

Preparation time (estimated):

- 5 minutes

Cooking time (estimated):

- 9 minutes

Instructions:

- Break eggs into a bowl, stir them into an egg paste, and set it aside for later use

- Heat up avocado oil in a frying pan with medium to high heat, lower the heat to medium to low, add in slices of cabbage, and sauté cabbage for 3 minutes
- Add 1-2 pinches of salt and mixed seeds and continue to sauté for 1-2 minutes
- Add egg paste into the pan, wait for about 10 seconds to allow time for the egg paste to start to become solid, and sauté every few seconds until egg paste is completely cooked
- Turn off heat, add in sesame oil, and mix well
- Serve

This dish is especially good for:

- Stimulating bowel movements
- Improving digestion
- Moisturizing and nourishing the skin and body
- Brightening up the skin
- Preventing cancer
- Relieving coughs
- Relieving constipation
- Nourishing the kidneys
- Improving urinary flow
- Expelling heat and detoxifying the body
- Relieving thirst

Papaya Coconut Milk

Ingredients:

- Young coconuts, 2

- Papaya, peeled, with seeds removed, and cut into small bitable chunks, 1 cup
- Baby spinach, 1 cup
- Clean water, 1 cup

Serving size:

- 2

Total cooking time (estimated):

- 20 minutes

Preparation time (estimated):

- 10 minutes

Cooking time (estimated):

- 10 minutes (of course, it may take you longer time if this is your first time to crack a coconut. So be prepared to give yourself more time for the learning process ;)

Instructions

- Crack 2 coconuts and add fresh coconut water and coconut meat into a blender
- Add papaya chunks, baby spinach, and water into the blender and blend away
- Pour the smoothie into a glass and serve

This dish is especially good for:

- Expelling heat
- Nourishing and hydrating the skin
- Relieving thirst
- Replenishing electrolytes
- Slowing down aging process
- Improving immunity

Notes:

- You can find tips on how to crack a coconut here in this video http://bit.ly/crack-a-coconut. Additionally, I personally find that if you slightly warm up the smoothie by cooking it with medium to low heat. Definitely give it a try if you want to feel the subtle difference.

Pumpkin Oatmeal Congee

Ingredients:

- Rolled oats, 1/2 cup
- Brown rice, 1/2 cup
- Pumpkin, peeled, pitted, and chopped into small bitable chunks, 4 cups
- Clean water, 6 cups
- Scallions, chopped, 1/4 cup
- Himalayan salt, to taste

Serving size:

- 4

Total cooking time (estimated):

- 65 minutes

Preparation time (estimated):

- 5 minute

Cooking time (estimated):

- 60 minutes

Instructions:

- Wash brown rice, add brown rice and 4 cups of water into a pot, and bring the water to boil
- Simmer for 30 minutes
- (While simmering) Add pumpkin chunks and 2 cups of water into a blender and blend them into a pumpkin paste
- (After simmering brown rice for 30 minutes) pour pumpkin paste into the congee and continue to simmer for 10 minutes
- Add rolled oats into pumpkin congee and continue to simmer for 15 minutes
- Turn off heat, add in scallions and 3-4 pinches of salt, and mix well
- Serve

This dish is especially good for:

- Replenishing and nourishing qi
- Detoxifying the body
- Improving immunity
- Nourishing and moisturizing the skin
- Improving digestion
- Calming the mind

Mint Lime Ginger Juice

Ingredients:

- Fresh ginger juice, 4 ounces
- Mint leaves, 1/2 cup
- Lime, pitted, 1
- Water, 4 cups

Serving size:

- 4

Total cooking time (estimated):

- 10 minutes

Preparation time (estimated):

- 5 minutes

Cooking time (estimated):

- 5 minutes

Instructions:

- Boil 4 cups of water
- (While boiling the water) cut the whole lime into small pieces (keep the skin, too)
- (While boiling the water) put lime pieces into a blender and blend them together into a lime paste
- (While boiling the water) evenly distribute lime paste into 4 glasses that can withhold high temperature of boiling water
- (While boiling the water) evenly distribute mint leaves and ginger juice into the same 4 glasses
- (When water is boiled) pour 1 cup of boiling water to each glass and mix well
- Serve when the mint lie ginger juice cools down

This dish is especially good for:

- Calming the mind
- Improving appetite
- Alleviating pain
- Improving immunity
- Brightening the skin
- Refreshing the mind

Rose Tea with Red Dates and Goji Berries

Ingredients:

- Dried rose buds, 5 pieces
- Red dates, pitted, 5 pieces
- Longan, 8 pieces
- Goji berries, 10 pieces
- Honey, 2 tsp (optional)
- Clean water, 2 cups

Serving size:

- 1

Total cooking time (estimated):

- 26 minutes (disregarding the time it takes to cool down this herbal tea)

Preparation time (estimated):

- 1 minutes

Cooking time (estimated):

- 25 minutes (disregarding the time it takes to cool down this herbal tea)

Instructions:

- Bring 2 cups of water to boil
- (While boiling the water) was rose buds, red dates, longan, and goji berries
- (When the water is boiling) add rose buds, red dates, longan, and goji berries into the water and simmer for 20 minutes

- Turn off heat
- If you want, you could add honey when this herbal tea cools down (when you don't feel that the temperature is burning your fingers)
- Serve

This dish is especially good for:

- Nourishing and hydrating the skin and the body
- Calming the mind
- Improving vision
- Enriching and replenishing qi

Notes:

- For me, this herbal is already sweet enough. So, I usually enjoy this herbal tea without adding honey. Of course, feel free to add a little honey to satisfy your sweet tooth. But, at the same time, make sure you moderate your intake of sweets as well.

Traditional Rose Tea

Ingredients:

- Dried rose buds, 5-10 pieces
- Jasmine tea leaves, 1 tsp (or you can use 1 jasmine tea bag)
- Clean water

Serving size:

- 1

Total cooking time (estimated):

- 16 minutes

Preparation time (estimated):

- 1 minute

Cooking time (estimated):

- 15 minutes

Instructions:

- Boil the water
- (While boiling the water) wash rose buds and jasmine tea leaves under running water and place them into a glass or cup that can hold high temperature of boiling water
- (When the water is boiled) pour the water into the glass or cup and let it sit for 10 minutes

This dish is especially good for:

- Nourishing and moisturizing the skin
- Calming the mind

Notes:

- I will leave it to you to decide the amount of water you want to boil, which depends on how much you would like to consume. If you choose to use a teabag to make your tea, then simply washing the dried rose buds without washing the teabag during preparation should be fine.

Celery Walnut Mix

Ingredients:

- Celery stalks, chopped, into small bitable pieces, 2 cups
- Red peppers, with seeds removed, sliced, 1 cup
- Walnuts, 1/2 cup
- Scallions, chopped, 1/4 cup

- Himalayan salt, to taste
- Avocado oil, 2 tbsp

Serving size:

- 3

Total cooking time (estimated):

- 15 minutes

Preparation time (estimated):

- 5 minutes

Cooking time (estimated):

- 10

Instructions:

- Heat up avocado oil with medium to high heat, lower the heat to medium, add in scallions, and sauté for 30-60 minutes
- Add in celery pieces, red pepper slices, and walnuts and sauté with medium to low heat for 5-7 minutes
- Add 2-3 pinches of salt and mix well
- Turn off heat and serve

This dish is especially good for:

- Replenishing blood and qi
- Nourishing the kidneys and the liver
- Relieving coughs
- Moisturizing the skin and the body
- Improving digestion
- Calming the mind
- Preventing cancer

- Nourishing yin energy
- Improving urinary flow

Chapter 29: Recipes for *Bailu* (Dew Starting to Form)

Lower humidity around this time of the year makes it necessary for you to consumer more foods that are moisturizing and hydrating to protect your skin and help your body with its regular functions. Common hydrating foods include Chinese yam, lily bulbs, lotus seeds, honey, pears, white fungus, white radish, sugar canes, Chinese water chestnuts, pumpkins, spinach, sesame seeds, and sticky rice.

In the following recipes, you will find out how you can take advantage of these ingredients to create delicious and nourishing dishes that your skin and body will thank you for.

Pumpkin Rice with Mix Seeds

Ingredients:

- Pumpkin, peeled, pitted, and chopped into small pieces, 2 cups
- Brown rice, 1 cup
- Mix seeds (I personally use spouted pumpkin seeds and sunflower seeds), 2 tbsp
- Clean water, 4 cups
- Himalayan salt, to taste

Serving size:

- 4

Total cooking time (estimated):

- 55 minutes

Preparation time (estimated):

- 5

Cooking time (estimated):

- 50 minutes

Instructions:

- Wash brown rice, add brown rice and 4 cups of water into a pot, and bring the water to boil
- Simmer for 20 minutes
- Add pumpkin chunks on the top of brown rice and continue to simmer for 20 minutes
- Sprinkle seeds on the top of pumpkin chunks and continue to simmer for 2-3 minutes
- Turn off heat, add 2-3 pinches of salt, and mix salts, seeds, pumpkin chunks, and brown rice together
- Serve

This dish is especially good for:

- Nourishing the spleen and the stomach
- Improving digestion
- Nourishing and hydrating the skin
- Preventing cancer
- Lowering blood sugar level
- Bringing down inflammation
- Detoxifying the body
- Relieving thirst
- Enriching and replenishing qi

Sugar Cane Juice with Water Chestnut and Mint Leaves

Ingredients:

- Sugar cane juice, 2 cups
- Water chestnuts, peeled and cut into small pieces, 1/4 cup
- Mint leaves, 3-4

Serving size:

- 1

Total cooking time (estimated):

- 6 minutes

Preparation time (estimated):

- 5 minutes

Cooking time (estimated):

- 1 minute

Instructions:

- Mix everything together and server right away!

This dish is especially good for:

- Nourishing the stomach and the lungs
- Expelling internal heat
- Hydrating the skin and the body
- Calming the mind
- Relieving thirst
- Relieving coughs
- Relieving constipation

Fried Water Chestnut with Black Fungus

Ingredients:

- Chinese water chestnuts, peeled and cut into thin slices, 1 cup
- Black fungus, 1/4 cup
- Clean water, 2 cups (for soaking black fungus)
- Green bell peppers, with seeds removed, cut into small pieces, 1/4 cup
- Red bell peppers, with seeds removed, cut into small pieces, 1/4 cup
- Cilantro, chopped, 1/4 cup
- Garlic, peeled and chopped, 2 cloves
- Avocado oil, 2 tbsp

Serving size:

- 2

Total cooking time (estimated):

- 25 minutes (plus 4 hours for soaking black fungus)

Preparation time (estimated):

- 15 minutes(plus 4 hours for soaking black fungus)

Cooking time (estimated):

- 10 minutes

Instructions:

- Soak black fungus in 2 cups of water for 4 hours
- Rinse black fungus under running water and drain fungus
- Heat up avocado oil, add garlic into the pot, and fry until garlic turns brown-ish

- Lower the heat to medium, add in slices of water chestnuts, and sauté for 1-2 minutes
- Add in black fungus, pieces of red and green peppers, and continue to sauté for 3-4 minutes
- Turn off heat, add in 1-2 pinches of salt and cilantro, and mix well
- Serve

This dish is especially good for:

- Adjusting pH levels in the body
- Strengthening the teeth
- Preventing cancer
- Relieving thirst
- Bringing down internal heat
- Hydrating the body and the skin

Pumpkin Coconut Paste

Ingredients:

- Pumpkin, peeled, pitted, and chopped into small pieces, 2 cups
- Young coconut, 1
- Clean water, 2 cups

Serving size:

- 2

Total cooking time (estimated):

- 25 minutes

Preparation time (estimated):

- 5 minutes

Cooking time (estimated):

- 20 minutes

Instructions:

- Place pumpkin chunks and 2 cups of water in a blender and blend the mixture into a pumpkin paste
- Pour it into a pot, bring it to boil, and then simmer for 20 minutes
- (While simmering) crack the young coconut, pour coconut water into the blender, put coconut meat into it, and blend the mixture into coconut milk
- (After simmering pumpkin paste for 20 minutes) pour coconut milk into pumpkin paste and stir well
- Turn off heat and sere

This dish is especially good for:

- Nourishing and hydrating the skin and the body
- Nourishing the spleen and the stomach
- Detoxifying the body
- Brightening up the skin
- Improving immunity
- Improving digestion
- Replenishing electrolytes inside the body

Mung Bean Pumpkin Soup

Ingredients:

- Mung beans, 1/2 cup

- Pumpkin, peeled, pitted, and cut into pieces, 2 cups
- Clean water, 4 cups

Serving size:

- 2

Total cooking time (estimated):

- 53 minutes

Preparation time (estimated):

- 5 minutes

Cooking time (estimated):

- 48 minutes

Instructions:

- Wash mung beans, add beans and 2 cups of clean water into the pot, bring the water to boil, and simmer for 20 minutes
- Add pumpkin chunks and 2 cups of water into mung bean soup, bring the water to boil, and simmer for 20 minutes
- Turn off heat and serve

This dish is especially good for:

- Nourishing and hydrating the skin and the body
- Nourishing the spleen and the stomach
- Detoxifying the body
- Brightening up the skin
- Improving immunity
- Improving digestion

Steamed Pumpkin with Red Dates and Lily Bulbs

Ingredients:

- Pumpkin, peeled, pitted, and cut into small pieces, 2 cups
- Red dates, pitted, 10 pieces
- Fresh lily bulbs, peeled into lily petals, 1/2 cup
- White sesame seeds, 1 tbsp
- Honey, 1 tbsp

Serving size:

- 2

Total cooking time (estimated):

- 40 minutes (disregarding the time for cooling down the dish)

Preparation time (estimated):

- 10 minutes

Cooking time (estimated):

- 30 minutes (disregarding the time for cooling down the dish)

Instructions:

- Add 2 cups of water to the bottom of a steamer and bring it to boil
- Place pumpkin chunks, lily petals, and red dates onto a plate and put the plate on the rack inside the steamer
- Steam with medium heat for 20 minutes
- Sprinkle white sesame on top of the pumpkin chunks, red dates, and lily petals and continue to steam for 1-2 minutes

- Turn off heat and slowly and carefully pour water inside the plate into a small bowl
- Add honey into the small bowl, stir well, and let honey water drip on the top of pumpkin chunks, lily petals, red dates, and white sesame seeds
- Serve when this dish cools down

This dish is especially good for:

- Nourishing and hydrating the skin and the body
- Nourishing the spleen and the stomach
- Detoxifying the body
- Brightening up the skin
- Improving immunity
- Improving digestion
- Calming the mind
- Enriching and replenishing the blood

Chines Yam and Barley Paste

Ingredients:

- Fresh Chinese yam, peeled and cut into small pieces, 1 cup
- Chinese barley, 1/2 cup
- Clean water, 4 cups

Serving size:

- 2

Total cooking time (estimated):

- 71 minutes

Preparation time (estimated):

- 3 minutes

Cooking time (estimated):

- 68 minutes

Instructions:

- Add Chinese yam, Chinese barley, and 4 cups of water into a pot, bring the water to boil, and simmer for 1 hour
- Turn off heat, pour everything into a blender and blend everything into a paste
- Serve

This dish is especially good for:

- Expelling internal heat
- Detoxifying the body
- Hydrating and brightening up the skin
- Driving dampness outside the body
- Improving urinary flow

Chinese Yam Spinach Goji Mix

Ingredients:

- Baby spinach, 6 cups
- Chinese yam, peeled and cut into small pieces, 1 cup
- Ginger, sliced, 2-3 slices
- Goji berries, 20 pieces
- Avocado oil, 2 tbsp
- Himalayan salt, to taste

Serving size:

- 2

Total cooking time (estimated):

- 13 minutes

Preparation time (estimated):

- 3 minutes

Cooking time (estimated):

- 10 minutes
- Instructions:
- Heat up avocado oil on a frying pan
- Add slices of ginger into the pan and cook with medium heat for about 1 minute
- Add in Chinese yam and cook for 3-4 minutes
- Lower the heat to medium to low and add in spinach and goji berries and cook for 3-4 minutes
- Turn off heat, add 1-2 pinches of salt, and mix well
- Serve

This dish is especially good for:

- Expelling internal heat
- Hydrating and brightening up the skin
- Enriching and replenishing qi
- Strengthening functions of the stomach and the spleen
- Improving digestion
- Relieving diarrhea

Mashed Chinese Yam

Ingredients:

- Fresh Chinese yam, peeled and cut into small chunks, 2 cups
- Clean water, 5 cups
- Himalayan salt, to taste

Serving size:

- 4

Total cooking time (estimated):

- 61 minutes

Preparation time (estimated):

- 3 minutes

Cooking time (estimated):

- 58 minutes

Instructions:

- Add 5 cups of clean water and Chinese yam into a pot, bring the water to boil, and simmer for 50 minutes
- Pour everything into a blender and blend mixture into a Chinese yam paste
- Pour the paste into a bowl, add 2-3 pinches of salt, and stir well
- Serve

This dish is especially good for:

- Expelling internal heat
- Hydrating and brightening up the skin
- Enriching and replenishing qi
- Strengthening functions of the stomach and the spleen
- Improving digestion
- Relieving diarrhea

Toasted Cashews with Spinach

Ingredients:

- Baby spinach, 8 cups
- Roasted cashews, 1/4 cup
- Himalayan salt, to taste
- Clean water, 4 cups
- Sesame oil, 2 tsp

Serving size:

- 2

Total cooking time (estimated):

- 9 minutes

Preparation time (estimated):

- 1 minutes

Cooking time (estimated):

- 8 minutes

Instructions:

- Bring the water to boil
- Add baby spinach into the water, stir well, and quickly cook for 1-2 minutes
- Drain the spinach and place spinach onto a plate
- Add 1-2 pinches of salt and mix well
- Add 2 tsp of sesame oil into spinach and mix well
- Add cashews into spinach and mix well
- Serve

This dish is especially good for:

- Improving digestion
- Improving immunity
- Nourishing yin energy inside the body
- Improving metabolism
- Slowing down aging process
- Relieving constipation
- Nourishing the skin to keep it brighten and smooth
- Treating anemia

Chapter 30: Recipes for *Qiufen* (Official Autumn)

As promised, this is a chapter of recipes that teach you to make lung-nourishing and moisturizing dishes while help you restore internal balance as well.

Now I'll invite you to quickly go back to Chapter 6 and learn which body type your body belongs to. Then, come back to this chapter and find the recipes that are designed for your own body type to help your body stay in balance.

Specifically speaking, I've prepared two recipes for each body type to help you get started.

Qi Deficiency

Symptoms: You constantly feel weak and tired and easily get sick.

Recipe 1: Green Pepper and Potato Slices

Ingredients:

- Green bell peppers, with seeds removed, sliced, 1 cup
- Potatoes, peeled and sliced, 2 cups
- Avocado oil, 2 tbsp
- Garlic, chopped, 4 cloves
- Himalayan salt, to taste
- Black pepper, grinded, to taste

Serving size:

- 3

Total cooking time (estimated):

- 27 minutes

Preparation time (estimated):

- 10 minutes

Cooking time (estimated):

- 17 minutes

Instructions:

- Heat up the oil, add garlic into the oil, and cook until garlic turns brown-ish
- Add potato slices into the pan and sauté with medium heat for 7-10 minutes
- Add in green pepper slices and continue to sauté for 3-4 minutes
- Turn off heat, add 2-3 pinches of salt and 2-3 pinches of grinded black pepper, and mix well
- Serve

Recipe 2: Curry Beef Potato

Ingredients:

- Grass-fed beef, cut into small bitable chunks, 10 ounces
- Potatoes, peeled and cut into small bitable chunks, 2 cups
- Tomatoes, cut into small bitable chunks, 1 cup
- Ginger, sliced, 3-4 slices
- Curry powder, 3 tbsp
- Himalayan salt, to taste
- Avocado oil, 1 tbsp

- Clean water, 4 cups (for quickly boiling the beef)
- Clean water, 4 cups (for making beef soup)

Serving size:

- 3

Total cooking time (estimated):

- 50 minutes

Preparation time (estimated):

- 10 minutes

Cooking time (estimated):

- 40 minutes

Instructions:

- Add 4 cups of water into a pot and bring it to boil
- Add beef chunks into boiling water, simmer for 10 minutes, drain beef, set it aside for later use
- Heat up avocado oil in the frying pan
- Add garlic into the pan and cook with medium to high heat until garlic turn brown-ish
- Add beef into the pan and sauté for 2-3 minutes
- Add 4 cups of clean water into the pan and bring the water to boil
- Add in potato chunks and simmer for 10 minutes
- Add in curry powder and tomato chunks and continue to simmer for 5 minutes (add more curry powder if needed)
- Turn off heat, add 2-3 pinches of salt, and mix well
- Serve

Yang Deficiency

Symptoms: You tend to have cold hands and feet.

Recipe 1: Ginger Sweet Potato Soup

Ingredients:

- Ginger juice, 4 ounces
- Sweet potatoes, peeled and cut into small bitable chunks, 2 cups
- Clean water, 3 cups
- Honey, 1 tbsp

Serving size:

- 2

Total cooking time (estimated):

- 48 minutes

Preparation time (estimated):

- 10 minutes

Cooking time (estimated):

- 38 minutes

Instructions:

- Add sweet potatoes chunk and 3 cups of water into a pot and bring the water to boil
- Simmer for 30 minutes
- Add in ginger juice, mix well, and continue to simmer for 2-3 minutes

- Turn off heat and add honey when the soup cools down
- Serve

Notes:

- In Chapter 9, you have learned that it is important to moderate the intake of pungent foods to avoid excess energy buildup in the lungs. But, that is only for general advice. Specifically speaking, if you have a yang deficiency body type, it is recommended that you consume more pungent foods than others.

- That's why I say advice offered in Chapter 9 is for your reference only. You will need to look into these general references as well as your body's unique conditions to come up with a detailed and customized dietary plan for your own self.

Recipe 2: Chives with Shrimps

Ingredients:

- Shrimps, peeled and with heads cut off, 1 cup
- Chives, cut into 2-inch pieces, 2 cups
- Garlic, peeled and chopped, 4 cloves
- Cooking wine, 1/4 cup
- Avocado oil, 2 tbsp
- Himalayan salt, to taste

Serving size:

- 3

Total cooking time (estimated):

- 20 minutes

Preparation time (estimated):

- 10 minutes

Cooking time (estimated):

- 10 minutes

Instructions:

- Heat up the oil in the frying pan
- Add garlic into the pan and cook with medium heat until garlic turns brown-ish
- Add shrimps into the pan and sauté until shrimps all turn red
- Add chives into the pan and sauté for 3-4 minutes
- Add in cooking wine and simmer for 1-2 minutes
- Turn off heat, add 2-3 pinches of salt, and mix well
- Serve

Yin Deficiency

Symptoms: It is likely that you have dry skin, warm hands and feet, a red face, dry eyes, and dry stool. You easily get thirsty.

Recipe 1: Hawthorn Berry Congee

Ingredients:

- Hawthorn berries, pitted, 1/4 cup
- Brown rice, 1/2 cup

- Clean water, 3 cups

Serving size:

- 1

Total cooking time (estimated):

- 46 minutes

Preparation time (estimated):

- 1 minute

Cooking time (estimated):

- 45 minutes

Instructions:

- Wash brown rice, add brown rice and water into a pot, and bring the water to boil
- Simmer for 35 minutes
- Add in hawthorn berries and continue to simmer for 5 minutes
- Turn off heat and serve

Recipe 2: Black Sesame Sticky Rice

Ingredients:

- Black sesame seeds, 2 tbsp
- Sticky rice, 1/2 cup
- Clean water, 2 cups
- Himalayan salt, to taste

Serving size:

- 2

Total cooking time (estimated):

- 51 minutes

Preparation time (estimated):

- 1 minute

Cooking time (estimated):

- 50 minutes

Instructions:

- Wash sticky rice, add sticky rice and water into a pot, and bring the water to boil
- Simmer for 40 minutes
- Add in black sesame seeds, mix well, and continue to simmer for 5 minutes
- Turn off heat, add in 1-2 pinches of salt, and stir well
- Serve

Blood Stasis

Symptoms: You easily get dark eye circles, and easily get bruises even you are only mildly hurt.

Recipe 1: Chives with Squid

Ingredients:

- Chives, cut into 2-inch pieces, 4 cups
- Squid, cut into 2-inch strips, 2 cup
- Clean water, 4 cups

- Avocado oil, 2 tbsp
- Himalayan salt, to taste

Serving size:

- 4

Total cooking time (estimated):

- 25 minutes

Preparation time (estimated):

- 5 minutes

Cooking time (estimated):

- 20 minutes

Instructions:

- Bring 4 cups of water to boil
- Boil strips of squid in boiling water for 30-60 seconds, drain them, run them under running water, drain them again, and set them aside on a plate for later use
- Add avocado oil into a frying pan and heat up the oil
- Turn the heat to medium to low, add in chives, and sauté for 3-5 minutes
- Add in strips of squid and continue to sauté for 5 minutes
- Add 3-4 pinches of salt, mix well and continue to sauté for 1-2 minutes
- Turn off heat and serve

Recipe 2: Hawthorn Berry Apple Tea

Ingredients:

- Organic apples, pitted and cut into small chunks, 2
- Hawthorn berries, pitted, 1 cup
- Clean water, 4 cups

Serving size:

- 2-4

Total cooking time (estimated):

- 4 minutes

Preparation time (estimated):

- 3 minutes

Cooking time (estimated):

- 1 minute

Instructions:

- Add apple chunks, pitted hawthorn berries, and 4 cups of water into a blender and blend away
- Pour the smoothie into glasses and serve

Dampness Heat

Symptoms: You have acne-prone skin and may have bad breaths from time to time.

Recipe 1: Winter Melon Needle Mushroom Soup

Ingredients:

- Winter melon, peeled and chopped into small chunks, 2 cups

- Needle mushrooms, 2 cups
- Chicken stock, 4 cups
- Himalayan salt, to taste

Serving size:

- 4

Total cooking time (estimated):

- 23 minutes

Preparation time (estimated):

- 3 minutes

Cooking time (estimated):

- 20 minutes

Instructions:

- Cut off the bottom of needle mushrooms, rinse them under running water, and drain them
- Add chicken stock into the pot and bring it to boil
- Add small chunks of winter melon and needle mushrooms into chicken stock and simmer for 15 minutes
- Turn off heat
- Add 3-4 pinches of salt and mix well
- Serve

Notes:

- Needle mushrooms are very popular in China. In case they sound strange to you, I've attached a photo for you. Usually the bottom of needle mushrooms will be discarded before use. That's why, in the instruction, I mention cutting off the bottom of needle mushrooms.

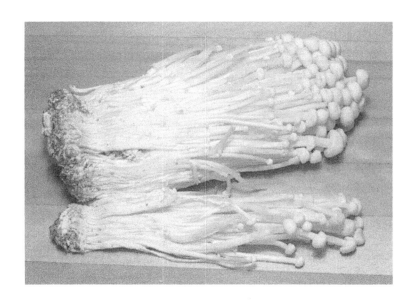

Recipe 2: Needle Mushrooms with Fried Eggs

Ingredients:

- Needle mushrooms, 2 cups,
- Organic eggs, 2
- Avocado oil, 2 tbsp
- Himalayan salt, to taste

Serving size:

- 2

Total cooking time (estimated):

- 11 minutes

Preparation time (estimated):

- 1 minute

Cooking time (estimated):

- 10 minutes

Instructions:

- Break 2 eggs into a bowl, stir them into an egg paste
- Cut off and discard the bottom of needle mushrooms
- Rinse the mushrooms under running water and drain them
- Add avocado oil on a frying pan, add mushrooms into the pan, and sauté with medium heat for 3-4 minutes
- Pour egg paste onto needle mushrooms, wait for about 30 seconds, and sauté mushrooms every few seconds until egg paste is fully cooked
- Turn off heat, add 1-2 pinches of salt, and mix well
- Serve

Qi Depression

Symptoms: You often feel depressed and suffer from insomnia.

Recipe 1: Peanut Butter Buckwheat

Ingredients:

- Buckwheat, ½ cup
- Peanut butter, 2 tbsp
- Clean water, 2 cups

Serving size:

- 2

Total cooking time (estimated):

- 31 minutes

Preparation time (estimated):

- 1 minute

Cooking time (estimated):

- 30 minutes

Instructions:

- Wash buckwheat, add clean water and buckwheat into a pot, and bring the water to boil
- Simmer for 25 minutes
- Turn off heat, add peanut butter into the pot, and mix well with buckwheat
- Serve

Recipe 2: Veggie Omelet

Ingredients:

- Organic eggs, 4 eggs
- Onions, chopped into small pieces, 1/4 cup
- Chives, chopped into 1-inch pieces, ½ cup
- Red bell peppers, with seeds removed, sliced, ½ cup
- White mushrooms, cut into small pieces, 1 cup
- Avocado oil, 2 tbsp
- Cilantro, chopped, 1/4 cup
- Himalayan salt, to taste

Serving size:

- 2

Total cooking time (estimated):

- 25 minutes

Preparation time (estimated):

- 10 minutes

Cooking time (estimated):

- 15 minutes

Instructions:

- Break eggs into a bowl, stir well into an egg paste, and set the bowl aside for later use
- Add avocado oil onto a frying pan and heat up the oil
- Add pieces of white mushrooms into the pan and sauté for 4 minutes
- Add chives into the pan and sauté for 3-4 minutes
- Add bell peppers and onions into the pan and continue to sauté for 3-4 minutes
- Pour egg paste over the mixed veggies, sprinkle cilantro on top of veggies, wait for about 30-40 seconds, and flip over the omelet to cook the other side
- Wait for about 30-40 seconds
- Turn off heat and sprinkle 2-3 pinches of salt on the top of the omelet
- Serve

Phlegm Dampness

Symptoms: You might be overweight and feel heavy in four limbs.

Recipe 1: White Radish Tomato Soup

Ingredients:

- Tomatoes, cut into small pieces, 4
- White radish, peeled and sliced into thin strips, 1 cup
- Clean water, 1 cup
- Miso paste, 1 tbsp

Serving size:

- 2

Total cooking time (estimated):

- 25 minutes

Preparation time (estimated):

- 5 minutes

Cooking time (estimated):

- 20 minutes

Instructions:

- Add water onto a small frying pan and bring the water to boil
- Lower to heat to medium, add in pieces of tomatoes, and cook for 5 minutes (frying pan is covered by a lid on top)
- Add in miso paste and white radish strips, lower the heat to medium to low, and simmer for 10 minutes
- Turn off heat and serve

Recipe 2: Sweet Potato Chinese Barley Congee

Ingredients:

- Sweet potatoes, peeled and cut into small bitable chunks, 2 cups

- Chinese barley, ½ cup
- Clean water, 3 cups

Serving size:

- 2

Total cooking time (estimated):

- 60 minutes

Preparation time (estimated):

- 5 minutes

Cooking time (estimated):

- 55 minutes

Instructions:

- Place chunks of sweet potatoes and 1 cup of water into a small pot (pot A) and bring the water to boil
- (While boiling sweet potatoes) wash Chinese barley and place barley and 2 cups of water into another pot (pot B) and bring the water to boil
- When water in pot A is boiled, lower the heat and simmer for 20 minutes
- When water in pot B is boiled, lower the heat and simmer for 40 minutes
- (After sweet potatoes are simmered for 20 minutes) pour sweet potatoes and water into a blender and blender sweet potatoes into a sweet potato paste
- (After Chinese barley is cooked for 40 minutes) pour sweet potatoes paste into Chinese barley congee, mix well, and continue to simmer for 10 minutes
- Turn off heat and serve

Special Diathesis

Symptoms: You easily get allergy and are sensitive to environmental changes.

Recipe 1: Rice & Barley Congee

Ingredients:

- Brown rice, 1/3 cup
- Black rice, 1/3 cup
- Chinese barley, 1/3 cup
- Clean water, 4 cups

Serving size:

- 4

Total cooking time (estimated):

- 56 minutes

Preparation time (estimated):

- 1 minute

Cooking time (estimated):

- 55 minutes

Instructions:

- Wash brown rice, black rice, and Chinese barley
- Add brown rice, black rice, Chinese barley, and water into a pot and bring the water to boil
- Simmer for 50 minutes
- Turn off hear and serve

Recipe 2: Carrot Brown Rice Paste

Ingredients:

- Baby carrots, 1 cup
- Brown rice, ½ cup
- Clean water, 3 cup
- Honey, 1 tbsp

Serving size:

- 2

Total cooking time (estimated):

- 48 minutes (disregarding the time needed for cooling down carrot brown rice paste)

Preparation time (estimated):

- 1 minute

Cooking time (estimated):

- 47 minutes (disregarding the time needed for cooling down carrot brown rice paste)

Instructions:

- Wash brown rice, add brown rice and water into a pot, and bring the water to boil
- Simmer or 25 minutes
- Add baby carrots into brown rice and continue to simmer for 15 minutes
- Turn off heat, pour brown rice congee and carrots into a blender, and blender everything into a paste
- Pour the paste into bowl

- Add honey when the paste cools down and mix well
- Serve

Gentleness

If your body type belongs to "gentleness", congratulations! That means you are currently having a healthy and balanced body. All you need to do is to pay attention to all the key dietary principles in autumn outlined in Chapter 5, incorporate them into your life, and stick with a balanced lifestyle. Below I've incorporated two types of Chinese herbal tea that nourish the lungs and moisturize your skin, two key activities you should do in this season.

Recipe 1: Orange Peel Ginger Tea

Ingredients:

- Dried orange peels, 1 tbsp
- Black tea, 1 tsp
- Fresh ginger, sliced, 3-4 slices
- Red dates, 3-4 pieces
- Hot water

Serving size:

- 1

Total cooking time (estimated):

- 15 minutes

Preparation time (estimated):

- 5 minutes

Cooking time (estimated):

- 10 minutes

Instructions:

- Place dried orange ginger peels, black tea leaves, ginger slices, red dates into a glass or cup that can hold high temperature of boiling water
- Add hot water into the glass or cup and let it sit for 10 minutes
- Enjoy

Notes:

- If you are not used to using black tea leaves to prepare tea, you can use black tea bags by using 1 bag at a time.

Recipe 2: Rose Peppermint Tea

Ingredients:

- Rose buds, 5-6 pieces
- Peppermint tea bag, 1
- Hot water

Serving size:

- 1

Total cooking time (estimated):

- 15 minutes

Preparation time (estimated):

- 5 minutes

Cooking time (estimated):

- 10 minutes

Instructions:

- Place rose buds and peppermint tea bag into a glass or cup that can hold high temperature of boiling water
- Add hot water into the glass or cup and let it sit for 10 minutes
- Enjoy

Chapter 31: Recipes for *Hanlu* (Dew Becoming Colder)

As you can tell from the name already, the temperature continues to drop. Usually, after *qiufen* (official autumn), the cold weathers become more distinct. TCM believes that, as weathers get colder, it is time to pay more attention to nourishing yin energy inside the body.

Based on this, starting from *hanlu*, you should emphasize more on consuming foods that can nourish yin. This kind of foods can moisturize and rejuvenate the skin and improve the quality of your sleep (which is the key to your overall health and increasing the level of energy and radiance reflected on the face). Enjoy the 10 recipes below that serve these purposes.

Sugar Cane Congee

Ingredients:

- Sugar cane juice, 1 cup
- Brown rice, ½ cup
- Clean water, 3 cups

Serving size:

- 2

Total cooking time (estimated):

- 50 minutes

Preparation time (estimated):

- 5 minutes

Cooking time (estimated):

- 45 minutes

Instructions:

- Wash brown rice, add brown rice and clean water into a pot, and bring the water to boil
- Simmer for 35 minutes
- Add Sugar cane juice into brown rice congee, stir well, and continue to simmer for 5 minutes
- Turn off heat and serve

This dish is especially good for:

- Moisturizing the skin
- Expelling internal heat
- Nourishing yin
- Moistening the throat
- Relieving coughs
- Relieving hangover
- Prevent cancer
- Relieving constipation

Hawthorn Berry Stick Rice Congee

Ingredients:

- Hawthorn berries, pitted, 1 cup
- Sticky rice, 1 cup
- Clean water, 2 cups (for soaking sticky rice)
- Clean water, 8 cups (for making this congee)

- Honey, 3 tbsp (optional)

Serving size:

- 6

Total cooking time (estimated):

- 63 minutes (plus 2hours for soaking sticky rice and disregarding the tie for cooling down hawthorn berry congee)

Preparation time (estimated):

- 3 minutes (plus soaking sticky rice for 2 hours)

Cooking time (estimated):

- 60 (disregarding the time for cooling down hawthorn berry congee)

Instructions:

- Soak sticky rice in 2 cups of clean water for 2 hours
- Wash them under running water and drain them
- Place sticky rice and 8 cups of clean water into a pot and bring the water to boil
- Simmer for 45 minutes
- Add in hawthorn berries, mix well, and continue to simmer for 15 minutes
- Turn off heat
- (Optional) add honey when congee cools down

This dish is especially good for:

- Nourishing the yin
- Improving digestion
- Improving appetite
- Slowing down aging process

- Preventing heart problems
- Improving heart functions
- Strengthening immunity
- Enriching and nourishing the blood

Notes:

- If you have recently been experiencing poor digestion, you can use brown rice instead of sticky rice. The result is that there is lack of chewiness as you switch to brown rice.

Lotus Leaf Hawthorn Berry Tea

Ingredients:

- Dried lotus leaves, cut into small pieces, 10 grams
- Hawthorn berries, pitted, 15 pieces
- Chinese barley, ½ cup
- Dried orange peels, 2 tbsp
- Honey, 1 tbsp
- Clean water, 4 cups

Serving size:

- 2-3

Total cooking time (estimated):

- 60 minutes (disregarding the time used for cooling down the tea at the final step)

Preparation time (estimated):

- 5 minutes

Cooking time (estimated):

- 55 minutes (disregarding the time used for cooling down the tea at the final step)

Instructions:

- Wash dried lotus leaves, pitted hawthorn berries, Chinese barley, and dried orange peels
- Add dried lotus leaves, pitted hawthorn berries, Chinese barley, dried orange peels, and 4 cups of water into a pot and bring the water to boil
- Simmer for 50 minutes
- Turn off heat
- Add honey when the tea cools down
- Serve

This dish is especially good for:

- Improving digestion
- Nourishing the skin and the body
- Brightening up the skin
- Nourishing yin
- Losing weight
- Nourishing the heart
- Slowing down aging process
- Preventing heart problems
- Strengthening immunity
- Enriching and nourishing the blood

Carrot Hawthorn Berry Juice

Ingredients:

- Baby carrots, 2 cups

- Hawthorn berries, pitted, 3-4 pieces

Serving size:

- 1

Total cooking time (estimated):

- 6 minutes

Preparation time (estimated):

- 3 minutes

Cooking time (estimated):

- 3 minutes

Instructions:

- Wash baby carrots and pitted hawthorn berries
- Place carrots and berries into juicer and keep the juice
- Serve

This dish is especially good for:

- Nourishing the yin
- Brightening up the skin
- Improving digestion
- Improving appetite
- Slowing down aging process
- Preventing heart problems
- Improving heart functions
- Strengthening immunity
- Enriching and nourishing the blood

Walnut Hawthorn Berry Milk

Ingredients:

- Walnuts, ½ cup
- Hawthorn berries, pitted, 10 pieces
- Honey, 1 tbsp
- Clean water, ½ cup (for blending walnuts into walnut milk)
- Clean water, 3 cups (for boiling hawthorn berries)

Serving size:

- 2

Total cooking time (estimated):

- 31 minutes

Preparation time (estimated):

- 4 minutes

Cooking time (estimated):

- 27 minutes

Instructions:

- Wash hawthorn berries, add berries and 3 cups of water into a pot, and bring the water to boil
- (While boiling the water) add walnuts and ½ cup of water into a blender and blend them into walnut milk
- (After water is boiled) simmer for 15 minutes
- Use a cheesecloth to filter out cooked hawthorn berries and keep the hawthorn berries juice
- Add walnut milk and hawthorn berries juice into a pot, mix well, and cook for 3-4 minutes with medium to low heat
- Turn off heat and add honey when the milk cools down
- Serve

This dish is especially good for:

- Nourishing the yin
- Nourishing the skin and hair
- Improving digestion
- Improving appetite
- Slowing down aging process
- Preventing heart problems
- Improving heart functions
- Strengthening immunity
- Enriching and nourishing the blood
- Improving brain functions

Chrysanthemum Black Tea Hawthorn Berry Tea

Ingredients:

- Chrysanthemum flowers, 1 tbsp
- Black tea leaves, 1 tsp
- Hawthorn berry, pitted and sliced, 1
- Hot water

Serving size:

- 1

Total cooking time (estimated):

- 22 minutes

Preparation time (estimated):

- 5 minutes

Cooking time (estimated):

- 17 minutes

Instructions:

- Wash chrysanthemum flowers, black tea leaves, and hawthorn berry slices
- Place ingredients into a glass or cup that can hold high temperature of boiling water
- Add boiling hot water into the glass or cup and let it sit for 15 minutes
- Enjoy

This dish is especially good for:

- Refreshing and calming the mind
- Reliving swelling
- Improving vision
- Nourishing the yin
- Nourishing the skin and hair
- Improving digestion
- Improving appetite
- Slowing down aging process
- Preventing heart problems
- Improving heart functions
- Strengthening immunity
- Enriching and nourishing the blood

Notes:

- If you are not used to preparing tea with tea leaves, you can use one black tea teabag. I personally like to use tea leaves, because they make the tea tastes lightly stronger, which I really enjoy.

Black & White Sesame Congee

Ingredients:

- Black sesame seeds, 1 tbsp
- White sesame seeds, 1 tbsp
- Brown rice, ½ cup
- Clean water, 2 cups

Serving size:

- 2

Total cooking time (estimated):

- 47 minutes

Preparation time (estimated):

- 2 minutes

Cooking time (estimated):

- 45 minutes

Instructions:

- Wash brown rice, add brown rice and water into a pot, and bring the water to boil
- Simmer for 35 minutes
- Add black and white sesame seeds into the congee and continue to simmer for 5 minutes
- Turn off heat and serve

This dish is especially good for:

- Nourishing the kidneys and the liver
- Enriching the blood
- Moisturizing the skin and the body
- Nourishing the hair
- Nourishing yin energy
- Slowing down aging process

- Brightening the skin
- Relieving constipation

Notes:

- Both black and white sesames are dense with nutrients. From a TCM's perspective, black sesame seeds have stronger healing properties. This is also in line with TCM's belief that, usually, the dark color the foods have, the more nourishing benefits they give the body.

American Ginseng Congee

Ingredients:

- American ginseng, sliced, 7-8 slices
- Brown rice, ½ cup
- Clean water, 4 cups

Serving size:

- 2

Total cooking time (estimated):

- 47 minutes

Preparation time (estimated):

- 2 minutes

Cooking time (estimated):

- 45 minutes

Instructions:

- Wash brown rice, add brown rice, American ginseng, and water into a pot, and bring the water to boil

- Simmer for 40 minutes
- Turn off heat and serve

This dish is especially good for:

- Slowing down aging process
- Improving brain functions
- Improving immunity
- Improving heart functions
- Nourishing yin energy
- Enriching blood and replenishing qi
- Beautifying the skin
- Nourishing the spleen and the stomach

The Super "Black" (with Black Beans, Black Sesame Seeds, and Black Rice)

Ingredients:

- Black beans, ½ cup
- Black rice, ½ cup
- Black sesame seeds, 2 tbsp
- Red dates, pitted, 4-6 pieces
- Clean water, 4

Serving size:

- 2

Total cooking time (estimated):

- 54 minutes

Preparation time (estimated):

- 2 minutes

Cooking time (estimated):

- 52 minutes

Instructions:

- Wash black beans and black rice
- Add black beans, rice, and water into a pot and bring the water to boil
- Simmer for 45 minutes
- Add sesame seeds and red dates into the pot and continue to simmer for 5 minutes
- Turn off heat
- Pour everything into a blender and blend away
- Pour the paste into a bowl
- Serve

This dish is especially good for:

- Enriching and replenishing blood
- Improving energy and stamina
- Nourishing the skin and hair
- Brightening up the skin
- Improving digestion
- Nourishing the kidneys
- Improving urinary flow
- Detoxifying the body
- Relieving and preventing constipation
- Rejuvenating the whole body
- Improving brain functions

Creamy Peanut Taro Coconut Soup

Ingredients:

- Raw peanuts, ½ cup
- Taro, peeled and cut into small bitable chunks, 1 cup
- Organic coconut cream, 2 tbsp
- Clean water, 1 cup (for soaking peanuts for 4 hours)
- Clean water, 4 cups

Serving size:

- 2

Total cooking time (estimated):

- 60 minutes

Preparation time (estimated):

- 5 minutes

Cooking time (estimated):

- 55 minutes (plus 4 hours for soaking peanuts)

Instructions:

- Soak peanuts for 4 hours
- Add peanuts and 2 cups water into a pot and bring the water to boil
- Simmer for 30 minutes
- Add taro chunks and 2 cups of water into the same pot and again bring the water to boil
- Simmer for 15 minutes
- Add coconut cream into the pot, mix well, and continue to simmer for 1-2 minutes
- Turn off heat and serve

This dish is especially good for:

- Nourishing and moisturizing the skin

- Improving brain functions
- Slowing down aging process
- Strengthening heart functions
- Reducing phlegm
- Relieving coughs
- Nourishing yin energy
- Nourishing qi
- Nourishing the lungs, the stomach, the spleen, and the heart

Chapter 32: Recipes for *Shuangjiang* (Frost Starting to Appear)

The focus of this *jieqi* is preventing respiratory diseases. To achieve this, all these three tasks – keeping the lungs in balance, hydrating the body, and nourishing yin energy – are important. Because of this, you should pay closer attention to these three areas at the same time on this *jieqi* to minimize the chance of developing respiratory diseases.

As a result, you could either revisit the chapters that talk about recipes which give you benefits in these three areas, or stay in this chapter where I am about to share with you more recipes which also serve the same purposes just to give you more options.

If you choose to revisit previous chapters to review recipes, here is a shortcut: you can find foods and related recipes that nourish the lungs on Chapter 27, familiarize yourself with moisturizing foods and related recipes in Chapter 29, and choose what to eat to nourish yin energy inside the body by revisiting Chapter 31.

If you choose to stay, then let's continue on our recipe journey now!

Mushroom Taro Pumpkin Stew

Ingredients:

- Pumpkin, peeled and cut into small bitable chunks, 2 cups
- Taro, peeled and cut into small bitable chunks, 2 cups
- Dried mushrooms, 12

- Scallions, chopped, 1/4 cup
- Coconut cream, 1/4 cup
- Avocado oil, 2 tbsp
- Himalayan salt, to taste
- Clean water, 1 cup (for soaking dried mushrooms)
- Clean water, 6 cups

Serving size:

- 4

Total cooking time (estimated):

- 37 minutes (plus 6-8 hours for soaking dried mushrooms)

Preparation time (estimated):

- 10 minutes (plus 6-8 hours for soaking dried mushrooms)

Cooking time (estimated):

- 27 minutes

Instructions:

- Wash mushrooms and soak them overnight for 6-8 hours
- Heat up avocado oil on a frying pan, lower the heat to medium, add in scallions, and sauté till you can smell scallions
- Add pumpkin chunks and taro chunks into the pan and fry till they are brown-ish
- Pour everything inside the frying pan into a pot and add mushrooms, water used for soaking mushrooms, and 6 cups of clean water into the same pot
- Bring the water to boil
- Simmer for 15 minutes or until pumpkin chunks and taro chunks become soft

- Add in coconut cream, mix well, and continue to simmer for 2 minutes
- Turn off heat and add 3-4 pinches of salt (add more salt if needed)
- Serve

This dish is especially good for:

- Improving digestion
- Lowering down blood sugar levels
- Nourishing and brightening up the skin
- Preventing cancer
- Detoxifying the body

Goji Pumpkin Paste

Ingredients:

- Pumpkin, peeled and cut into small pieces, 2 cups
- Sticky rice, 1/4 cup
- Longan, 10 pieces
- Goji berries, 20 pieces
- Clean water, 4 cups
- Himalayan salt, to taste

Serving size:

- 2

Total cooking time (estimated):

- 68 minutes

Preparation time (estimated):

- 5 minutes

Cooking time (estimated):

- 63 minutes

Instructions:

- Wash sticky rice, add rice into 1 cup of water, and bring the water to boil
- Simmer for 30 minutes
- Add pumpkin chunks, Longan, and 3 cups of water into sticky rice congee and bring the water to boil
- Add goji berries into the congee and continue to simmer for 5 minutes
- Simmer for 15 minutes
- Turn off heat
- Pour everything into a blender and blend it into a pumpkin paste
- Pour the paste into a bowl, add 2 pinches of salt, and mix well
- Serve

This dish is especially good for:

- Improving digestion
- Lowering down blood sugar levels
- Nourishing and brightening up the skin
- Preventing cancer
- Detoxifying the body
- Nourishing yin energy inside the body
- Improving vision

Peanut Walnut Milk

Ingredients:

- Raw peanuts, ½ cup
- Walnuts, ½ cup
- Clean water, 2 cup
- Honey, 1 tbsp

Serving size:

- 2

Total cooking time (estimated):

- 56 minutes

Preparation time (estimated):

- 1 minute

Cooking time (estimated):

- 55 minutes

Instructions:

- Add peanuts and water into a pot and bring the water to boil
- Simmer for 40 minutes
- Add walnuts into the water and continue to simmer for 3-4 minutes
- Turn off heat
- Pour everything in the pot into a blender and blend away
- Cover a cheesecloth over a bowl and pour the milk onto the cloth
- Fold the cheesecloth, squeeze the milk into the bowl, and keep the milk
- Add honey into the milk and mix well
- Serve

This dish is especially good for:

- Improving memory
- Nourishing the spleen and the stomach
- Slowing down aging process
- Nourishing the skin
- Reducing swelling
- Nourishing the lungs
- Reducing phlegm
- Relieving coughs
- Enriching and nourishing qi

Spinach Black Fungus

Ingredients:

- Dried black fungus, ½ cup
- Baby spinach, 8 cups,
- Garlic, chopped, 2 cloves
- Avocado oil, 2 tbsp
- Sesame oil, 2 tsp
- Himalayan salt, to taste
- Clean water, 2 cups (for soaking black fungus)

Serving size:

- 2-3

Total cooking time (estimated):

- 13 minutes (plus 4 hours for soaking black fungus)

Preparation time (estimated):

- 3 minute (plus 4 hours for soaking black fungus)

Cooking time (estimated):

- 10 minutes

Instructions:

- Soak black fungus in water for 4 hours
- Wash black fungus under running water and drain fungus
- Add avocado oil onto a frying pan and heat up the oil
- Lower the heat to medium, add in chopped garlic, and cook until garlic turns brown-ish
- Add in soaked black fungus and sauté for 3-4 minutes
- Lower the heat to medium to low, add in baby spinach, and sauté for 4-5 minutes (or when spinach becomes soft)
- Turn off heat, add in sesame oil and 2 pinches of salt , and mix well
- Serve

This dish is especially good for:

- Enriching and replenishing the blood
- Detoxifying the body
- Nourishing the stomach and the kidneys
- Improving qi
- Lowering blood lipid levels
- Improving immunity
- Losing weight
- Strengthening heart functions
- Slowing down aging process
- Improving digestion
- Nourishing yin

Cucumber Slices Black Fungus Mix

Ingredients:

- Black fungus, ½ cup
- Cucumber, sliced into thin strips, 2 cups
- Olive oil, 2 tbsp
- Himalayan salt, to taste
- Apple cider vinegar, 1 tbsp
- Clean water, 2 cups (for soaking black fungus)
- Clean water, 2 cups (for boiling black fungus)

Serving size:

- 2 - 3

Total cooking time (estimated):

- 20 minutes (plus 4 hours for soaking black fungus)

Preparation time (estimated):

- 5 minutes (plus 4 hours for soaking black fungus)

Cooking time (estimated):

- 15 minutes

Instructions:

- Soak black fungus in water for 4 hours
- Rinse black fungus under running water and drain fungus
- Add 2 cups of water into a pot and bring it to boil
- Add soaked black fungus into boiling water, cook for 5 minutes, take black fungus out of the water, and drain the fungus
- Add cooked black fungus and cucumber strips into a bowl and mix well

- Add olive oil, apple cider vinegar, and 2-3 pinches of salt into the bowl and mix well
- Serve

This dish is especially good for:

- Enriching and replenishing the blood
- Detoxifying the body
- Nourishing the stomach and the kidneys
- Improving qi
- Lowering blood lipid levels
- Improving immunity
- Losing weight
- Reducing swelling
- Detoxifying the body
- Expelling internal heat
- Relieving sore throats
- Driving out dampness

Chicken Breast with Black Fungus

Ingredients:

- Organic chicken breast, cut into thin slices, 1 cup
- Green bell peppers, with seeds removed, cut into strips, 1 cup
- Red bell peppers, with seeds removed, cut into strips, 1 cup
- Dried black fungus, 1/3 cup
- Clean water, 2 cups (for soaking chicken breast)
- Himalayan salt, to taste

Serving size:

- 2

Total cooking time (estimated):

- 23 minutes (plus 4 hours for soaking black fungus)

Preparation time (estimated):

- 10 minute (plus 4 hours for soaking black fungus)

Cooking time (estimated):

- 13 minutes

Instructions:

- Soak black fungus for 4 hours in 2 cups of water
- Heat up a frying pan, add slices of chicken breast into the pan, and cook with medium to high heat until chicken breast turns brown-ish
- Lower the heat the medium, add black fungus into the pot, and sauté for 3-4 minutes
- Lower the heat to medium to low, add green and red bell peppers into the pot, and sauté for 3-4 minutes
- Turn off heat
- Add 2 pinches of salt and mix well
- Serve

This dish is especially good for:

- Enriching and replenishing the blood
- Detoxifying the body
- Nourishing the stomach and the kidneys
- Improving qi
- Lowering blood lipid levels
- Improving immunity
- Losing weight

Cilantro with Black Fungus

Ingredients:

- Dried black fungus, 1/3 cup
- Cilantro, chopped, 1/3 cup
- Onions, cut into small pieces, ½ cup
- White sesame seeds, 1 tbsp
- Clean water, 2 cups (for soaking dried black fungus)
- Clean water , 3 cups (for boiling black fungus)
- Himalayan salt, to taste
- Sesame oil, 2 tsp
- Olive oil, 1 tbsp

Serving size:

- 2

Total cooking time (estimated):

- 20 minutes (plus 4 hours for soaking dried black fungus)

Preparation time (estimated):

- 5 minutes (plus 4 hours for soaking dried black fungus)

Cooking time (estimated):

- 15 minutes

Instructions:

- Soak black fungus in water for 4 hours
- Rinse black fungus under running water, drain fungus, and put fungus in a bowl for later use
- Heat up a frying pan, add white sesame seeds into the pan,

cook with medium to low heat for 3-4 minutes (or until white sesame seeds turn brown-ish), and place white sesame seeds into a different small bowl for later use
- Add 3 cups of water into a pot and bring the water to boil
- Add black fungus into water and boil fungus for 3-4 minutes
- Take fungus out of water and drain the fungus
- Add black fungus, cilantro, onions, white sesame seeds, sesame oil, and 2 pinches of salt into a bowl and mix well
- Serve

This dish is especially good for:

- Enriching and replenishing the blood
- Detoxifying the body
- Nourishing the stomach and the kidneys
- Improving qi
- Lowering blood lipid levels
- Improving immunity
- Losing weight
- Nourishing yin

Banana Lily White Fungus Soup

Ingredients:

- Banana, peeled and sliced, 1
- Dried white fungus, 1
- Lily bulbs, peeled into lily petals, ½ cup
- Goji berries, 20 pieces
- Honey, 1 tbsp

- Clean water, 2 cups (for soaking dried white fungus)
- Clean water, 3 cups

Serving size:

- 2

Total cooking time (estimated):

- 60 minutes (plus 6-8 hours for soaking white fungus and disregarding the time needed for cooling down the soup)

Preparation time (estimated):

- 5 minutes (plus 6-8 hours for soaking white fungus and disregarding the time needed for cooling down the soup)

Cooking time (estimated):

- 55 minutes (disregarding the time needed for cooling down the dish or for placement in the fridge)

Instructions:

- Soak dried white fungus overnight (about 6-8 hours)
- Rinse white fungus under running water and cut it into small pieces
- Add pieces of white fungus and 3 cups of water into a pot and bring the water to boil
- Simmer for 30 minutes
- Add lily petals into water and continue to simmer for 5 minutes
- Add banana slices and goji berries into the soup and continue to simmer for 10 minutes
- Turn off heat
- Add honey when the soup cools down and stir well
- Serve

This dish is especially good for:

- Moisturizing and nourishing the lungs
- Relieving coughs
- Calming the mind
- Nourishing the skin
- Preventing cancer
- Moistening the throat
- Improving vision
- Stimulating bowel movements

Colorful Fried Mix Veggies

Ingredients:

- Lotus roots, peeled and sliced, 1 cup
- Water chestnuts, peeled and sliced, ½ cup
- Fresh Chinese yam, peeled and sliced, 1 cup
- Lily bulbs, peeled into lily petals, ½ cup
- Red bell peppers, with seeds removed, cut into small pieces, ½ cup
- Dried black fungus, 1/4 cup
- Snow beans, both ends of the beans cut off, 1 cup
- Avocado oil, 3 tbsp
- Garlic, chopped, 5 cloves
- Clean water, 4 cups (for cooking mix veggies)
- Clean water, 2 cups (for soaking black fungus)
- Himalayan salt, to taste

Serving size:

- 4

Total cooking time (estimated):

- 27 minutes (plus 6-8 hours for soaking dried black fungus)

Preparation time (estimated):

- 10 minutes (plus 6-8 hours for soaking dried black fungus)

Cooking time (estimated):

- 17 minutes

Instructions:

- Soak dried black fungus into 2 cups of water overnight (about 6-8 hours)
- Rinse black fungus under running water, drain fungus, and place fungus in a bowl for later use
- Add 4 cups of water into a pot and bring the water to boil
- Add lotus roots, Chinese yam, black fungus, and snow beans into water and cook for 3-4 minutes
- Take the veggies out and drain them
- Heat up avocado oil on a frying pan
- Lower the heat to medium, add garlic into the pan, and cook garlic until it turns brown-ish
- Add mix veggies, lily petals, water chestnuts, and red bell pepper pieces into the pan and cook with medium to low heat for 3-4 minutes
- Turn off heat
- Add 3-4 pinches of salt and mix well
- Serve

This dish is especially good for:

- Moisturizing and nourishing the lungs
- Relieving coughs
- Calming the mind
- Nourishing the skin

- Preventing cancer
- Moistening the throat
- Improving immunity
- Stimulating bowl movements
- Expelling internal heat and dampness
- Brightening up the skin
- Nourishing yin energy inside the body
- Detoxifying the body

Black Sesame Paste

Ingredients:

- Black sesame seeds, 1/4 cup
- Sticky rice, 1/4 cup
- Clean water, 1 cup
- Honey, 2 tsp

Serving size:

- 1

Total cooking time (estimated):

- 48 minutes (disregarding the time needed for cooling down the paste)

Preparation time (estimated):

- 1 minute

Cooking time (estimated):

- 47 minutes (disregarding the time needed for cooling down the paste)

Instructions:

- Wash sticky rice, add rice and water into a pot, and bring the water to boil
- Simmer for 35 minutes
- Mix in sesame seeds and continue to simmer for 5 minutes
- Pour everything into a blender and blend away
- Pour sesame paste into a bowl
- Add honey when the paste cools down
- Serve

This dish is especially good for:

- Nourishing the kidneys
- Enriching and replenishing blood
- Moisturizing the skin and the body
- Nourishing the hair
- Nourishing yin energy inside the body

Part 3-4: Winter Eating Recipes

Chapter 33: Recipes for *Lidong* (Arrival of Winter)

As a reminder, you have learned from Chapter 6 already: it is recommended to protect the kidneys in this *jieqi*. Below are a series of kidney-nourishing choices that can also harness the yang energy inside.

Curry Goat Meat with Chinese Yam

Ingredients:

- Goat meat, cut into small chunks, 1 cup
- Chinese yam, peeled and sliced, 1 cup
- Baby carrots, cut into small pieces, 1 cup
- Curry powder, 2 tbsp
- Coconut cream, 2 tbsp
- Clean water, 3 cups
- Himalayan salt, to taste

Serving size:

- 2

Total cooking time (estimated):

- 65 minutes

Preparation time (estimated):

- 10 minutes

Cooking time (estimated):

- 55 minutes

Instructions:

- Add goat meat and 2 cup of water into a pot (pot A) and bring the water the boil
- Add Chinese yam and 1 cup of water into another pot (pot B) and bring the water to boil
- For pot A, when the water is boiled, add baby carrot slices into the pot and simmer for 50 minutes
- For pot B, when the water is boiled, simmer for 30 minutes, add Chinese yam and water into a blender and blend everything into a Chinese yam paste, pour the paste into pot A (which is still being used to cook goat meat and baby carrots at the moment), and mix well
- Add curry powder and coconut cream into pot A and stir well
- Let it sit until you have simmered the foods in pot A for 50 minutes after water is boiled
- Turn off heat, add 2-3 pinches of salt, and mix well
- Serve

This dish is especially good for:

- Nourishing the spleen and the kidneys
- Giving the body warm energies
- Treating diarrhea caused by cold weathers in winter
- Driving out dampness
- Expelling internal heat
- Nourishing and hydrating the skin

Goat Meat Brown Rice Congee

Ingredients:

- Goat meat, cut into small chunks, 1 cup
- Brown rice, 1/4 cup
- Ginger, peeled and sliced, 2-3 slices
- Red dates, pitted, 5 pieces
- Clean water, 2 cups
- Himalayan salt, to taste

Serving size:

- 2

Total cooking time (estimated):

- 58 minutes

Preparation time (estimated):

- 3 minutes

Cooking time (estimated):

- 55 minutes

Instructions:

- Wash brown rice, add brown rice, goat meat, ginger and clean water into a pot, and bring the water to boil
- Add red dates into the congee, mix well, and simmer for 50 minutes
- Turn off heat, add 1-2 pinches of salt, and stir well
- Serve

This dish is especially good for:

- Nourishing the spleen and the kidneys
- Giving the body warm energies
- Nourishing qi and blood
- Warming up the body (including the spleen and the stomach)
- Treating shortness of breath
- Nourishing and brightening up the skin
- Improving stamina
- Improving appetite

Notes:

- Despite the nourishing benefits of congee, I try to minimize the amount of brown rice here. As too many starches (which are what brown rice is primarily made of) can affect the digestion of protein (the nutritional value the goat meat brings to you)

Black Sesame Peanut Congee

Ingredients:

- Black sesame seeds, 2 tbsp
- Raw peanuts, ½ cup
- Brown rice, ½ cup
- Clean water, 3 cups

Serving size:

- 3

Total cooking time (estimated):

- 57 minutes

Preparation time (estimated):

- 2 minutes

Cooking time (estimated):

- 55 minutes

Instructions:

- Wash brown rice, add peanuts, brown rice, and water into a pot, and bring the water to boil
- Add in black sesame seeds and simmer for 50 minutes
- Turn off heat and serve

This dish is especially good for:

- Nourishing the skin and hair
- Warming up the body
- Nourishing the stomach and the spleen
- Preventing heart problems
- Nourishing the lungs
- Moisturizing the body
- Detoxifying the body
- Reducing phlegm
- Nourishing qi

Honey Sesame Chicken

Ingredients:

- Organic chicken breast, cut into small chunks, 1 cup

- Organic soy sauce, 1 tbsp
- Cooking wine, 1 tbsp
- White sesame seeds, 2 tbsp
- Honey, 1-2 tbsp
- Sesame oil, 2 tsp
- Basil leaves, 1/3 cup
- Himalayan salt, to taste

Serving size:

- 2

Total cooking time (estimated):

- 15 minutes (plus 60 minutes for marinating the chicken breast)

Preparation time (estimated):

- 5 minutes (plus 60 minutes for marinating the chicken breast)

Cooking time (estimated):

- 10 minutes

Instructions:

- Add chunks of chicken breast, soy sauce, and cooking wine into a bowl, mix well, and let it sit for 1 hour
- Heat up the pan with medium to high heat, add everything in the bowl into a pan, and sauté for 5 minutes
- Lower the heat to medium to low, add sesame seeds, honey, and basil leaves into the pan, mix well, and continue to sauté for 4-5 minutes

- Turn off heat, add sesame oil and 1-2 pinches of salt, and mix well
- Serve

This dish is especially good for:

- Warming up the body
- Improving immunity and stamina
- Nourishing organs inside the body
- Strengthening bones
- Improving qi and blood circulation
- Treating malnutrition
- Treating anemia
- Reducing swelling

Bamboo Shoot Beef Mushroom Stew

Ingredients:

- Bamboo shoots, sliced, 1 cup
- Button mushrooms, sliced, 2 cups
- Dried mushrooms, 5-6 pieces
- Grass-fed beef, 1 cup
- Pumpkin, peeled and cut into thin slices, 2 cups
- Black pepper, grinded, 2 tsp
- Himalayan salt, 1 tsp
- Avocado oil, 1 tbsp
- Clean water, ½ cup

Serving size:

- 3-4

Total cooking time (estimated):

- 32 minutes (plus 6-8 hours for soaking dried mushrooms and marinating beef slices for 10 minutes)

Preparation time (estimated):

- 15 minutes (plus 6-8 hours for soaking dried mushrooms and marinating beef slices for 10 minutes)

Cooking time (estimated):

- 17 minutes

Instructions:

- Wash mushrooms and soak dried mushrooms overnight (for about 6-8 hours)
- Remove mushroom stems, cut mushrooms into thin slices, place them in a bowl for later use
- Mix beef slices with black pepper and salt and let it sit for 10 minutes
- Add 1 tbsp of avocado oil in a frying pan and heat up the oil
- Add marinated beef slices into the pan and sauté with medium to high heat until beef slices are 80% cooked
- Add in bamboo shoots, all sliced mushrooms, and pumpkin slices into the pan, mix them well with beef, and sauté with medium heat for 2-3 minutes
- Add ½ cup of water and stew with medium to low heat for 10 minutes
- Turn off heat and serve

This dish is especially good for:

- Improving appetite

- Improving digestion
- Detoxifying the body
- Nourishing, hydrating, and brightening up the skin
- Improving immunity
- Enriching qi and blood
- Lowering blood sugar levels

Notes:

- Do not limit yourself to only trying button mushrooms and dried mushrooms. You can choose whatever mushrooms you love to make this dish.

Cumin Beef with Broccoli

Ingredients:

- Grass-fed beef, sliced, 1 cup
- Broccoli, cut into small bitable florets, 3 cups
- Scallions, cut into small pieces, 1/4 cup
- Ginger, sliced, 2-3 slices
- White sesame seeds, 1 tsp
- Avocado oil, 1 tbsp
- Cumin powder, 1 tsp
- Himalayan salt, to taste
- Sesame oil, 2 tsp
- Clean water, 1/3 water

Serving size:

- 3

Total cooking time (estimated):

- 22 minutes

Preparation time (estimated):

- 10 minutes

Cooking time (estimated):

- 12 minutes

Instructions:

- Heat up avocado oil on a frying pan
- Add ginger slices into the pan and heat up ginger slices
- Add beef slices into the pan and sauté with medium to high heat until they are cooked
- Add cumin power into the pan, mix it well with beef, and continue to sauté for 1-2 minutes
- Mix in broccoli florets and white sesame seeds and sauté with medium to low heat for 1-2 minutes
- Add in 1/3 cup of clean water, scallions, and 2-3 pinches of salt, mix well, and simmer for 1-2 minutes
- Turn off heat, mix in sesame oil, and stir well
- Serve

This dish is especially good for:

- Improving immunity
- Nourishing the stomach and the spleen
- Nourishing qi and blood
- Reducing phlegm
- Relieving thirst
- Treating anemia
- Treating shortness of breaths

- Improving appetite
- Improving digestion
- Driving out dampness outside the body

Onion Beef Slices with Black Pepper

Ingredients:

- Onions, peeled and sliced, 1 cup
- Grass-fed beef, cut into 2-inch strips, 1 cup
- Cooking wine, 1 tbsp
- Organic soy sauce, 2 tsp
- Ginger, chopped into small pieces, 1 tbsp
- Black peppers, grinded, 2 tsp
- Himalayan salt, to taste
- Avocado oil, 2 tbsp

Serving size:

- 2-3

Total cooking time (estimated):

- 16 minutes (plus 20 minutes for marinating beef)

Preparation time (estimated):

- 7-8 minutes (plus 20 minutes for marinating beef)

Cooking time (estimated):

- 8 minutes

Instructions:

- Mix beef with cooking wine, soy sauce, ginger, and grinded black peppers, and let it sit for 20 minutes
- Heat up 1 tbsp of avocado oil on a frying pan, add marinated beef into the pan, and sauté with medium to high heat until beef turns colors from red to brown
- Place cooked beef on a place and set it aside for later use
- Heat up 1 tbsp of avocado oil on a frying pan, add onion slices into the pan, and sauté with medium heat until they start to become soft
- Mix beef into onion slices, stir well, and continue to sauté with medium heat for 1 minute
- Turns off heat, add in 2-3 pinches of salt, and serve

This dish is especially good for:

- Improving immunity
- Nourishing the stomach and the spleen
- Nourishing qi and blood
- Reducing phlegm
- Relieving thirst
- Treating anemia
- Bring down inflammation
- Coping with low mood or depression
- Preventing cancer

Beef Peas Mix

Ingredients:

- Peas, 1 cup
- Grass-fed beef, cut into small bitable pieces, 1 cup

- Scallions, 1/4 cup
- Ginger, sliced, 1 tbsp
- Cooking wine, 1 tbsp
- Organic soy sauce, 2tsp
- Sesame oil, 2 tsp
- Black peppers, grinded, 2 tsp
- Himalayan salt, to taste
- Avocado oil, 1 tbsp
- Clean water, 2 cups

Serving size:

- 2-3

Total cooking time (estimated):

- 23 minutes (plus 20 minutes for marinating beef)

Preparation time (estimated):

- 5 minutes (plus 20 minutes for marinating beef)

Cooking time (estimated):

- 18 minutes

Instructions:

- Mix beef with cooking wine, soy sauce, ginger, and grinded black peppers, and let it sit for 20 minutes
- Bring 2 cups of water to boil
- Soak peas in boiling water for 30 seconds, rinse them under running tap water, place them in a bowl, and set aside for later use
- Add avocado oil onto a frying pan and heat it up

- Add beef into the pan and sauté with medium to high heat until beef is cooked
- Mix in peas and scallions and sauté with medium to low heat for 3-4 minutes
- Turn off heat, add sesame oil, and mix well
- Serve

This dish is especially good for:

- Improving immunity
- Nourishing the stomach and the spleen
- Nourishing qi and blood
- Reducing phlegm
- Relieving thirst
- Treating anemia
- Improving digestion
- Improving immunity

Needle Mushrooms Beef Rolls

Ingredients:

- Grass-fed beef, sliced, 1 cup
- Cooking wine, 1 tbsp
- Organic soy sauce, 2 tsp
- Ginger, chopped into small pieces, 1 tbsp
- Black peppers, grinded, 2 tsp
- Himalayan salt, to taste
- Avocado oil, 2 tbsp
- Needle mushrooms, 1.5 cup
- Clean water, 1/3 cup

Serving size:

- 2-3

Total cooking time (estimated):

- 20 minutes (plus 20 minutes for marinating the beef)

Preparation time (estimated):

- 5 minutes (plus 20 minutes for marinating the beef)

Cooking time (estimated):

- 15 minutes

Instructions:

- Cut off the bottom of needle mushrooms, rinse them under running water, drain them, and set them aside for later use
- Mix beef with cooking wine, soy sauce, ginger, and grinded black peppers, and let it sit for 20 minutes
- Place a few needle mushrooms on each beef slice, use each slice of beef as a wrap to wrap up needle mushrooms, and use a toothpick to make sure that needle mushrooms are tightly wrapped in beef slices and that mushrooms won't fall out
- Add avocado oil onto a frying pan and heat up the oil
- Place mushroom beef rolls into the pan and fry them with medium heat
- Flip the rolls over every few seconds to make sure all sides of the rolls are cooked evenly
- When the color of all beef slices turns from red to brown, add 1/3 water into the pan, and simmer for 3-4 minutes (with a lid on top of the pan)

- Turn off heat and serve

This dish is especially good for:

- Improving immunity
- Nourishing the stomach and the spleen
- Nourishing qi and blood
- Reducing phlegm
- Relieving thirst
- Treating anemia
- Fighting fatigue
- Bringing down inflammation
- Prevent cancer
- Prevent heart problems

Notes:

- Needle mushrooms are very popular in China. In case they sound strange to you, I've attached a photo for you. Usually the bottom of needle mushrooms will be discarded before use. That's why, in the instruction, I mention cutting off the bottom of needle mushrooms.

Pineapple Fried Beef

Ingredients:

- Grass-fed beef, sliced, 1 cup
- Pineapple, peeled and cut into small pieces, 1 cup
- Green bell peppers, with seeds removed, sliced, 1
- Organic egg, 1
- Cooking wine, 1 tbsp
- Organic soy sauce, 2 tsp

- Ginger, chopped into small pieces, 1 tbsp
- Black peppers, grinded, 2 tsp
- Himalayan salt, to taste
- Avocado oil, 2 tbsp
- Clean water, 1/3 cup

Serving size:

- 2-3

Total cooking time (estimated):

- 45 minutes

Preparation time (estimated):

- 2 minutes

Cooking time (estimated):

- 42 minutes

Instructions:

- Break the egg and stir it into an egg paste
- Mix beef with egg paste, cooking wine, soy sauce, ginger, and grinded black peppers, and let it sit for 20 minutes
- Add 1 tbsp of avocado oil on to a frying pan and heat up the oil
- Add marinated beef slices into the pan, sauté with medium to high heat until beef slices all turn brown, and place them on a plate
- Add 1 tbsp of avocado oil into the pan, add in green pepper slices and pineapple chunks, sauté with medium heat for 2-3 minutes

- Add beef slices and 1/3 cup of water into the pan and simmer for 1-2 minutes (with lid on top of the pan)
- Turn off heat, add 1-2 pinches of salt, and stir well
- Serve

This dish is especially good for:

- Improving immunity
- Nourishing the stomach and the spleen
- Nourishing qi and blood
- Reducing phlegm
- Relieving thirst
- Treating anemia
- Improving appetite
- Brightening up the skin
- Improving digestion
- Expelling internal heat
- Warming up the body
- Nourishing the heart and the spleen

Chapter 34: Recipes for *Xiaoxue* (Beginning to Snow)

As mentioned earlier, this is a time when one can easily have low mood or depression. The following options will help you boost your mood and help fight depression. Enjoy!

Oatmeal Sesame Paste

Ingredients:

- Rolled oats, 1 cup
- Sesame seeds, 4 tbsp
- Clean water, 4 cups
- Himalayan salt, to taste

Serving size:

- 2

Total cooking time (estimated):

- 27 minutes

Preparation time (estimated):

- 1 minute

Cooking time (estimated):

- 26 minutes

Instructions:

- Mix rolled oats in water and bring the water to boil
- Add in sesame seeds, mix well, and simmer for 20 minutes
- Turn off heat, add in 1-2 pinches of salt, and mix well

- Pour everything into a blender and blend it into a paste
- Pour the paste into a bowl and serve

This dish is especially good for:

- Prevent heart problems
- Losing weight
- Improving digestion
- Enriching qi and blood
- Nourishing and moisturizing the body
- Slowing down aging process
- Boosting your mood

Notes:

- If you are allergic to gluten like me, you could use gluten-free rolled oats.

Chinese Yam Red Dates Oatmeal Congee

Ingredients:

- Chinese yam, peeled and sliced, 1 cup
- Rolled oats, 1 cup
- Red dates, pitted, 6 pieces,
- Goji berries, 20 pieces,
- Clean water, 5 cups
- Himalayan salt, to taste

Serving size:

- 2-3

Total cooking time (estimated):

- 30 minutes

Preparation time (estimated):

- 5 minutes

Cooking time (estimated):

- 25 minutes

Instructions:

- Add Chinese yam, rolled oats, and water into a pot and bring the water to boil
- Add red dates and goji berries into the pot and simmer for 20 minutes
- Turn off heat, add 1-2 pinches of salt, and mix well
- Serve

This dish is especially good for:

- Nourishing the spleen and the stomach
- Improving appetite
- Enriching and replenishing qi and blood
- Preventing anemia
- Speeding up wound healing process
- Nourishing the lungs and the kidneys
- Expelling dampness
- Calming the mind

Pumpkin Oatmeal Paste

Ingredients:

- Pumpkin, peeled and sliced, 2 cups
- Brown rice, 1/4 cup

- Rolled oats, 1 cup
- Goji berries, 20 pieces,
- Clean water, 6 cups
- Miso paste, 1 tbsp

Serving size:

- 3-4

Total cooking time (estimated):

- 51 minutes

Preparation time (estimated):

- 1 minutes

Cooking time (estimated):

- 50 minutes

Instructions:

- Wash brown rice, add rolled oats, brown rice, pumpkin slices, and 2 cups of water into a pot , and bring the water the boil
- Add in goji berries into the mix and simmer for 50 minutes
- Turn off heat, pour everything into a blender, and blend it into a paste
- Pour the paste into a bowl
- Add miso paste into the paste and stir well
- Serve

This dish is especially good for:

- Improving digestion
- Detoxifying the body
- Nourishing and hydrating the skin and the body
- Improving vision

- Calming the mind

Rice Oatmeal Congee with Walnut

Ingredients:
- Brown rice, 1/4 cup
- Black rice, 1/4 cup
- Chinese barley, 1/4 cup
- Millet, 1/4 cup
- Rolled oats, 1/4 cup
- Walnuts, ½ cup
- Red dates, pitted, 10 pieces
- Goji berries, 30 pieces
- Clean water, 5 cups

Serving size:
- 3-4

Total cooking time (estimated):
- 57 minutes

Preparation time (estimated):
- 2 minutes

Cooking time (estimated):
- 55 minutes

Instructions:
- Wash brown rice, black rice, Chinese barley and millet
- Add brown rice, black rice, Chinese barley, millet, rolled oats, and water into a pot and bring the water to boil

- Add walnuts, red dates, and goji berries into the congee and simmer for 50 minutes
- Turn off heat and serve

This dish is especially good for:

- Improving digestion
- Nourishing the skin
- Hydrating the body
- Calming the mind
- Enriching and replenishing qi and blood
- Driving dampness
- Improving urinary flow
- Improving vision

Black Rice Oatmeal Congee

Ingredients:

- Brown rice, 1/3 cup
- Black rice, 1/3 cup
- Rolled oats, 1/3 cup
- Lotus roots, peeled and cut into small chunks, 1 cup
- Walnuts, ½ cup
- Clean water, 5 cups

Serving size:

- 3-4

Total cooking time (estimated):

- 55 minutes

Preparation time (estimated):

- 5 minutes

Cooking time (estimated):

- 50 minutes

Instructions:

- Wash brown rice and black rice
- Add brown rice, black rice, rolled oats, and 4 cups of water into a pot and bring the water to boil
- Simmer for 30 minutes
- (While simmering) add lotus root chunks and 1 cup of water into a blender and blend it into a lotus root paste
- (After simmering for 30 minutes) add lotus root paste and walnuts into the congee and continue to simmer for 15 minutes
- Turn off heat and mix well
- Serve

This dish is especially good for:

- Nourishing the qi and blood
- Warming up the body
- Nourishing the spleen, the stomach, the lungs, and the kidneys
- Improving vision
- Slowing down aging process
- Nourishing yin energy inside the body
- Calming the mind
- Clearing out internal heat

Peanut Cilantro

Ingredients:

- Cilantro, 4 cups
- Raw peanuts, ½ cup
- Himalayan salt, to taste
- Sesame oil, 2 tsp
- Clean water, 2 cups (for soaking peanuts)
- Clean water, 2 cups (for boiling peanuts)
- Avocado oil, 2 tbsp

Serving size:

- 2

Total cooking time (estimated):

- 40 minutes (plus 120 minutes for soaking peanuts)

Preparation time (estimated):

- 120 minutes for soaking peanuts

Cooking time (estimated):

- 40 minutes

Instructions:

- Soak peanuts in 2 cups of water for 2 hours
- Add another 2 cups of water in a pot and bring the water to boil
- Add peanuts into the water and simmer for 30 minutes
- (While simmering the peanuts) add avocado oil onto a frying pan and heat up the oil
- (While simmering the peanuts) add 4 cups of cilantro into the pan and sauté with medium to low heat for 1-2 minutes
- (While simmering the peanuts) turn off heat and place cilantro in a bowl for later use

- (After simmering the peanuts for 30 minutes) drain peanuts and place them in a bowl
- Add peanuts and cilantro onto a pan and sauté with medium to low heat for 1-2 minutes
- Turn off heat, add 1-2 inches of salt and sesame oil, and mix well
- Serve

This dish is especially good for:

- Improving memory
- Slowing down aging process
- Nourishing the skin and the body
- Preventing heart problems
- Nourishing the spleen, the lungs, and the stomach
- Reducing phlegm
- Nourishing qi
- Relieving coughs
- Treating malnutrition
- Boosting the mood

Cilantro Potato

Ingredients:

- Potatoes, peeled and cut into strips, 2 cups
- Cilantro, 2 cups
- Black sesame seeds, 2 tbsp
- Scallions, chopped, ½ cup
- Himalayan salt, to taste
- Clean water, 4 cups

- Avocado oil, 2 tbsp

Serving size:

- 3-4

Total cooking time (estimated):

- 28 minutes

Preparation time (estimated):

- 5 minutes

Cooking time (estimated):

- 23 minutes

Instructions:

- Bring 4 cups of water to boil
- Add potato strips into boiling water and cook for 7-10 minutes
- Drain potato strips
- Add avocado oil into a frying pan and heat up the oil
- Add scallion into the pan and cook with medium to low heat for 1-2 minutes
- Add potato strips and sesame seeds into the pan and sauté for 1-2 minutes
- Add cilantro into the pan and sauté for 1-2 minutes
- Turn off heat, add 2-3 pinches of salt and sesame oil into the dish, and mix well
- Serve

This dish is especially good for:

- Boosting the mood
- Warming up the body
- Improving immunity

- Improving digestion
- Improving qi
- Improving digestion
- Preventing constipation

Beef Mixed with Cilantro

Ingredients:

- Grass-fed beef, cut into strips, 1 cup
- Cilantro, 4 cups
- Avocado oil, 1 tbsp
- Himalayan salt, to taste

Serving size:

- 2

Total cooking time (estimated):

- 15 minutes

Preparation time (estimated):

- 5 minutes

Cooking time (estimated):

- 10 minutes

Instructions:

- Heat up avocado oil on a frying pan
- Add beef into the pan and sauté with medium to high heat until beef turns from red to brown
- Mix in cilantro and sauté with medium to low heat for 4-5 minutes

- Turn off heat, add 1-2 pinches of salt (add more if needed), and mix well
- Serve

This dish is especially good for:

- Nourishing the spleen and the kidneys
- Giving the body warm energies
- Nourishing qi and blood
- Warming up the body (including the spleen and the stomach)
- Treating shortness of breath

Carrot Cilantro Mix

Ingredients:

- Baby carrots, cut into thin slices, 1 cup
- Ginger, chopped, 1 tbsp
- Cilantro, chopped, 1 cup
- Clean water, 1/3 cup
- Himalayan salt, to taste
- Avocado oil, 1 tbsp

Serving size:

- 1-2

Total cooking time (estimated):

- 15 minutes

Preparation time (estimated):

- 5 minutes

Cooking time (estimated):

- 10 minutes

Instructions:

- Heat up avocado oil on a pan
- Add baby carrots and ginger into the pan and sauté with medium heat for 3-4 minutes
- Add cilantro into the mix and sauté with medium to low heat for 2-3 minutes
- Add 1/3 cup of clean water in the pan and simmer for 2-3 minutes
- Turn off heat, add 1-2 pinches of salt, and mix well
- Serve

This dish is especially good for:

- Lowering down blood lipid levels
- Nourishing qi
- Nourishing the heart
- Preventing heart problems
- Nourishing and brightening up the skin

Cilantro Celery Tofu Mix

Ingredients:

- Celeries, sliced, 1 cup
- Tofu, cut into small bitable chunks, 1 cup
- Cilantro, 1 cup
- Dried black fungus, 1/3 cup
- Himalayan salt, to taste

- Sesame oil, 2 tsp
- Avocado oil, 2tbsp
- Clean water, 2 cups (for soaking black fungus)

Serving size:

- 2

Total cooking time (estimated):

- 18 (plus 4 hours for soaking black fungus)

Preparation time (estimated):

- 5 minutes (plus 4 hours for soaking black fungus)

Cooking time (estimated):

- 13 minutes

Instructions:

- Soak black fungus for 4 hours
- Rinse black fungus under running water and darin fungus
- Add 2 tbsp of avocado oil on a frying pan and heat up the oil
- Add tofu chunks into the pan and sauté with medium heat till they become golden
- Add black fungus into the pan and sauté for 2-3 minutes
- Mix in celery slices and cilantro and sauté with medium to low heat for 3-4 minutes
- Turn off heat, add 2 pinches of salt and sesame oil, and mix well
- Serve

This dish is especially good for:

- Enriching the blood
- Nourishing the stomach, the kidneys, and the heart

- Preventing heart problems
- Detoxifying the body
- Improving digestion

Chapter 35: Recipes for *Daxue* (Getting More Snow)

Yes, in cold winter, you will need to consume a lot of warm foods to give the body enough energy. But, at the same time, consuming foods with cooling properties from time to time is also important, too, as this can help the body drive out excess heat buildup over the course of the season. *Daxue* is the time to remind you to not forget the importance of keeping the body "cool" while warming up the body. Below are 10 recipe ideas for raw and low-calories dishes which you can make once in a while to help the body stay in balance without suffering from internal excess heat.

Honey Lotus Juice

Ingredients:

- Lotus roots, peeled and cut into small chunks, 2 cups
- Honey, 2 tsp

Serving size:

- 1

Total cooking time (estimated):

- 22 minutes

Preparation time (estimated):

- 5 minutes (disregarding the time for cooling down lotus juice)

Cooking time (estimated):

- 17 minutes (disregarding the time for cooling down lotus juice)

Instructions:

- Add lotus root chunks into a juicer
- Keep the juice
- Add the juice to a pot, bring the juice to boil, and simmer for 15 minutes
- Turn off heat and mix in honey when juice cools down
- Serve

This dish is especially good for:

- Removing bruises
- Expelling internal heat
- Relieving thirst
- Strengthening the spleen
- Improving appetite
- Nourishing the blood
- Treating diarrhea
- Hydrating the skin

Tofu Kelp Soup

Ingredients:

- Dried tofu, cut into small bitable chunks, 1 cup
- Kelp, cut into 2-inch strips, 1 cup
- Dried mushrooms, 6 pieces
- Ginger, peeled and sliced, 3-4 pieces
- Clean water, 1 cup (for soaking dried mushrooms)
- Clean water, 3 cups

- Avocado oil, 2 tbsp
- Himalayan salt to taste

Serving size:

- 2

Total cooking time (estimated):

- 44 minutes (plus 6-8 hours for soaking dried mushrooms)

Preparation time (estimated):

- 4 minutes (plus 6-8 hours for soaking dried mushrooms)

Cooking time (estimated):

- 40 minutes

Instructions:

- Wash dried mushrooms and soak mushrooms overnight in 1 cup of water for about 6-8 hours
- Keep the water used for soaking mushrooms and cut soaked mushrooms into thin slices
- Heat up avocado oil on a frying pan with medium to high heat
- Add tofu chunks into the pan and fry them with medium heat until they start to turn golden
- Add mushroom slices, kelp strips, ginger slices, 3 cups of water, and the water used for soaking dried mushroom earlier into the pan and bring the water to boil
- Simmer for 30 minutes
- Turn off heat and add 1-2 pinches of salt (add more if needed)

This dish is especially good for:

- Preventing cancer

- Improving memory
- Keeping a sharp and focused mind
- Strengthening liver functions
- Treating diabetes
- Preventing heart diseases
- Promoting longevity

Kelp Mung Bean Congee

Ingredients:

- Sticky rice, ½ cup
- Mung beans, 1/4 cup
- Kelp, cut into small 2-inch strips, 1/2 cup
- Orange peels, chopped, 4 tbsp
- Clean water, 4 cups
- Ginger, chopped, 2 tbsp
- Himalayan salt, to taste

Serving size:

- 2

Total cooking time (estimated):

- 17 minutes

Preparation time (estimated):

- 5 minutes

Cooking time (estimated):

- 12 minutes

Instructions:

- Wash sticky rice, mung beans, and kelp
- Add sticky rice, mung beans, kelp, orange peels, ginger, and 4 cups of water into a pot and bring the water to boil
- Simmer for 40 minutes
- Turn off heat and add 1-2 pinches of salt (add more if needed)
- Serve

This dish is especially good for:

- Clearing internal heat
- Nourishing the lungs
- Healing acne skin
- Driving out dampness
- Brightening up the skin
- Nourishing qi and yin energy

Kelp Sesame Mix

Ingredients:

- Kelp, cut into 2-inch strips, 1 cup
- White sesame seeds, 2 tbsp
- Sesame oil, 2 tsp
- Organic soy sauce, 1-2 tsp
- Clean water, 2 cups

Serving size:

- 2

Total cooking time (estimated):

- 28 minutes

Preparation time (estimated):

- 3 minutes

Cooking time (estimated):

- 25 minutes

Instructions:

- Bring 2 cups of water to boil
- (While boiling water) heat up a frying pan with medium to high heat
- (While boiling water) lower the heat to medium, add sesame seeds into the pan, sauté until you can smell white sesame seeds and they start to turn brown-ish
- (While boiling water) turn off heat and place sesame seeds in a bowl for later use
- (When the water is boiled) add kelp strips into boiling water and cook for 15 minutes
- Drain kelp strips and place them in a bowl
- Mix kelp strips and white sesame seeds together
- Add soy sauce and sesame oil into the same bowl and mix well
- Serve

This dish is especially good for:

- Nourishing hair and skin
- Detoxifying the body
- Reducing swelling
- Driving out excess heat inside the body
- Preventing heart diseases

Kelp Celery Peanut Mix

Ingredients:

- Kelp, cut into 2-inch strips, ½ cup
- Celeries, cut into thin slices, ½ cup
- Peanut, ½ cup
- Sesame oil, 2 tsp
- Cilantro, chopped, 1/4 cup
- White sesame seeds, 2 tbsp
- Himalayan salt, to taste
- Clean water, 2 cups (for cooking peanuts)
- Clean water, 2 cups (for cooking kelp and celeries)

Serving size:

- 2

Total cooking time (estimated):

- 48 minutes

Preparation time (estimated):

- 8 minutes

Cooking time (estimated):

- 40 minutes

Instructions:

- Add peanuts and 2 cups of water into a pot and bring the water to boil
- Simmer for 30 minutes
- (While simmering peanuts) add another 2 cups of water into a different pot and bring the water the boil
- (While simmering peanuts) add celery slices and kelp strips

into boiling water and cook for 3-4 minutes
- (While simmering peanuts) drain celery slices and kelp strips and set them aside for later use
- (While simmering peanuts) heat up a frying pan with medium to high heat
- (While simmering peanuts) lower the heat to medium, add white sesame seeds into the pan, sauté until they start to turn brown-ish
- (While simmer peanuts) turn off heat and place sesame seeds into a bowl for later use
- (After simmering peanuts for 30 minutes) turn off heat and drain peanuts
- Mix peanuts with kelp strips and celery slices and rinse them under cool boiled water to bring down the temperature of the mixture
- Drain peanuts, kelp strips, and celery slices and place the mixture into a bowl
- Add sesame seeds, sesame oil, cilantro, and 1-2 inches of salt into the bowl and mix well
- Serve

This dish is especially good for:

- Expelling internal excess heat
- Nourishing the skin and hair
- Nourishing yin energy
- Improving appetite
- Improving digestive
- Lowering down blood sugar levels
- Detoxifying the body

American Ginseng Pear Stew

Ingredients:

- American ginseng, sliced, 1/4 cup
- Pears, peeled, pitted, and cut into small bitable chunks, 2
- Honey, 2-4 tsp
- Clean water, 4 cups

Serving size:

- 2

Total cooking time (estimated):

- 34 minutes (disregarding the time needed for cooling down the stew)

Preparation time (estimated):

- 3 minutes

Cooking time (estimated):

- 65 (disregarding the time needed for cooling down the stew)

Instructions:

- Bring 4 cups of water to boil
- Add ginseng and chunks of pears into boiling water and stew for 45 minutes
- Turn off heat and let it sit for another 15 minutes
- Add honey when the stew is not burning hot and mix well
- Serve

This dish is especially good for:

- Nourishing the spleen, the lungs, heart, and the kidneys

- Enriching and replenishing the qi and blood
- Calming the mind
- Nourishing yin energy inside the body

Goji Chrysanthemum Ginseng Tea

Ingredients:

- Dried white chrysanthemum flowers, 1 tbsp
- Goji berries, 10 pieces
- American ginseng, sliced, 4-5 slices
- Hot water

Serving size:

- 1

Total cooking time (estimated):

- 16 minutes

Preparation time (estimated):

- 5 minutes

Cooking time (estimated):

- 11 minutes

Instructions:

- Add chrysanthemum flowers, goji berries, and ginseng into a glass or cup that can hold boiling hot water
- Add 1/4 cup of hot water into the container and pour out the water to rinse ingredients
- Add 1 cup of hot water and let it sit for 10 minutes
- Serve (refill when needed)

This dish is especially good for:

- Enriching and replenishing yin energy
- Improving vision
- Bringing down internal heat
- Hydrating the skin
- Detoxifying the liver
- Bringing down blood pressure levels
- Preventing cancer
- Improving heart functions
- Refreshing the mind

Lotus Ginseng Soup

Ingredients:

- Lotus seeds, with embryos removed, 1/4 cup
- American ginseng, sliced, 4-5 slices
- Clean water, 1.5 cups
- Honey, 2 tsp

Serving size:

- 1

Total cooking time (estimated):

- 27 minutes (disregarding the time for cooling down the soup)

Preparation time (estimated):

- 2 minutes

Cooking time (estimated):

- 25 minutes (disregarding the time for cooling down the soup)

Instructions:

- Add lotus seeds and ginseng into water and bring the water to boil
- Simmer for 20 minutes
- Turn off heat and add honey when the soup cools down
- Serve
- This dish is especially good for:
- Nourishing qi and yin energy
- Strengthening spleen functions
- Calming the mind
- Clearing out internal heat

Millet Red Dates Ginseng Congee

Ingredients:

- Red dates, pitted, 6 pieces,
- Millet, ½ cup
- American ginseng, sliced, 7-8 slices
- Clean water, 3 cups

Serving size:

- 2

Total cooking time (estimated):

- 57 minutes

Preparation time (estimated):

- 2 minutes

Cooking time (estimated):

- 55 minutes

Instructions:

- Add millet, ginseng slices, and red dates into water and bring the water to boil
- Simmer for 50 minutes
- Turn off heat and serve

This dish is especially good for:

- Hydrating the skin
- Enriching and replenishing blood
- Nourishing qi and yin energy
- Calming the mind
- Treating insomnia
- Nourishing the spleen and the stomach

Pumpkin Mung Bean Soup

Ingredients:

- Pumpkin, peeled and cut into small bitable chunks, 2 cups
- Mung beans, ½ cup
- Himalayan salt, to taste
- Honey, 1 tbsp
- Clean water, 4 cups

Serving size:

- 2

Total cooking time (estimated):

- 40 minutes (disregarding the time for cooling down the soup)

Preparation time (estimated):

- 5 minutes

Cooking time (estimated):

- 35 minutes (disregarding the time for cooling down the soup)

Instructions:

- Wash mung beans, add beans into 2 cups of water, and bring the water to boil
- (While boiling the water) add 2 cups of pumpkin and 2 cup of water into a blender and blend away
- (When the water is boiled) pour pumpkin paste into mung bean soup and simmer for 30 minutes
- Turn off heat, add 1 pinch of salt, and mix well
- Add honey when the soup cools down and mix well
- Serve

This dish is especially good for:

- Improving digestion
- Detoxifying the body
- Nourishing the skin
- Lowering blood sugar levels
- Preventing cancer
- Losing weight
- Strengthening spleen and stomach functions
- Driving out excess heat and dampness

Chapter 36: Recipes for *Dongzhi* (Official Winter)

This *jieqi* brings your attention from consuming high-calories foods to a more balanced diet with more varieties. It reminds you that: in a season when consuming lots of foods with high calories is very important, it is also crucial to not forget to get nutrients from different food sources (such as vitamins, minerals, and enzymes from vegetables) to help the body stay in balance and get all the nutrients needed.

More fruits and vegetables (especially dark leafy green) should be introduced. Below you can find 10 recipes that can inspire you of different ways to consume more vegetables to make your cooking experience and life more fun!

White Red Green Veggie Mix

Ingredients:

- Potatoes, peeled and cut into 2-inch strips, 1 cup
- Baby carrots, sliced, 1 cup
- Green bell peppers, with seeds removed and sliced, 1 cup
- Scallions, chopped, 1/4 cup
- Apple cider vinegar, 1-2 tbsps
- Avocado oil, 2 tbsp
- Himalayan salt, to taste
- Sesame oil, 2 tsp

Serving size:

- 2

Total cooking time (estimated):

- 29 minutes

Preparation time (estimated):

- 15 minutes

Cooking time (estimated):

- 14 minutes

Instructions:

- Heat up a frying pan with avocado oil
- Lower the heat to medium, add scallions into the pan, and sauté for 30-40 seconds
- Add potatoes strips into the pan and sauté for 3-4 minutes
- Add sliced carrots into the pan and continue to sauté for 3-4 minutes
- Lower the heat to medium to low, add apple cider vinegar and 2 pinches of salt, mix well, and continue to sauté for 1-2 minutes
- Add green pepper slices into the pan and continue to sauté for 1-2 minutes
- Turn off heat, add sesame seed oil, and mix well
- Serve

This dish is especially good for:

- Nourishing the spleen and the stomach
- Driving out dampness
- Bringing down inflammation
- Detoxifying the body
- Improving digestion
- Bringing down blood sugar levels
- Nourishing qi and blood

- Reducing swelling
- Improving immunity
- Slowing down aging process
- Relieving constipation
- Improving stamina
- Relieving joint pains
- Treating eczema

Green Yellow Red White Veggie Garden

Ingredients:

- Peas, ½ cup
- Corns, ½ cup
- Baby carrots, cut into small bitable pieces, ½ cup
- Potatoes, peeled and cut into small bitable chunks, ½ up
- Cucumbers, cut into small bitable chunks, ½ cup
- Ginger, chopped, 3 tbsp
- Scallions, chopped, 1/4 cup
- Avocado oil, 3 tbsp
- Himalayan salt, to taste
- Clean water, 2 cups

Serving size:

- 3-4

Total cooking time (estimated):

- 30 minutes

Preparation time (estimated):

- 15 minutes

Cooking time (estimated):

- 15 minutes

Instructions:

- Add 2 cups of water into a pot and bring the water to boil
- Add carrot pieces and potato chunks into boiling water and cook for 3 minutes
- Turn off heat and drain carrot pieces and potato chunks
- Heat up avocado oil on a frying pan with medium to high heat
- Lower the heat to medium, add ginger and scallions into the pan, and sauté for 1 minutes
- Add carrot pieces, potato chunks, peas, corns, and cucumber chunks into the pan and continue to sauté for 3-4 minutes
- Turn off heat and add 3 pinches of salt (add more if needed)
- Serve

This dish is especially good for:

- Nourishing the skin
- Improving digestion
- Strengthening stomach functions
- Relieving coughs
- Improving immunity
- Preventing cancer
- Preventing heart diseases
- Nourishing qi

Garlic Mushroom Broccoli

Ingredients:

- Dried mushrooms, 6 pieces
- Broccoli, cut into small florets, 2 cups
- Red bell peppers, with seeds removed, cut into small pieces, ½ cup
- Garlic, chopped, 3-4 cloves
- Avocado oil, 2 tbsp
- Sesame oil, 2 tsp
- Himalayan salt, to taste
- Clean water, 1/3 water

Serving size:

- 2

Total cooking time (estimated):

- 20 (plus 6-8 hours for soaking dried mushrooms)

Preparation time (estimated):

- 8 minutes (plus 6-8 hours for soaking dried mushrooms)

Cooking time (estimated):

- 12 minutes

Instructions:

- Soak dried mushrooms overnight for about 6-8 hours
- Rinse mushrooms under running water and drain them
- Cut soaked mushrooms into thin slices
- Heat up avocado oil on a frying pan with medium to high heat
- Lower the heat to medium and add garlic into the pan

- Sauté until garlic turns brown-ish
- Add mushrooms into the pan and sauté for 5 minutes
- Lower the heat to medium to low and add broccoli and red bell pepper pieces into the pan and sauté for 1 minute
- Add 1/3 cup of water into the veggies and simmer for 1 minute
- Turn off heat, add 2 pinches of salt, and mix well
- Add sesame oil into the mixed veggies and mix well
- Serve

This dish is especially good for:

- Nourishing the kidneys
- Improving brain functions
- Improving memory
- Strengthening stomach and spleen functions
- Detoxifying the liver
- Preventing cancer
- Improving immunity
- Improving metabolism

Mixed Veggie Stew

Ingredients:

- Corns, ½ cup
- Winter melons, peeled and cut into small chunks, 1 cup
- Chinese yam, peeled and sliced, ½ cup
- Broccoli, cut into small florets, 2 cups
- Dried mushrooms, 10 pieces
- Lettuces, chopped into small pieces, 2 cups

- Baby carrots, sliced, 1 cup
- Clean water, 5 cups
- Clean water, 1 cup (for soaking dried mushrooms)
- Miso paste, 2 tbsp
- Avocado oil, 1 tbsp
- Sesame oil, 1 tbsp

Serving size:

- 5

Total cooking time (estimated):

- 58 minutes (plus 6-8 hours for soaking dried mushrooms)

Preparation time (estimated):

- 15 minutes (plus 6-8 hours for soaking dried mushrooms)

Cooking time (estimated):

- 43 minutes

Instructions:

- Wash dried mushrooms and soak them in 1 cup of clean water overnight for 6-8 hours
- Keep the water and cut soaked mushrooms into thin slices
- Add corns, winter melon chunks, Chinese yam, mushrooms slices, baby carrot slices, 5 cups of water, and 1 cup of water used for soaking dried mushrooms into a pot and bring the water to boil
- Add avocado oil into the pot, mix well, and stew with medium heat for 30 minutes
- Add miso paste into the stew and mix well
- Add broccoli florets and lettuce into the stew, mix well, and stew with medium to low heat for 2-3 minutes

- Turn off heat, add sesame oil, and mix well
- Serve

This dish is especially good for:

- Improving immunity
- Improving appetite
- Strengthening stomach functions
- Improving digestion
- Relieving coughs
- Bringing down internal heat and excess dampness
- Preventing heart diseases and cancer
- Reducing swelling

Fried Mushrooms with Chives and Tofu Skin

Ingredients:

- Dried mushrooms, 6 pieces
- Bamboo shoots, cut into 2-inch strips, 1 cup
- Chives, cut into 2-inch pieces, 2 cups
- Tofu skin, sliced into thin strips, 2cups
- Avocado oil, 2 tbsp
- Himalayan salt, to taste
- Clean water, 2 cups

Serving size:

- 2-3

Total cooking time (estimated):

- 25 minutes (plus 6-8 hours for soaking dried mushrooms)

Preparation time (estimated):

- 10 minutes (plus 6-8 hours for soaking dried mushrooms)

Cooking time (estimated):

- 15 minutes

Instructions:

- Wash and soak dried mushrooms in 2 cups of clean water overnight for 6-8 hours
- Rinse soaked mushrooms under running water and drain them
- Cut mushrooms into thin slices
- Heat up avocado oil in a frying pan with medium to high heat
- Lower the heat to medium and add mushrooms slices and bamboo shoots into the pan and sauté for 5 minutes
- Add tofu skin strips into the mix and continue to sauté for 3-4 minutes
- Add chives into the pan and sauté with medium to low heat for 2-3 minutes
- Turn off heat, add 2-3 pinches of salt into the pan, and mix well
- Serve

This dish is especially good for:

- Boosting the mood
- Losing weight
- Nourishing the kidneys and the stomach
- Enriching qi and blood

Fried Lily Bulbs with Broccoli

Ingredients:

- Broccoli, cut into small bitable florets, 2 cups
- Lily bulbs, peeled into lily petals, 1 cup
- Himalayan salt, to taste
- Avocado oil,
- Garlic, chopped, 3-4 cloves

Serving size:

- 2

Total cooking time (estimated):

- 10 minutes

Preparation time (estimated):

- 5 minutes

Cooking time (estimated):

- 5 minutes

Instructions:

- Heat up avocado oil on a frying pan with medium to high heat
- Add garlic into the pan and sauté until garlic turns brownish
- Lower the heat to medium to low, add broccoli florets and lily petals into the pan, and sauté for 2-3 minutes
- Turn off heat, add 1-2 pinches of salt into the mix, and stir well
- Serve

This dish is especially good for:

- Improving appetite
- Improving digestion

- Improving immunity
- Slowing down aging process
- Speeding up healing process in skin
- Nourishing the skin
- Preventing cancer

Macadamia Nuts with Mix Veggies

Ingredients:

- White radish, peeled and chopping into small pieces, 1 cup
- Red bell peppers, with seeds removed, cut into small pieces, 1 cup
- Cucumbers, chopped into small pieces, ½ cup
- Chinese water chestnuts, peeled and cut into small pieces, ½ cup
- Celeries, sliced, 1 cup
- Macadamia nuts, ½ cup
- Avocado oil, 3 tbsp
- Himalayan salt, to taste
- Clean water, 2 cups

Serving size:

- 3-4

Total cooking time (estimated):

- 45 minutes

Preparation time (estimated):

- 15 minutes

Cooking time (estimated):

- 30 minutes

Instructions:

- Add 2 cup of water into a pot and bring the water to boil
- Add white radish into boiling water and cook for 10 minutes
- Drain white radish
- Add avocado oil into a frying pan and heat up with oil with medium to high heat
- Lower the heat to medium, add nuts into the pan, and sauté for 2-3 minutes
- Lower the heat to medium to low, add red bell peppers, cucumber, water chestnuts, and sliced celeries into the pan, and sauté for 3-4 minutes
- Add white radish into the mix and continue to sauté for 3-4 minutes
- Turn off heat, add 3-4 pinches of salt, and mix well
- Serve

This dish is especially good for:

- Expelling lung heat inside the body
- Nourishing the lungs
- Removing phlegm
- Improving urinary flow
- Detoxifying the body
- Reducing swelling
- Relieving bloating
- Reliving sore throats

Eggplant Potato Bell Pepper Mix

Ingredients:

- Potato, peeled and sliced, 1 cup
- Eggplant, sliced, 1 cup
- Green bell pepper, with seeds removed and sliced, 1 cup
- Red bell pepper, with seeds removed and sliced, 1 cup
- Scallions, chopped, 1/4 cup
- Garlic, chopped, 4-5 cloves
- Avocado oil, 3 tbsp
- Himalayan salt, to taste
- Black pepper, grinded, to taste
- Clean water, 1/3 water

Serving size:

- 3-4

Total cooking time (estimated):

- 35 minutes

Preparation time (estimated):

- 15 minutes

Cooking time (estimated):

- 20 minutes

Instructions:

- Heat up avocado oil on a frying pan with medium to high heat
- Lower the heat to medium, add garlic and scallions into the pan, and sauté until garlic turns brown-ish
- Add potato slices into the pan and cook till they become

soft
- Place them on a plate and set them aside for later use
- Add eggplant slices into the pan and cook until they become soft
- Mix in green and red bell pepper slices and continue to sauté for 3-4 minutes
- Add potato slices into the mix and continue to sauté for 2-3 minutes
- Add 1/3 cup of water and simmer for 2-3 minutes
- Turn off heat, add 3-4 pinches of salt and 2-3 pinches of grinded black pepper, and mix well
- Serve

This dish is especially good for:

- Nourishing the stomach and the spleen
- Detoxifying the body
- Bringing down inflammation
- Lowering blood sugar levels
- Nourishing the blood
- Reducing swelling
- Improving qi
- Improving immunity
- Slowing down aging process
- Improving digestion
- Relieving constipation
- Fighting fatigue
- Relieving joint pains

Fried Mung Bean Sprouts with Chives

Ingredients:

- Mung bean sprouts, 4 cups
- Chives, 2 cups
- Avocado oil, 2 tbsp
- Himalayan salt, to taste
- Apple cider vinegar, 1 tbsp
- Ginger, chopped, 1 tbsp

Serving size:

- 2

Total cooking time (estimated):

- 12 minutes

Preparation time (estimated):

- 2 minutes

Cooking time (estimated):

- 10 minutes

Instructions:

- Wash mung bean sprouts and chives separately and drain them
- Add 2 tbsp of avocado oil into the pan and heat up the oil with medium to high heat
- Lower the heat to medium, add ginger into the pan, and sauté for 1 minutes
- Lower the heat to medium to low, add mung bean sprouts into the pan, and cook for 1 minutes
- Add chives into the pan and continue to sauté for 2-3 minutes
- Add apple cider vinegar and continue to sauté for 30 seconds
- Turn off heat, add 1-2 pinches of salt, and mix well
- Serve

This dish is especially good for:

- Improving digestion

- Relieving constipation
- Preventing cancer in the digestive system
- Preventing heart diseases
- Expelling internal
- Detoxifying the body
- Improving urinary flow
- Reducing swelling
- Driving out internal dampness
- Bringing down inflammation

Napa Cabbage Tofu Stew

Ingredients:

- Tofu, chopped into small bitable pieces, 2 cups
- Napa cabbage, sliced, 4 cups
- Avocado oil, 2 tbsp
- Sesame oil, 2 tsp
- Himalayan salt, to taste
- Ginger, sliced, 2 tbsp
- Scallions, 1/4 cup
- Clean water, 3 cups

Serving size:

- 2

Total cooking time (estimated):

- 25 minutes

Preparation time (estimated):

- 5 minutes

Cooking time (estimated):

- 20 minutes

Instructions:

- Heat up the pan with avocado oil with medium to high heat
- Lower the heat to medium, add scallions and ginger into the pan, and sauté for 1 minutes
- Lower the heat to medium to low, add cabbage into the pan, and sauté until cabbage becomes soft
- Add 3 cups of water and tofu into the pan
- Bring the water the boil
- And simmer for 10 minutes
- Turn off heat, add 1-2 pinches of salt and sesame oil, and mix well
- Serve

This dish is especially good for:

- Preventing heart problems
- Improving brain functions
- Nourishing yin energy inside the body
- Bringing down internal heat
- Nourishing and hydrating the skin
- Expelling internal heat

Chapter 37: Recipes for *Xiaohan* (Starting to Get Freezing Cold)

As mentioned in Chapter 6, around this time you can focus on introducing more herbs into your daily life to further warm up and nourish the body. So, enjoy the following 10 recipes featuring different herbs.

Steamed Egg with Longan

Ingredients:

- Organic eggs, 2
- Longan, 12 pieces
- Clean water, ½ cup (for blending longan)
- Clean water 2 cups (for adding water a steamer)
- Honey, 1 tbsp

Serving size:

- 1-2

Total cooking time (estimated):

- 21 minutes

Preparation time (estimated):

- 1 minute

Cooking time (estimated):

- 20 minutes

Instructions:

- Add ½ cup of water and longan into a blender and blend away into a longan paste
- Crack two eggs into a bowl, mix well, and stir them into an egg paste
- Add longan paste into the egg paste and mix well
- Add 2 cups of water into the bottom of a steamer and bring it to boil
- Place the bowl with longan and egg paste onto the rack of the steamer and steam with medium to high heat for 10 minutes
- Take the bowl out and drip honey on top when steamed egg cools down
- Serve

This dish is especially good for:

- Nourishing qi
- Enriching yin energy inside the body
- Improving immunity
- Warming up with the body
- Hydrating and nourishing the skin
- Nourishing the blood

Pumpkin Longan Red Date Paste

Ingredients:

- Pumpkin, peeled and cut into small bitable chunks, 2 cups
- Longan, 12 pieces
- Red dates, pitted, 5-6 pieces
- Clean water, 3 cups

- Honey, 1 tbsp

Serving size:

- 2

Total cooking time (estimated):

- 42 minutes (disregarding the time for cooling down pumpkin paste)

Preparation time (estimated):

- 5 minutes

Cooking time (estimated):

- 37 minutes (disregarding the time for cooling down the paste)

Instructions:

- Add pumpkin chunks and longan into 3 cups of water and bring the water to boil
- Add red dates into the soup and simmer for 30 minutes
- Turn off heat
- Pour everything into a blender and blender it into a paste
- Pour into a bowl and add honey when pumpkin paste cools down
- Serve

This dish is especially good for:

- Enriching and replenishing qi and blood
- Improving digestion
- Nourishing and hydrating the skin
- Warming up the body
- Nourishing the spleen and the stomach
- Detoxifying the body

- Improving immunity
- Lowering down blood sugar levels and high blood pressure levels
- Losing weight

Red Dates Longan Ginger Tea

Ingredients:

- Longan, 8 pieces
- Red dates, pitted, 6 pieces
- Ginger, sliced, 3-4 slices
- Clean water, 2 cups

Serving size:

- 1

Total cooking time (estimated):

- 36 minutes

Preparation time (estimated):

- 1 minute

Cooking time (estimated):

- 35 minutes

Instructions:

- Add longan, ginger, and water into a pot and bring the water to boil
- Add red dates into the tea and simmer for 30 minutes
- Turn off heat and serve

This dish is especially good for:

- Enriching and replenishing blood
- Hydrating and nourishing the skin
- Warming up with the body
- Nourishing the stomach and the lungs

Red Dates Longan Astragalus Tea

Ingredients:

- Red dates, pitted, 5-6 pieces
- Longan, 8 pieces
- Astragals, sliced, 1/4 cup
- Goji berries, 10 pieces
- Clean water, 2 cups

Serving size:

- 2

Total cooking time (estimated):

- 51 minutes

Preparation time (estimated):

- 1 minutes

Cooking time (estimated):

- 50 minutes

Instructions:

- Add longan and astragalus into 2 cups of water and bring the water to boil
- Simmer for 40 minutes
- Add red dates and goji berries into the soup and continue

to simmer for 5 minutes
- Turn off heat and serve

This dish is especially good for:

- Enriching and replenishing blood
- Hydrating and nourishing the skin
- Warming up with the body
- Nourishing the stomach and the lungs
- Improving vision
- Replenishing qi
- Improving qi circulation

Goat Meat Soup with Longan, Chinese Yam, Dates, and Goji Berries

Ingredients:

- Goat meat, cut into small bitable chunks, 1 cup
- Goji berries, 10 pieces
- Chinese yam, ½ cup
- Longan, 10 pieces
- Chinese dates, pitted, 5 pieces
- Clean water, 2 cups (for quickly boiling goat meat)
- Clean water 3 cups
- Himalayan salt, to taste

Serving size:

- 2

Total cooking time (estimated):

- 205 minutes

Preparation time (estimated):

- 5 minutes

Cooking time (estimated):

- 200 minutes

Instructions:

- Bring 2 cups of water to boil
- Add goat meat into boiling water and quickly cook the meat for 1-2 minutes
- Drain goat meat
- Add goat meat, longan, and Chinese yam into 3 cups of water, and bring the water to boil
- Pour everything into a slow cooker and stew with low heat for 3 hours
- Add Chinese dates and goji berries and continue to stew for 5-10 minutes
- Turn off heat, add 1-2 pinches of salt, and mix well
- Serve

This dish is especially good for:

- Enriching and replenishing qi and blood
- Warming up the body
- Treating shortness of breaths
- Improving immunity
- Improving stamina

Ginger Dates Tea

Ingredients:

- Red dates, 6 pieces
- Longan, 6-8 pieces
- Ginger, sliced, 4-5 pieces
- Clean water, 2 cups
- Honey, 2 tsp

Serving size:

- 2

Total cooking time (estimated):

- 41 minutes

Preparation time (estimated):

- 1 minute

Cooking time (estimated):

- 40 minutes

Instructions:

- Add ginger and longan into water and bring the water to boil
- Simmer for 30 minutes
- Add red dates into the tea and continue to simmer for 5 minutes
- Turn off heat and add honey when tea cools down
- Serve

This dish is especially good for:

- Enriching and replenishing qi and blood
- Warming up the body
- Fighting colds
- Nourishing the stomach and the lungs
- Nourishing and hydrating the skin

-   Improving heart functions
-   Preventing heart diseases

Chicken Soup with Carrots, Chinese Yam, and Dates

Ingredients:

-   Organic chicken breast, sliced, 1 cup
-   Baby carrots, sliced, 1 cup
-   Chinese yam, sliced, ½ cup
-   Chinese dates, pitted, 8 pieces
-   Dried mushrooms, 6 pieces
-   Goji berries, 10 pieces
-   Ginger, chopped, 2 tbsp
-   Scallions, chopped, 1/4 cup
-   Himalayan salt, to taste
-   Clean water, 2 cups
-   Clean water, 1 cup (for soaking dried mushrooms)

Serving size:

-   2

Total cooking time (estimated):

-   60 minutes (plus 6-8 hours for soaking dried mushrooms)

Preparation time (estimated):

-   15 minutes (plus 6-8 hours for soaking dried mushrooms)

Cooking time (estimated):

-   45 minutes

Instructions:

- Wash dried mushrooms and soak mushrooms in 1 cup of water overnight (about 6-8 hours)
- Keep the water and cut mushrooms into thin slices
- Heat up a frying pan, add chicken breast into the pan, and cook with medium to high heat until chicken breast turns brown-ish
- Add mushrooms into the pan and sauté with medium heat for 4-5 minutes
- Add sliced baby carrots, Chinese yam, ginger, 2 cups of water, and 1 cup of water for soaking dried mushrooms earlier on into the pan
- Bring the water to boil and simmer for 30 minutes
- Add Chinese dates, scallions, and 2-3 pinches of salt into the soup and continue to cook for 5 minutes
- Turn off heat and serve

This dish is especially good for:

- Warming up the body
- Improving immunity
- Nourishing the skin
- Nourishing yin energy inside the body
- Nourishing the lungs and the stomach
- Enriching and replenishing blood
- Nourishing qi and improving qi circulation
- Brightening up and nourishing the skin
- Improving vision

Astragalus Bass Soup

Ingredients:

- Bass, sliced, 1 cup
- Astragalus, 1/4 cup
- Red dates, pitted, 6-8 pieces
- Goji berries, 10 pieces
- Ginger, chopped, 2 tbsp
- Cooking wine, 2 tbsp
- Himalayan salt, to taste
- Clean water, 3 cups

Serving size:

- 2

Total cooking time (estimated):

- 38 minutes

Preparation time (estimated):

- 5 minutes

Cooking time (estimated):

- 33 minutes

Instructions:

- Add 3 cups of clean water into a pot and bring the water to boil
- Add astragalus, longan, and ginger into boiling water and simmer for 20 minutes
- Add red dates and fish fillets into the soup and cook with medium heat for 5-6 minutes
- Add cooking wine and continue to cook for 1 minutes
- Turn off heat, add 1-2 pinches of salt into the soup, and stir well
- Serve

This dish is especially good for:

- Treating anemia
- Nourishing the liver, the spleen, and the kidneys
- Strengthening spleen functions
- Nourishing qi
- Improving digestion
- Warming up the body

Steamed Bass

Ingredients:

- Bass, sliced, 2 cups
- Scallions, chopped, 1/4 cup
- Ginger, 2 tbsp
- Garlic, chopped, 2 cloves
- Organic soy sauce, 1 tbsp
- Apple cider vinegar, 1 tbsp
- Avocado oil, 2 tbsp
- Goji berries, 10 pieces
- Sesame oil, 2 tsp
- Clean water, 2 cups

Serving size:

- 2

Total cooking time (estimated):

- 25 minutes

Preparation time (estimated):

- 10 minutes

Cooking time (estimated):

- 15 minutes

Instructions:

- Add 2 cups of clean water into the bottom of a steamer and bring it to boil
- (While boiling water) mix fish fillets with goji berries and 1 tbsp of avocado oil and place them on a plate
- (When the water is boiled) place the plate with fish fillets onto the rack of the steamer and steam with medium to high heat for 6 minutes
- Take fish fillets out of the steamer
- Heat up a frying pan with 1 tbsp f avocado oil with medium to high heat
- Lower the heat to medium, add ginger and garlic into the pan, and sauté until garlic turns brown-ish
- Lower the heat to medium to low, add scallions, organic soy sauce, and apple cider vinegar into the pan, and sauté for 1-2 minutes
- Turn off heat, add sesame oil, mix well with the sauce in the frying pan, and quickly pour sauce evenly on the fish fillets
- Serve

This dish is especially good for:

- Treating anemia
- Nourishing the liver, the spleen, and the kidneys
- Strengthening spleen functions
- Nourishing qi
- Improving digestion
- Warming up the body

Astragalus Red Date Shrimp Stew

Ingredients:

- Shrimps, peeled, 1 cup
- Astragalus, 1/4 cup
- Red dates, 10 pieces
- Ginger, chopped, 2 tbsp
- Clean water, 3 cups
- Himalayan salt, to taste

Serving size:

- 2

Total cooking time (estimated):

- 32 minutes

Preparation time (estimated):

- 2 minutes

Cooking time (estimated):

- 30 minutes

Instructions:

- Add shrimps, astragalus, ginger, and clean water into a pot and bring the water to boil
- Simmer for 20 minutes
- Add red dates into the soup and continue to simmer for 5 minutes
- Turn off heat, add 1-2 pinches of salt, and mix well
- Serve

This dish is especially good for:

- Nourishing the spleen
- Replenishing qi and improving qi circulation
- Warming up the body
- Reducing swelling
- Driving out dampness
- Improving urinary flow
- Treating insomnia

Chapter 38: Recipes for *Dahan* (Coldest Time of the Year)

"Now this is not the end. It is not even the beginning of the end. But it is, perhaps, the end of the beginning."

I found that Winston Churchill's quote describes what I want to say well – *dahan*, the last *jieqi* of winter, also suggests the coming of a new year because spring comes right after it.

To best prepare for the coming of spring, remember to slowly cut down the intake of high-calories food but consume more pungent foods, as pungent foods have the same movements of the season spring: the upward and outward movements.

If you are still confused about food movements, you can revisit Chapter 4.

Additionally, *dahan* is also a time when people are very likely to catch a cold. Eating foods that can prevent and fight colds also helps at this time, too.

Therefore, in the following recipe section, I've incorporated five recipes with pungent flavors and five more recipes that focus on prevent and fight colds.

Stir-fried Chinese Yam with Ginger and Goji

Ingredients:

- Chinese yam, sliced, 1 cup
- Goji berries, 20 pieces

- Ginger, chopped, 2 tbsp
- Avocado oil, 2 tbsp
- Himalayan salt, to taste
- Clean water, 2 cups
- Clean water, 1/4 cup (for soaking goji berries)

Serving size:

- 2

Total cooking time (estimated):

- 21 minutes

Preparation time (estimated):

- 5 minutes

Cooking time (estimated):

- 16 minutes

Instructions:

- Soak goji berries in 1/4 cup of clean water
- (While soaking goji berries) bring 2 cups of water to boil
- (While soaking goji berries) add Chinese yam into boiling water and cook for 1 minute
- (While soaking goji berries) turn off heat and take out Chinese yam
- (While soaking goji berries) heat up avocado oil on a frying pan with medium to high heat
- (While soaking goji berries) lower the heat to medium, add ginger into the pan, and sauté ginger until you can smell ginger flavor
- (While soaking goji berries) add Chinese yam into the pan and sauté Chinese yam for 4-5 minutes
- Take goji berries out of clean water

- Lower the medium to low, add 2 pinches of salt and goji berries into the pan, and sauté for 2-3 minutes
- Turn off heat and serve

This dish is especially good for:

- Improving digestion
- Strengthening the spleen and the stomach
- Nourishing the kidneys
- Nourishing the lungs
- Relieving coughs
- Lowering down blood sugar levels
- Relieving bloating
- Detoxifying the body
- Slowing down aging process
- Fighting colds
- Relieving stomachache and diarrhea

Ginger Scallion Garlic Shrimp

Ingredients:

- Shrimps, peeled, 1 cup
- Ginger, chopped, 3 tbsp
- Apple cider vinegar, 1 tbsp
- Organic soy sauce, 1 tbsp
- Garlic, chopped, 3-4 cloves
- Scallions, 1/4 cup
- Sesame oil, 2 tsp
- Clean water, 2 cups
- Avocado oil, 2 tbsp

Serving size:

- 2-3

Total cooking time (estimated):

- 15 minutes

Preparation time (estimated):

- 5 minutes

Cooking time (estimated):

- 10 minutes

Instructions:

- Bring the water to boil
- Add shrimps into boiling water and boil shrimps until they become red
- Drain shrimps and place them on a plate
- Heat up avocado oil on a frying pan with medium to high heat
- Lower the heat to medium, add ginger and garlic, and sauté until garlic turns brown-ish
- Lower the heat to medium to low, add apple cider vinegar, soy sauce, and scallions and mix well
- Turn off heat, add sesame oil, and mix well
- Pour sauce evenly onto shrimps
- Serve

This dish is especially good for:

- Detoxifying the body
- Warming up the body
- Slowing down aging process
- Fighting colds
- Nourishing the spleen, the stomach, and the lungs

- Relieving coughs
- Relieving diarrhea

Sour Spicy Chicken Soup

Ingredients:

- Organic chicken breast, cut into small bitable pieces, 1 cup
- Cilantro, chopped, ½ cup
- Himalayan salt, to taste
- Sesame oil, 2 tsp
- Red chili oil, 1-2 tsp
- Ginger, chopped, 2 tbsp
- Apple cider vinegar, 1 tbsp
- Clean water, 3 cups

Serving size:

- 2

Total cooking time (estimated):

- 47 minutes

Preparation time (estimated):

- 7 minutes

Cooking time (estimated):

- 40 minutes

Instructions:

- Add chicken breast into water and bring the water to boil
- Add ginger into the soup and simmer for 30 minutes
- Add cilantro, red chili oil, and apple cider vinegar into the

soup and continue to simmer for 5 minutes

- Turn off heat, and 1-2 pinches of salt and sesame oil, and mix well

- Serve

This dish is especially good for:

- Fighting colds
- Warming up the body
- Nourishing the lungs, the spleen, and the stomach
- Improving digestion
- Improving digestion
- Nourishing qi

Notes:

- Some people really enjoy the spicy kick inside the mouth because of the additional of red chili oil. However, if you have acne-prone skin, it is recommended that you avoid or minimize the intake of red chili oil or chili peppers.

- According to TCM, people with acne prone skin usually have a body type called dampness heat body type, which means that there is excess dampness and heat accumulated inside the body. Red chili oil has warm energies and usually brings up a lot of heat inside the body. That's why you should definitely moderate the intake of this ingredient.

- If you want to know more about your own body type and how that can affect what you eat to help you achieve optimal health, beauty, and a calm mind, you can visit the bonus chapter that goes with this book: http://bit.ly/sign-up-for-bonus-chapter.

Ginger Chicken

Ingredients:

- Organic chicken breast, cut into thin 2-inch strips, 1 cup
- Organic egg, 1
- Ginger, sliced, 4-5 slices
- Cooking wine, 2
- Himalayan salt,
- Sesame oil, 2 tsp
- Avocado oil, 1 tbsp

Serving size:

- 2

Total cooking time (estimated):

- 12 minutes

Preparation time (estimated):

- 5 minutes

Cooking time (estimated):

- 7 minutes

Instructions:

- Wash chicken breast
- Crack the egg into a bowl and stir it into an egg paste
- Pour egg paste into chicken breast and mix well
- Heat up a frying pan with medium to high heat

- Add chicken breast into the pan and stir fry until chicken turns red
- Turn off heat and place chicken breast onto a place
- Add avocado oil into the frying pan and heat up the oil with medium to high heat
- Add ginger into the pan and cook for 30-40 seconds
- Lower the heat to medium to low, add cooking wine, 1-2 pinches of salt, and sesame oil into the pan, and mix well
- Turn off heat and pour the sauce onto chicken breast on a plate
- Serve

This dish is especially good for:

- Slowing down aging process
- Detoxifying the body
- Nourishing the stomach, the spleen, and the lungs
- Fighting colds
- Nourishing the heart
- Nourishing qi
- Enriching and replenishing blood
- Treating anemia
- Fighting fatigue
- Strengthening the body

Ginger Pineapple Beef

Ingredients:

- Grass-fed beef, cut into 2-inch strips, 1 cup
- Ginger, chopped, 2 tbsp

- Apple cider vinegar, 1 tbsp
- Pineapple, peeled and sliced, ½ cup
- Red chili oil, 2 tsp (optional)
- Garlic, chopped, 3-4 cloves
- Scallions, chopped, 1/4 cup
- Cooking wine, 2 tbsp
- Avocado oil, 1 tbsp
- Himalayan salt, to taste

Serving size:

- 2

Total cooking time (estimated):

- 27 minutes

Preparation time (estimated):

- 15 minutes

Cooking time (estimated):

- 12 minutes

Instructions:

- Heat up avocado oil in a frying pan with medium to high heat
- Add garlic and ginger into the pan and cook until garlic turns brown-ish
- Add beef into the pan and cook until beef turns from red to brown
- Lower the heat to medium, add apple cider vinegar, pineapple slices, and cooking wine into the pan, mix well, and sauté for 2-3 minutes
- Lower the heat to medium to low, add red chili oil, sesame oil, and 1-2 pinches of salt into the pan, mix well, and

continue to sauté for 2-3 minutes
- Turn off heat and serve

This dish is especially good for:

- Improving immunity
- Warming up the body
- Nourishing the stomach and the spleen
- Nourishing and replenishing qi
- People who suffer from shortness of breaths
- Reducing phlegm
- Enriching and replenishing blood
- Treating anemia
- Reducing swelling
- Relieving thirst

Notes:

- As mentioned above in the "Ginger Chicken" section, if you have acne-prone skin, you might want to avoid consuming red chili oil as it may cause you to break out more often.

Reishi Mushrooms Ginger Herbal Tea

Ingredients:

- Reishi mushrooms, peeled into small pieces, ½ cup
- Ginger, sliced, 4-5 slices
- Red dates, pitted, 6-8 pieces
- Honey, 1 tbsp
- Clean water, 3-4 cups

Serving size:

- 2

Total cooking time (estimated):

- 67 minutes (disregarding the time for cooling down herbal tea)

Preparation time (estimated):

- 2 minutes

Cooking time (estimated):

- 65 minutes (disregarding the time for cooling down herbal tea)

Instructions:

- Add reishi mushrooms and ginger into water and bring the water to boil
- Simmer for 50 minutes
- Add red dates into the pan and continue to simmer for 10 minutes
- Turn off heat and add honey when the tea cools down
- Serve

This dish is especially good for:

- Fighting colds
- Improving immunity
- Nourishing organs inside the whole body
- Hydrating the skin
- Slowing down aging process

Steamed Egg Paste with Ginger and Goji

Ingredients:

- Organic egg, 2
- Ginger, chopped, 2 tbsp
- Goji berries, 10 pieces
- Clean water, ½ cup (for adding it into an egg paste later on)
- Clean water, 2 cups (for steaming the egg paste)
- Honey, 1 tbsp

Serving size:

- 1-2

Total cooking time (estimated):

- 22 minutes (disregarding the time for cooling down the egg paste)

Preparation time (estimated):

- 1 minute

Cooking time (estimated):

- 21 minutes (disregarding the time for cooling down the egg paste)

Instructions:

- Crack the egg into a bowl and stir it into an egg paste
- Add ginger, goji berries, and ½ cup of water into the egg paste and stir well
- Add 2 cups of water into a steamer and bring it to boil
- Place the egg paste on the rack of the steamer and steam the egg paste with medium to high heat for 15 minutes
- Turn off heat and add drip honey on top when the steamed egg paste starts to cool down
- Serve

This dish is especially good for:

- Hydrating and nourishing the skin
- Detoxifying the body
- Warming up the body
- Improving immunity
- Fighting colds
- Bringing down internal inflammation

Ginger Purple Yam Soup

Ingredients:

- Purple yam, peeled and chopped into small bitable chunks, 1 cup
- Ginger, sliced, 4-5 slices
- Goji berries, 15 pieces,
- Clean water, 3-4 cups
- Honey, 1 tbsp

Serving size:

- 2

Total cooking time (estimated):

- 60 minutes (disregarding the time for cooling down the soup)

Preparation time (estimated):

- 5 minutes

Cooking time (estimated):

- 55 minutes (disregarding the time for cooling down the soup)

Instructions:

- Add purple yam and ginger into water and bring the water to boil
- Simmer for 40 minutes
- Add goji berries into the soup and continue to simmer for 10 minutes
- Turn off heat and ad honey when the soup cools down
- Serve

This dish is especially good for:

- Fighting cancer
- Fighting fatigue
- Slowing down aging process
- Enriching and replenishing blood
- Protecting the liver
- Nourishing the heart and preventing heart problems
- Improving digestion
- Bringing down inflammation
- Fighting colds

White Fungus Orange Peel Ginger Pear Stew

Ingredients:

- White fungus, 1
- Orange peels, 2 tbsp
- Ginger, sliced, 4-5 slices
- Goji berries, 15 pieces
- Honey, 1 tbsp
- Pear, peeled and cut into small bitable chunks, 2 cups

- Clean water, 3-4 cups
- Clean water, 2 cups (for soaking white fungus)

Serving size:

- 2 - 3

Total cooking time (estimated):

- 57 minutes (plus 4 hours for soaking white fungus, disregarding the tie for cooling down the tea)

Preparation time (estimated):

- 5 minutes (plus 4 hours for soaking white fungus)

Cooking time (estimated):

- 52 minutes (disregarding the time for cooling down the tea)

Instructions:

- Soak white fungus in 2 cups of clean water for 4 hours
- Rinse white fungus under running water and cut it into small pieces
- Add pieces of white fungus, orange peels, ginger, and pear chunks into 3-4 cups of water and bring the water to boil
- Simmer for 40 minutes
- Add goji berries into the soup and continue to simmer for 5 minutes
- Turn off heat and add honey when the soup cools down
- Serve

This dish is especially good for:

- Nourishing the spleen and the stomach
- Improving appetite
- Improving digestion
- Nourishing the qi

- Bringing down inflammation
- Nourishing yin energy
- Nourishing the skin
- Fighting colds

Ginger Sticky Rice Congee

Ingredients:

- Ginger, chopped, 2 tbsp
- Scallions, chopped, 1/4 cup
- Sticky rice, 1/2 cup
- Clean water, 2 cups
- Miso paste, 1 tbsp

Serving size:

- 2-3

Total cooking time (estimated):

- 55 minutes

Preparation time (estimated):

- 5 minutes

Cooking time (estimated):

- 50 minutes

Instructions:

- Add ginger and sticky rice into 2 cups of water and bring the water to boil
- Simmer for 40 minutes

- Add scallions into the congee and continue to simmer for 5 minutes
- Turn off heat, add miso paste into the congee, and mix well
- Serve

This dish is especially good for:

- Warming up the body
- Driving coldness out of the body
- Fighting colds
- Nourishing the stomach and the lungs
- Detoxifying the body

Check Out My Other Books

"Now this is not the end.

It is not even the beginning of the end.

But it is, perhaps, the end of the beginning."

--- Winston Churchill

Congratulations on finishing the book! I sincerely hope that you enjoyed the book as much as I was writing them.

Seasonal eating is only a fraction of Chinese Food Therapy. If you would like to get a comprehensive picture of Food Therapy, I would recommend you check out my book: *Food As Medicine: Traditional Chinese Medicine-Inspired Healthy Eating Principles with Action Guide, Worksheet, and 10-Week Meal Plan to Restore Health, Beauty, and Mind:* http://bit.ly/food-as-medicine.

There, I try my best to simplify the concept, summarize the essence of Traditional Chinese Medicine and Food Therapy, and provide you with an action guide to help you kick off your fun TCM experiments in the kitchen. The more-than-2,000-year-old Chinese Food Therapy is more than just seasonal eating. So, I'd highly recommend you get this book and reap more benefits from TCM for the health of yourself and your family.

In addition, throughout the seasonal eating book, I have been mentioning the healing benefits of Chinese herbs. If you are interested in learning more about them, you could check out my other book that gives you an introductory understanding of Chinese herbs and 10 herbs you could get started with:

http://bit.ly/chinese-herbs.

I am constantly learning and updating my knowledge about TCM and Food Therapy. If you would like to get a free updated version of this book – plus my personal insights, experiments, and learnings on the same topic along the way as well as a Bonus Chapter that helps you understand your own body and how to find the right foods that fit only your body type, don't forget to subscribe to my mailing list: http://bit.ly/sign-up-for-bonus-chapter.

I look forward to having you in the journey to explore the wonders of TCM and Food Therapy together with you.

Last but not least, if you like this book, I'd greatly appreciate it if you could leave me a review (http://bit.ly/seasonal-healthy-eating-review) at Amazon to help others discover the book, so that other people can benefit from the content as well.

To your ultimate health and beauty,

Tracy

Appendix A: Foods of Five Energies

(You can have a print-ready Word document of this appendix here: http://bit.ly/seasonal-eating-appendixes.)

Cold	Cool	Neutral	Warm	Hot
Sugarcane, chrysanthemum flower, bitter melon, lotus root, water chestnut, kudzu root, watermelon, banana, mulberry, kelp, lettuce, watercress, orange peel, octopus, crab, sprout, honeysuckle	Millet, wheat, Chinese barley, eggplant, cucumber, winter melon, cauliflower, broccoli, celery, mustard green, napa cabbage, spinach, lily bulb, pea, mung bean, pear, papaya, tea leaf, tofu, mushroom, needle mushroom	Brown rice, taro, sweet potato, potato, cabbage, carrot, red bean, peanut, kidney bean, pistachio, soy milk, grape, black sesame seed, black fungus, black rice, black bean	Chive, cilantro, onion, mint, lichi, peach, cherry, chestnut, pumpkin, sticky rice, red date, walnut, lobster, fish, lamb, chicken, coffee, alcohol, cigarette, hawthorn berry	Chili pepper, ginger, black pepper

Appendix B: Foods of Five Flavors

(You can have a print-ready Word document of this appendix here: http://bit.ly/seasonal-eating-appendixes.)

Sour	Sweet	Bitter	Pungent	Salty
Lemon, lime, tomato, pineapple, green apple, strawberry, orange, grapefruit, hawthorn berry, plum, mango, vinegar, grape	Papaya, pear, apple, honey, red date, mushroom, taros, sweet potato, potato, pumpkin, brown rice, wheat, black bean, red bean, soy bean, cherry, lotus seed, grape, corn, sugarcane, peanut, chestnut, beet	Bitter melon, tea leaf, coffee, lettuce, arugula, broccoli rabe, mustard green, turmeric	Garlic, ginger, chili pepper, onion, scallion, radish, horse-radish, Brussels sprout, curry	Seaweed, kelp, pork, crab, shrimp, Himalayan salt, miso paste

Appendix C: Foods of Five Colors

(You can have a print-ready Word document of this appendix here: http://bit.ly/seasonal-eating-appendixes.)

Red	White	Yellow	Green	Black
Red radish, red bell pepper, apple, cherry, watermelon, red chili pepper, red date, pomegranate, tomato, red bean, goji berry, cauliflower, strawberry, persimmon, pork, beef, lamb	Chinese yam, lily bulb, lotus root, lotus seed, Chinese barley, white radish, potato, tofu, white bean, white fungus, button mushroom, pear, water chestnut, taro, onion, garlic, egg, goat cheese, milk, white radish, white sesame seed, lichi, fish, chicken, almond, winter melon, whitebait, sticky rice, peanut	Ginseng, brown rice, quinoa, millet, sweet potato, pineapple, mango, pumpkin, papaya, lemon, chestnut, ginger root, turmeric, curry, buckwheat, teff, amaranth, walnut, chick pea, oat, chrysanthemum, orange, banana, corn, needle mushroom, bamboo shoot, grapefruit, soy bean, tangerine, egg yolk, carrot	Collard greens, broccoli, lettuce, mustard green, broccoli rabe, arugula, baby spinach, spinach, cabbage, sprout, green bell pepper, lime, mung bean, kale, celery, asparagus, cucumber, green tea, mocha, scallion, cilantro, parsley, basil, thyme, rosemary, green pea, chive, avocado, kiwi fruit, Brussel sprout, bitter melon, water spinach, watercress	Black rice, black sesame seed, black fungus, black bean, seaweed, kelp, algae, blackberry, mulberry, eggplant, mushroom, dark purple grape, purple cabbage

Appendix D: Foods of Four Movements

(You can have a print-ready Word document of this appendix here:
http://bit.ly/seasonal-eating-appendixes.)

Upwards	Outwards	Downwards	Inwards
Usually applying to foods with hot or warm energies, and foods with sweet or pungent flavors (see "Appendix A: Foods of Five Energies" and "Appendix B: Foods of Five Flavors" for reference). Examples: ginger, scallions, chili peppers, garlic, and horse-radishes		Usually applying to foods with cold or cool energies, and foods with bitter, sour, or salty flavors (see "Appendix A: Foods of Five Energies" and "Appendix B: Foods of Five Flavors" for reference). Examples: bitter melons, plums, and honeysuckle flowers	

Appendix E: Foods with Different Organic and Common Actions

(You can have a print-ready Word document of this appendix here: http://bit.ly/seasonal-eating-appendixes.)

Food	Good for What Organ(s)?	Common Actions
Chinese yam	Spleen, stomach, kidneys	Improving digestion, losing weight, lowering down blood lipid levels and blood sugar levels
Lotus seed	Spleen, kidneys, heart	Calming the mind, relieving insomnia and palpitation, treating diarrhea
Mustard greens	Lungs, stomach, kidneys	Reducing phlegm, relieving coughing, improving appetite, improving digestion, relieving constipation
Sesame seeds	Stomach, liver, kidneys	Promoting red blood cell growth, relieving dizziness, nourishing hair, lowering down blood sugar levels, nourishing the skin, slowing down aging process
Bitter melon	Heart, liver, spleen, lungs	Clearing summer heat, improving vision, lowering down blood sugar levels, healing acne breakouts, fighting fatigue, calming the mind, relieving thirst, losing weight, detoxifying the body
Cherry	Spleen, stomach, liver	Promoting red blood cell production, preventing anemia, improving immunity, improving brain functions, nourishing the skin, potentially helping remove wrinkles
Mung bean	Live, kidneys	Fighting bacteria, preventing bacteria growth, lowering down blood lipid levels, preventing cancer, healing acne breakouts, brightening up the skin, improving appetite, preventing and treating heat stroke in summer, detoxifying the body
Kelp	Liver, kidneys	Helping fight radiation, lowering down blood pressure, improving immunity, lowering down blood sugar levels, relieving swelling, preventing heart problems, nourishing hair and skin, losing weight, lowering down aging process, preventing cancer, relieving constipation
Taro	Stomach, kidneys, spleen	Improving appetite, bringing down inflammation, improving qi and energy flow inside the body, improving immunity, relieving constipation
Kudzu root	Lungs, stomach, spleen	Relieving thirst, detoxifying the body, relieving diarrhea

Food	Good for What Organ(s)?	Common Actions
Ginger	Heart, lungs, stomach, spleen	Relieving coughing, dealing with nausea, relieving bloating and constipation,
Goji berry	Liver, kidneys	Improving vision, slowing down aging process, fighting fatigue, preventing cancer,
Chestnut	Spleen, stomach, kidneys	Preventing heart problems, slowing down aging process, preventing and lowering down blood sugar levels, preventing osteoporosis
Watermelon	Heart, lungs, bladders, stomach, spleen, liver	Clearing summer heat, improving urinary flow, relieving thirst, calming the mind, nourishing and brightening up the skin, hydrating the body, nourishing hair
Mushroom	Liver, stomach	Improving immunity, preventing cancer, lowering down blood sugar and blood lipid levels, improving digestion, relieving constipation
Chinese barley	Spleen, lungs, kidneys	Brightening up the skin, healing acne breakouts, improving urinary flow, improving blood and energy flow inside the body, reducing swelling
Lotus root	Heart, kidneys, stomach, spleen, lungs	Calming the mind, slowing down aging process, improving digestion, relieving diarrhea, relieving constipation, enriching and producing blood, reducing bruises
Celery	Stomach, lungs, liver	Lowering down blood pressure, detoxifying the body, preventing cancer, relieving hangover, improving digestion, reducing swelling, improving urinary flow, brightening up the skin, calming the mind, relieving insomnia
Longan berry	Heart, spleen, stomach	Relieving palpitation and insomnia, nourishing the skin, slowing down aging process, enriching and nourishing blood
Red date	Spleen, stomach	Nourishing the skin, enriching and producing blood, slowing down aging process, brightening up the skin, fighting fatigue

Appendix F: Foods for Nine Body Types

(You can have a print-ready Word document of this appendix here: http://bit.ly/seasonal-eating-appendixes.)

Body Type	Symptoms	Recommended Foods
Yin deficiency	It is likely that you have dry skin, warm hands and feet, a red face, dry eyes, and dry stool. You easily get thirsty.	Black bean, black sesame, lily bulb, tofu, soy milk, pork, white fungus, black fungus, squid, sesame oil, tomato, grape, orange, tangerine, water chestnut, banana, apple, mulberry, sugarcane, clam, persimmon, duck's egg, duck *Moderate the intake of lamb, shrimp, chive, red chili pepper, scallion, and ginger.*
Yang deficiency	You tend to have cold hands and feet.	More sweet foods (e.g. brown rice, sweet potato, and potato) and pungent foods (e.g. garlic, ginger, and scallion) that give the body warm energies. Beside, also consider shrimp, walnut, and royal jelly. You can refer to "Food of Fiver Flavors" and "Food of Fiver Energies" for more options.
Qi deficiency	You constantly feel weak and tired and easily get sick.	Brown rice, millet, soy bean, white bean, snow pea, broad bean, potato, Chinese yam, sweet potato, mushroom, carrot, goose, lotus seed, chestnut, shrimp, eel, ginseng *Moderate the intake of buckwheat, grapefruit, raw white radish, orange, and water spinach.*
Qi depression	You easily get dark eye circles, and easily get bruises even you are only mildly hurt.	Oatmeal, cilantro, white radish, scallion, rose tea, garlic, onion, bitter melon, kelp, seaweed, algae, carrot, orange, tangerine, hawthorn berry *Meanwhile, make sure you get enough sleep and physical activities; and participate in group activities and stay connected.*
Blood stasis	You have acne-prone skin and may have bad breaths from time to time.	Seaweed, hawthorn berry, black bean, soy bean, mushroom, eggplant, mango, papaya, seaweed, kelp, algae, white radish, carrot, orange, tangerine, grapefruit, peach, plum, vinegar, rose pedal, green tea, mocha, brown sugar, wine *Moderate the intake of oily foods especially those with saturated fat from animals.*

Body Type	Symptoms	Recommended Foods
Dampness heat	You often feel depressed and suffer from insomnia.	Bitter melon, mung bean, mustard green, winter melon, cucumber, water spinach, watercress, watermelon, millet, Chinese barley, kudzu root, lotus seed, red bean, napa cabbage, celery, cabbage, purple cabbage, lotus root *Moderate the intake of walnut, lamb, goose, eel, cilantro, chili pepper, alcoholic beverage, oily and fried foods, foods prepared by hotpot, and barbecued foods.*
Phlegm dampness	You might be overweight and feel heavy in four limbs.	Winter melon, Chinese barley, seaweed, radish, scallion, garlic, kelp, seaweed, algae, olive, bamboo shoot, white radish, orange, horseradish, Chinese yam *Moderate the intake of red date, plum, persimmon, and sweet, oily, and sticky foods in general.*
Special diathesis	You easily get allergy and are sensitive to environmental changes.	A plant-based diet is recommended *Make sure you cut down the intake of alcoholic beverages, pungent foods, beef, goose, eggplant, chili pepper, coffee, strong tea, and seafood like shrimp, fish, and crab.*
Gentleness	You have a healthy and balanced body.	It is recommended you continue to have a well-balanced plant-based diet.

Appendix G: Cooking Oils Smoking Points

(You can have a print-ready Word document of this appendix here: http://bit.ly/seasonal-eating-appendixes.)

Cooking Oils / Fats	Smoke Point °C	Smoke Point °F
Unrefined flaxseed oil	107°C	225°F
Unrefined safflower oil	107°C	225°F
Unrefined sunflower oil	107°C	225°F
Unrefined corn oil	160°C	320°F
Unrefined high-oleic sunflower oil	160°C	320°F
Extra virgin olive oil	160°C	320°F
Unrefined peanut oil	160°C	320°F
Semi-refined safflower oil	160°C	320°F
Unrefined soy oil	160°C	320°F
Unrefined walnut oil	160°C	320°F
Hemp seed oil	165°C	330°F
Butter	177°C	350°F
Semi-refined canola oil	177°C	350°F
Coconut oil	177°C	350°F
Unrefined sesame oil	177°C	350°F
Semi-refined soy oil	177°C	350°F
Vegetable shortening	182°C	360°F
Lard	182°C	370°F
Macadamia nut oil	199°C	390°F
Canola oil (Expeller Pressed)	200°C	400°F
Refined canola oil	204°C	400°F
Semi-refined walnut oil	204°C	400°F

Cooking Oils / Fats	Smoke Point °C	Smoke Point °F
High quality (low acidity) extra virgin olive oil	207°C	405°F
Sesame oil	210°C	410°F
Cottonseed oil	216°C	420°F
Grapeseed oil	216°C	420°F
Virgin olive oil	216°C	420°F
Almond oil	216°C	420°F
Hazelnut oil	221°C	430°F
Peanut oil	227°C	440°F
Sunflower oil	227°C	440°F
Refined corn oil	232°C	450°F
Palm oil	232°C	450°F
Palm kernel oil	232°C	450°F
Refined high-oleic sunflower oil	232°C	450°F
Refined peanut oil	232°C	450°F
Semi-refined sesame oil	232°C	450°F
Refined soy oil	232°C	450°F
Semi-refined sunflower oil	232°C	450°F
Olive pomace oil	238°C	460°F
Extra light olive oil	242°C	468°F
Rice Bran Oil	254°C	490°F
Soybean oil	257°C	495°F
Refined Safflower oil	266°C	510°F
Avocado oil	271°C	520°F

Made in the USA
Las Vegas, NV
09 September 2022

54982147R00282